Toward an Ethic of Citizenship

From Elective Government to a Culture of Democracy

William K. Dustin

ISBN 978-7344402-1-8

About the Cover

The symbol of the Ethic of Citizenship consists of the
yin and yang balanced on the scales of justice. The yin
and yang represent the numerous polarities and
contradictions of our modern society. The scales
represent the various theories of justice through which
we attempt to resolve these contradictions. The
tension between the individual and community is one
of the most fractious of these polarities, and it is
through an Ethic of Citizenship that we can bring it
into balance. In a similar vein, the symbol represents
the tensions inherent in the paradox of freedom. The
combination of a universal symbol that originated in
the east with a universal symbol that originated in the
west also represents the integration of the eastern and
western philosophical traditions

DEDICATED TO
Susan

Synopsis

Citizenship is defined as that secular ethic that defines membership and participation in the political community and provides the cooperative context for political competition. This definition is used to develop a model for the political construction of the next evolutionary stage of citizenship in an elective government that has achieved a rudimentary level of representation. The model consists of two major dimensions–the homeostatic and hermeneutic–and citizenship is the nexus of their intersection. The homeostatic dimension mediates the tension between the individual and community; the hermeneutic dimension involves shaping the evolutionary path into the future through the interpretation of the culture-history of our past into the context of the present. Citizenship is also considered in terms of its individual and collective attributes. The development of citizenship along these lines is seen as leading to the creation of a culture of democracy.

The model of citizenship is used to provide the context for the development of the idea of representation as the highest obligation of citizenship and to provide a critique of election. Since education is critical for the development of citizenship, the model is also applied to the system of education. Finally, the state of Minnesota is used as an example of how the model can be translated into practice. The main theme running throughout the work is the idea that citizenship can be politically developed as the mediating mechanism necessary to establish social and ecological balance.

The ultimate liberty is the freedom and ability to think for oneself.

To the Reader and Acknowledgments

When I mentioned to acquaintances that I was writing a book on citizenship, the response I received most often associated the idea of citizenship with immigration. This response indicates that those of us who inherited our citizenship by virtue of birth take it for granted and that it is mainly of concern only to those who are trying to acquire it. This sorry state of affairs has perhaps been caused by, or at least aggravated by, the political manipulation of citizenship for ideological ends which is commonly reflected in the pathetic state of citizenship education in many of our public schools. When I began my research for this book, I discovered, not surprisingly, that contrary to this public perception, citizenship is a multi-dimensional concept with considerable nuance and paradox. It does not fit easily into the thought patterns of a culture dominated by polar thinking along a single dimension. Therefore, much of what follows is written at a fairly high level of abstraction for which I make no apology. Abstraction is necessary to lay the theoretical and philosophical foundation for the practical constitutional changes I am proposing. I am asking that you, the reader, engage the concept of citizenship at this abstract theoretical level to better position yourself for an evaluation of its proposed implementation in practice.

The intellectual debt I owe to many thinkers spanning the centuries will be evident from the citations. Here I wish to acknowledge my debt to David Morris of the Institute for Local Self Reliance for reading the manuscript and offering some valuable comments. Harry Boyte of the Center for Democracy and Citizenship at the University of Minnesota's Humphrey Institute suggested additional sources, several quite recent, that were very useful. Finally, I owe a debt of gratitude to my wife Susan, for her consistent and constant encouragement and support during the two plus years it took me to complete this project. She not only encouraged me to seek a leave of absence from my job, but also served as an invaluable listener for my ideas at the various stages of their development and offered assistance in many little ways that allowed me the time to work on the project. The value of her love and support is incalculable. I must emphasize my sole responsibility for any asininities that remain.

Twenty Years of Failure

In the councils of government, we must guard against the acquisition of unwarranted influence, whether sought or unsought, by the military-industrial complex. The potential for the disastrous rise of misplaced power exists and will persist. We must never let the weight of this combination endanger our liberties or democratic processes. We should take nothing for granted. Only an alert and knowledgeable citizenry can compel the proper meshing of the huge industrial and military machinery of defense with our peaceful methods and goals, so that security and liberty may prosper together.
Dwight Eisenhower[1]

In nature there are no rewards or punishments, just consequences.
Robert Green Ingersoll

      This book was first published in 1999 with the hope that the new century would usher in progress toward genuine democratic governance. Hence the original subtitle "Creating a Culture of Democracy for the 21st Century". Creating a democracy begins with politics, but to survive and thrive, it must establish itself throughout the entire society as a political culture. The purpose of the book was to develop a model of citizenship that, hopefully, would initiate this transformation. Unfortunately, we are regressing in the opposite direction and the idea of democracy is receding into history.

---

[1] If anyone had the knowledge and insight to issue this warning it certainly was President/General Dwight D. Eisenhower.

The 21st Century began with the contested election of Bush vs. Gore which was settled by a decision of the Supreme Court. Then we had the terrorist attacks of 9/11 in 2001 and the financial crisis of 2008. The trend away from the idea of democracy was well under way. Fear is the enemy of democracy because it opens opportunity for autocrats to seize positions of power. The Republican Party has been in the process of attempting to establish one party rule since at least 1980 with its attacks on government. The Democratic Party aided and abetted them with its doctrine of "political correctness". The corporate control of the government has continued the policy of endless wars while the real threat of climate change is ignored with attacks on science. The second decade of the century ended with numerous incidents of murder by police, racial and civic unrest, a raging worldwide pandemic, and the Republican Party illegitimately refusing to concede power; all of which exploded into an attack upon the nation's capitol. Fascism is on the rise worldwide and the idea of democracy is in the grave.

The simple fact is that we were never a democracy. The Constitution of the United States was specifically designed to severely restrict political representation. Although some of these restrictions have been eased over the years, the fact remains that our government does not represent its citizens, and at this writing there are movements seeking to impose new restrictions upon it. The constitutional barriers to representation have been exacerbated by the corporate control of the political process where corporate representation has displaced citizen representation. What we have is economic politics, not political economy.

The corporation is a creation of government, but like Frankenstein's monster, it has taken control of its creator. In its multi-national form, it has impacted governments worldwide. (The birthplace of many corporations is the home state of our President.) The idea of free markets in its current form has its origins in Adam Smith's *Wealth of Nations* published in 1776. The idea of *laissez faire* revolves around the notion that private vices can lead to public virtues. There may have been some truth in this idea when Smith wrote. Remember he was talking about the baker, brewer, and candlestick maker, not IBM, GE, and Raytheon. In fact, I do not think he held the British East India Company in high regard, but his concept of the "invisible hand" has been used to set corporate entities free in the market. And since unregulated competitive markets will lead to monopoly power, we need government. While government has had some success in preventing monopoly, it is basically unable to resist corporate influence because of corporate dominance of the economy. The ultimate result is that the nation's capital is a seething cauldron of corruption, a condition mirrored in the various state capitals.

Corruption of governmental processes is so pervasive that it is accepted as normal. Most of it has been legalized through corporate lobbyists writing the legislation which is used to regulate their clients. The citizens are dimly aware of this corruption but feel powerless to do anything about it. A metaphor for good government is a smooth-running operating system: it keeps the system secure, it prevents the applications from interfering with one another while allowing them to do what they were designed to do, it runs in the background, and it is transparent. In short, it is boring. Real world government is the exact opposite. It is an extremely noisy enterprise in which all sorts of corporate entities compete with one another to secure advantage through leverage over governmental institutions. In the process they have turned the activities of government into a major entertainment enterprise. When voters vote, they are voting for those individuals who are the most entertaining. This is government by Weber's charismatic authority, and it is no way to achieve democratic governance. Bureaucratic authority isn't desirable either because it eventually leads to rule bound paralysis. If the source of governmental authority is to be derived from its citizens, then democracy is required, and democracy requires a method to secure citizen political representation.

This book is about how to achieve citizen representation. The arena of democratic political representation is the legislature. The importance of this fact is made clear in the United States Constitution where Article I is more than twice as long as Article II and Article III combined. Today, however, the legislative branch has yielded its powers to the executive, and the executive has control over the judiciary through its power of appointment. The legislature was not designed to represent the citizenry at large, but a small subset thereof who were white male property owners. This was the so-called "natural aristocracy" which was supposed to be corruption free because of their property ownership. The falsity of this idea is now clear: extreme wealth disparity is becoming more extreme under the law of accumulating returns. The result is the capture of governmental institutions through legalized corruption.

The idea of the "natural aristocracy" evolved into the idea of a governing meritocracy. The failure of this idea is now clear. From Robert McNamara's "whiz kids" and the Vietnam debacle to Donald Rumsfeld's Iraq War, we have had one foreign policy failure after another. Our regime changes and support of dictators around the world have provided constant blowback decades later, Iran being a perfect example. Our war on drugs has done nothing but feed organized crime and misery in Latin America. And environmental degradation resulting from our use of the planet as a source and sink continues with the ever-rising temperature and pollution.

The citizens are angry about this corruption, but they do not have a clear vision of the source of their anger. This creates the conditions for the political manipulation of this anger by political actors of all stripes. Talk radio was a major amplifier of this anger which spread to television and social media. Political correctness provided fuel for this anger. A prime example of political correctness is speech about Israel. You cannot express legitimate criticisms of

Israel's policies toward the Palestinians without being accused of being an anti-Semite. The same phenomenon applies to speech about any group, race, or class. Immigration was another area where anger was politically manipulated. But the real source of the anger is that we have whole classes of citizens that are politically unrepresented, and they are unrepresented because the whole idea of citizenship status has been shifted from citizens as natural persons to" citizens" as corporate entities. Some of this anger just culminated in the attack upon the nation's capitol building aided and abetted by the President.

The purpose of this book is to restore citizenship and representation to natural persons. The model of citizenship developed here is loosely based on the eukaryotic cell where the governing functions of the cell reside in the nucleus and metabolic and other functions are carried out in the cytoplasm. Instead of hubristically trying to dominate nature, we need to learn from it. We are part of nature and "human nature" is subject to the same laws as the rest of nature. It is through science that we learn from nature, and if we fail to stop the assault on the scientific enterprise, we will certainly suffer the consequences. One of the things we are learning about the biological world is that, even though there is competition, on the whole it is cooperative. Our success as a species has been the result of our ability to cooperate. Genuine political representation will begin to control our dysfunctional competition by containing it within a cooperative context. That is much more vital today than when this book was first published in 1999.

The problem of governance has defied solution since ancient times which explains, in the western context, our constant referral back to Plato and Aristotle. The first two decades of the 21st Century, after all the horrors of the 20th, make one thing clear. The time for solving the problem of governance is now. Unfortunately, it is now evident that the ideas presented here focus on what could have been rather than what could be.

Preface

As we cross the threshold of the new millennium, it behooves us to look back and view the territory we have traversed in reaching our present destination. Looking out over the political-social landscape, it appears lush and vibrant, but as the morning mists of deception dissipate with the rising sun, the sulfurous stench of rotting political parties creates a nauseous sensation and the distortion and contortion of the landscape immediately become apparent. From the twisted mountain peaks of gerrymandered legislative districts to the convoluted canyons of the internal revenue code and the eutrophied oceans of bureaucratic stagnation, the landscape is desolate and barren, eroded by rivers of money, ravaged by the excesses of competition and privatization, the evidence of pollution and corruption are everywhere. When we look for the inhabitants of this hostile environment, we find that the public space has been abandoned to corrupt politicians and roving gangs of aimless youth locked in the stupor of addiction while the rest of the population has broken up into antagonistic ethnic groups that have hidden themselves within walled enclaves of privacy and false security that malignantly spread outward across the barren terrain. Without the nurturing sustenance of an ethic of balance and harmony, the land has lost its ability to support civilized life.

As we approach the new millennium with the hope of delivery into a promised land, it is wise to learn from the despoiled landscape of our past. A promised land is not a mythical destination that is ordained for us by our creator; it can only be achieved by our collective volition and determination. Our choices will determine whatever the new millennium holds for us and the generations to come after us. The vacuous espousal of ideals through political pontification will not create the landscape of our future; it can only be built upon an ethical infrastructure of citizenship created through shared values expressed in concrete action.

Introduction

It is interesting to contemplate an entangled bank, clothed with many plants of many kinds, with birds singing on the bushes, with various insects flitting about, and with worms crawling through the damp earth, and to reflect that these elaborately constructed forms, so different from each other, and dependent on each other in so complex a manner, have all been produced by laws acting around us. These laws, taken in the largest sense, being Growth with Reproduction, Inheritance which is almost implied by reproduction; Variability from the indirect and direct action of the external conditions of life, and as a consequence to Natural Selection, entailing Divergence of Character and the Extinction of less improved forms. Thus, from the war of nature, from famine and death, the most exalted object which we are capable of conceiving, namely, the production of the higher animals, directly follows. There is grandeur in this view of life, with its several powers, having been originally breathed into a few forms or into one; and that, whilst this planet has gone cycling on according to the fixed law of gravity, from so simple a beginning endless forms most beautiful and most wonderful have been, and are being, evolved.

Charles Darwin

The LORD God planted a garden in Eden, in the east, and placed there the man whom He had formed. And from the ground the LORD God caused to grow every tree that was pleasing to the sight and good for food, with the tree of life in the middle of the garden, and the tree of knowledge of good and bad.

...

The LORD God took the man and placed him in the garden of Eden, to till it and tend it. And the LORD God commanded the man, saying, "Of every tree of the garden you are free to eat; but as for the tree of knowledge of good and bad, you must not eat of it; for as soon as you eat of it, you shall die."

...

And the LORD God said, "Now that the man has become like one of us, knowing good and bad, what if he should stretch out his hand and take also from the tree of life and eat, and live forever!' So the LORD God banished him from the Garden of Eden, to till the soil from which he was taken. He drove the man out and stationed east of the garden of Eden the cherubim and the fiery ever-turning sword, to guard the way to the tree of life.

Genesis Ch 2, V 8-10, V 15-7   Ch 3,V 22-24

Unlike other species whose evolution is dependent upon random variation and the survival of those forms most adapted to the environment, our species has developed consciousness and knowledge which have enabled us to begin to direct our own evolution[2]. Yet our evolution has not only been uneven; it has been bifurcated. On the one hand we have achieved remarkable advances in science and technology, but these advances have occurred in a socio-political context within which our evolution has been truncated. (Eisler, 1987) Because of this bifurcation in our evolution, we have become alienated from nature which means that our relationships are out of balance. Unless we restore this balance, and do it fairly soon, our uneven evolution may bring a premature end to our future on this planet[3].

It is through relationships that we as individuals participate in the process of living and contribute, either positively or negatively, to the evolution of our species. Evolution of the species is the driving force in the biological world, and it is here, I suggest, that man can find meaning in his existence. By living our lives in such a manner as to promote the evolution of our species while preserving the interdependent web of life of which we are a part, we contribute to the process of creation which was set in motion billions of years ago and continues to unfold with the passage of time. Since the species is

---

[2] Huston Smith (1958), in his classic book on the world's religions, wrote that there were three ways to promote change: (1) political action, (2) change man's genetic makeup, and (3) develop a new creed. When he wrote this in the 1950's, he argued that developing a new creed was most effective because political action had never been very effective and changing man's genetic makeup was impossible. Now, a few short decades later, the impossible is becoming a reality. As we begin to intervene in our own evolution by tinkering with our genetic makeup, it is imperative that we do so within an ethical context that will insure that such tinkering does in fact promote the long term well being and evolution of our species.

[3] For an insightful discussion on the meaning of extinction, see Jonathan Schell (1982 particularly Ch. II). Although Schell was writing about the result of nuclear war, his arguments apply equally well to the ecological crisis we have created. Nuclear war, after all, is the ultimate assault on the natural environment. While its effects are virtually immediate, some of these same effects - e.g. the destruction of the ozone layer - are already occurring as a result of our more subtle assaults on the environment.

2

potentially immortal, it is through our contributions to its development that we build on the achievements of those who came before us to pass on improvements to those who will come after. In so doing we can achieve a modicum of individual immortality.

Our relationships fall into three categories: with ourselves, with others, and with nature. The function of ethics is to structure and guide our relationships in all three categories to promote individual and collective flourishing in an environment that will ensure the continued survival and maturation of the species. A balanced relationship with ourselves means that we tend to the needs of the body, mind, and spirit. Although this statement seems platitudinous, the fact is that even though we have achieved a high degree of economic success, a large number of us are abusing our bodies[4], failing to educate our minds, and ignoring our spirit. The needs of the body are met by giving it nourishment, exercise, and rest. Education, a lifelong process, is the primary means through which we meet the needs of the mind. Once we stop learning, we are for all practical purposes, dead. The needs of the spirit are met through various practices, religious and others, that affect our attitudes[5]. A healthy relationship with ourselves is a necessary condition for a healthy relationship with others, for it is not possible to love another unless we first love ourselves.

It is through our relationships with each other that we develop as individuals and transmit the values and knowledge that

---

[4] Our bodies are being abused not only through the indulgences such as tobacco and drugs, but also through our pollution of the natural environment. One result of this is genetic deterioration, a form of negative evolution. See Clark, 1977 pp. 220-230.

[5] See Victor Frankl (1992) for a discussion of attitudes and freedom. See Paul Schmidt (1961) for a discussion of attitudes as a source of religious knowledge. Schmidt discusses knowledge by description and knowledge by acquaintance. He concludes that attitudes is the one category of knowledge by description within which religious knowledge is possible.

make civilization possible. We are born into this thing called "society" which consists of various institutions that are designed to structure our relationships so that we may effectively cope with each other. These institutions are given to us by the generations that came before us, and we can adapt their design for ourselves before passing them on to the generations yet to come. Unfortunately, the design and adaptation of social institutions to meet collective and individual human needs has been no easy matter, and more often than not, these institutions have either broken down or failed to adapt to changing conditions resulting in anomie - a state or normlessness akin to the Hobbesian "state of nature" in social contract theory.

A healthy relationship with nature is necessary if we are to survive as a species (after all survival is a necessary condition for evolution) and to experience and appreciate that which transcends mortal existence. We in the west have been brought up with the biblical injunction that man is to subjugate nature and have dominion over it. As a result, we have exhibited an attitude that I call biological hubris - a failure to recognize that we are part of an interdependent web of existence. Our banishment from the Garden of Eden is symbolic of our alienation from nature. Only recently have we begun to develop a dim awareness of the fact that the planet we occupy is fragile and needs to be protected. Ethical behavior in our relationship to nature will take the form of stewardship for our planet so that we preserve its natural beauty and habitability for generations yet unborn. We need to integrate the Native American's appreciation of the mystery of the natural world with our scientific world view to create a new ethic which places our role in the Great Living System in proper perspective. By so doing we will hopefully earn our re-admittance to the Garden of Eden.

In addition to our relationship with ourselves, others, and the natural environment, there is another set of relationships I need to mention, and that is our relationship to the intangible realm of ideas.

4

Ideas[6], and idea systems, not only transcend and connect the other three categories of relationship, but they connect us to our past and lead us to our future. It is through ideas that we define, explain, and understand our other relationships. What differentiates human evolution from other forms of biological evolution is that human evolution has left the realm of the gene to the realm of ideas, and ideas are making it possible to manipulate the natural world right down to the realm of the gene.

It is instructive at this point to consider the following thought experiment: suppose that after the passage of several more generations man's knowledge has progressed to the point where it

---

[6] Ideas, values, sentiments, and emotions are all interrelated aspects of the human experience and arise in the nervous system. It has been discovered that the human digestive tract contains numerous neurons and may function as a second brain. Thus, the term 'gut reaction' may have an actual neurological source. The implications of this notion of a second brain is that not all knowledge may be cerebral. Intuition may be a second source of knowledge. (Blakeslee, 1996)

A useful metaphor in discussing ideas has been the "free marketplace of ideas". This metaphor was (and is) very useful (particularly in free speech cases) in emphasizing the fact that the free expression and exchange of ideas, even hideous ideas, is a basic right necessary to the maintenance and development of democratic institutions and scientific and cultural progress. It is also useful in discussing responsible behavior regarding the exchange of ideas - e.g. the notion of "responsible citizenship in the marketplace of ideas." Gutmann and Thompson (1996) point out that this is a misleading metaphor because markets are not suitable mechanisms for distinguishing between information that is important and information that is not important in discussing public policy. Nor do they provide effective fora for collective action based on anything greater than citizens' fleeting judgments. A more useful metaphor, perhaps, is the "ecology of ideas". This metaphor implies that ideas and systems of ideas are complex entities that mirror the complexity of the universe they seek to describe and understand. It also accounts for the evolution of knowledge which we see in the continued revision and refinement of various scientific and philosophical theories. The evolutionary nature of this process is captured in Thomas Kuhn's (1962) notion of the paradigm shift.

actually becomes possible to re-create individuals that lived in prior generations by reproducing their DNA sequences exactly and imbuing them with their previous consciousness[7]. This is a contingent event that depends upon (1) the survival of our species and (2) an evolutionary path that develops along an ethical and intellectual dimension that makes the outcome possible. Obviously, this is a wild speculation, but it raises some interesting questions. If we believed in a contingent immortality of this type, what type of a society, what institutions, and what public policies would we create to increase the probability of this outcome? Since the choice of who will be re-created will rest with individuals in the distant future whose knowledge and very existence are contingent upon the actions and cultural developments achieved in prior generations, what choices would we be making today individually and collectively? Would we be using our resources towards ends that promote human progress or would we continue to use them for more immediate gratification? How would our priorities change between such things as entertainment and education, utility maximization and distributive justice, cooperation and competition? What attitudes would we have toward other species and the natural environment and the continued exponential growth of the human population? Finally, how will we define human progress? What are the ethical principles that need to be practiced to make progress possible?

This idea of an immortality contingent upon the successful outcome of human evolution raises two problems with many of our current beliefs–(1) the "messiah complex" and (2) the idea that salvation is individual. The idea of a messiah that will come and save the world allows us to avoid responsibility for some of the things we

---

[7] As this is being written, the issue of human cloning has become technically possible which thrust the issue into the forefront on the political agenda. This caught most people by surprise because the techniques to do it were not expected to be available for decades.

6

do, particularly in areas that affect the natural environment and future generations. A modern variant of the messiah complex is the idea that technological solutions will become available to correct the mistakes of the past and present. This attitude allows the assumption that we can afford to risk the future for the sake of immediate economic gain. The idea of individual salvation is more religious in nature, but the emphasis on the individual ignores the fact that we are embedded in society. The idea of the salvation of the individual being tied not only to individual action, but the successful outcome for the whole gives new meaning to the idea of responsibility. Responsibility is then located not solely within the individual, but within his or her relationships, and when it is so located, it begins to bridge the gap between the individual and the community. The implications of a belief such as this can perhaps be appreciated by considering the activities of some of those who believe the opposite. Many acts of terrorism result from the belief that the terrorist is an immortal living in a mortal world that he seeks to destroy.[8]

---

[8] See Arendt (Arendt, 1979) Arendt (1968) also argues that for the Greeks and Romans the idea of immortality had much more to do with activity than belief. The body politic was founded because of man's need to overcome his mortality. Outside the body politic not only was man's life insecure because of its exposure to violence of others, but it was also meaningless and without dignity because there was absolutely no opportunity to leave a trace behind it. "Immortality is what nature possesses without effort and without anybody's assistance, and immortality is what the mortals therefore must try to achieve if they want to live up to the world into which they were born, to live up to the things which surround them and to whose company they are admitted for a short while. The connection between history and nature is therefore by no means an opposition. History receives into its remembrance those mortals who through deed and word have proved themselves worthy of nature, and their everlasting fame means that they, despite their mortality, may remain in the company of the things that last forever." (1968:48)

In this book I am going to examine the meaning and function of citizenship[9]. In the modern world citizenship is an abstract concept that defines an individual's membership in that collectivity known as the nation state and his participation in it. It is an individual attribute and a collective practice. It defines the fundamental political relationship. My purpose in examining citizenship is based on the belief that at this stage of our socio-political evolution in western civilization, citizenship is the fundamental organizing principle through which we can expand the frontiers of democracy to achieve in practice what we espouse in theory. I am going to use my own position as a citizen of the United States and the State of Minnesota in particular as a point of reference for this analysis. Since the ideas of democracy have reached a fairly high degree of institutional expression in the United States, it follows that the American experience provides a suitable context within which to examine citizenship. The United States is a particularly fertile environment within which to develop various ideas of citizenship because it is a federal system and a multicultural society. As a federal system, it provides various laboratories within which ideas can be tested. As a multicultural society, it has the ingredients necessary to meet the challenge of the integration of diversity. If the theory and practice of citizenship cannot be realized in a society such as the United States which has achieved a fairly high degree of political participation on the part of its citizens, it is doubtful that it can be achieved anywhere.

Citizenship, I will argue, can be developed to provide the ethical context which will establish the balance and harmony we need if we are to achieve our democratic ideals. I shall begin by examining the development of citizenship as a unique feature of Western Civilization. Then I shall present a model of citizenship

---

[9] The idea of citizenship can be described as fuzzy around the edges and squishy in the middle. I hope to make the edges less fuzzy and the middle less squishy.

8

and discuss how it can be applied in practice. Citizenship is an evolving concept, and I am going to look at the next possible stage of its evolution. Our society is radically out of balance because we have devoted most of our resources toward defining ourselves as private persons acting in a competitive market and have failed to develop our public personas acting in a cooperative capacity as citizens. In short, commercial values constitute our highest secular ethic, and we define ourselves by the position we hold in some corporate entity and the wealth we accumulate. If, instead, we allow citizenship to become our highest secular ethic, and we define ourselves as having a primary role as citizen with a secondary role as private person, the ideals of democracy will become achievable in the next century.

Chapter I

The Meaning of Citizenship

There can be no patriotism without liberty, no liberty without virtue, no virtue without citizens; create citizens, and you have everything you need; without them you have nothing but debased slaves, from the rulers of the State downwards. To form citizens is not the work of a day, and in order to have men it is necessary to educate them when they are children.

J. J. Rousseau

Democracy is everywhere; democracy is nowhere. Virtually every nation on the face of the earth today claims to be a democracy. Yet democracy - a government of the people, by the people, and for the people - has never been achieved except in some of the pre-literate societies. The dilemma of democracy is that it is universally proclaimed, yet its ideals are universally rejected in practice. However, those ideals are aspired to and derive from ideas that have a long tradition in western civilization. Citizenship is the companion of democracy. Without citizenship there can be no democracy, and it is through the development of citizenship that democracy becomes possible.

Citizenship is a concept that is western in its origins. Although it can be argued that the concept originated in the city states of ancient Greece, it has also been argued that citizenship is a consequence of the French Revolution and the modernization arising out of the Industrial Revolution. (Turner & Hamilton, 1994) Another view is that there have been two citizenships with the first lasting from the time of the Greek city states until the French Revolution and the second being in existence since then to the present.

(Riesenberg, 1992) The term is defined in *Webster's Encyclopedic Unabridged Dictionary of the English Language* as (1) the state of being vested with the rights, privileges, and duties of a citizen, and (2) the character of an individual viewed as a member of society; behavior in terms of the duties, obligations, and functions of a citizen. A citizen is defined as (1) a native or naturalized member of a state or nation who owes allegiance to its government and is entitled to its protection (distinguished from *alien*), and (2) an inhabitant of a city or town, esp. one entitled to its privileges or franchises. Although the first definition of citizen is fairly universal throughout the modern world, it is immediately obvious that *citizenship* has a much different meaning in the United States as opposed to China, for example. Citizenship is a concept that has been evolving both historically and in theory. This chapter will review this development along both dimensions and conclude with a discussion of the future development of the idea.

Historical Development

The idea of citizenship arose in the city states of ancient Greece, particularly Athens, and was then carried over into the Roman Republic and Empire. With the decline of the Roman Empire, the idea of citizenship, although transformed by Christianity, flourished in the Italian merchant cities. After the Renaissance, however, citizens became subjects and the idea of citizenship nearly disappeared; but the development of cities and towns led to a rebirth of the idea to distinguish the resident of the city from the subjects who resided outside. Citizenship had territorial boundaries which for millennia were defined by the city. It was not until the modern era that these boundaries moved beyond the city and encompassed the nation-state. (Isin, 1997) The idea of citizenship achieved its modern transformation as a result of the

French and American Revolutions which established republican governments in Europe and the Americas.

In ancient Greece citizenship had elements of privilege that were earned, but for the most part it was regarded as a form of property and a birthright. The Assembly (*ekklesia*) was open to all citizens (women and slaves were not citizens) and each had one vote. The Assembly controlled basic decisions, but it in turn was controlled by a representative council, the *boule*. This body was responsible for foreign affairs and civic defense, and it was controlled in turn by the *prytaneis* which was a type of executive committee. Finally, the *epistatai* presided over the *prytaneis* and each member of the *espistatai* served for a day as the chairman of the executive committee. The *boule* consisted of five hundred members chosen by lot and every citizen could expect to be a member at least once during his lifetime. Administrative tasks were shared widely by citizens who held office briefly and then retired, and unpaid volunteers performed many of the minor tasks. The basic principle of political leadership that had developed by the middle of the fifth century was that no citizen is better qualified than any other citizen to direct public policy - i.e., Greek citizens are the state. There was little distinction between public and private because there were hardly any limits on the claims the state could make on the citizenry. However, the citizens received substantial advantages from their citizenship[10], and therefore they restricted its limits. (Gouldner, 1965).

---

[10] Many of these advantages resulted from the Athenian community perspective that incorporated egalitarian measures directly into its articulation of civil status. Such measures included selecting some offices to be filled by lot and paying officeholders for their services, allowing the appeal of judicial decisions to a popular tribunal, requiring wealthy citizens to provide expensive liturgies or services to the community, discouraging conspicuous private consumption, and by subsidizing brothels to ensure that every heterosexual male citizen had access to a sexual partner regardless of wealth. (Tétreault, 1998)

While ancient Greece left us with the legacy of participatory democracy, Rome left a law of citizenship that provided an institutional reality of a society that worked for many centuries. (Riesenberg, *op. cit.*: 56) Whereas Greece had one class of citizens beneath which there were several categories excluded from citizenship, Roman citizenship was based on the categories of patricians and plebeians. The patricians constituted about ten percent of the population at the beginning of the Roman Republic and they governed the plebes - free men, but citizens of a lesser status. Citizenship to the patrician meant the possession of large tracts of agricultural land and control of the magistracies which guaranteed access to virtue, honor, and state contracts. For the plebeian, citizenship meant some standing in the human community and recognition by their patrician betters that they merited the law's protection regarding their property, persons, and honor. It also meant access into Rome's structure of magistracies and assemblies. Many plebes had been educated in Rome's moral code that stressed responsibility and service.

Through patronage Rome's dual citizenship permitted oligarchy to work behind the republican facade which allowed the great families to retain control for generation after generation. The Roman elite was skillful in granting its allies and conquered peoples some or all the rights of citizenship. They used patronage to control the political side of citizenship while allowing many thousands commercial and personal privileges. (*Ibid.*:64 -5) Thus Roman citizenship was used to confer special rights and make one man more equal than another which illustrates the use of citizenship in promoting discrimination. But because Roman citizenship entailed private rights without concomitant public obligations, the empire eventually fell. In the words of Thomas Hill Green:

The citizens of the Roman empire were loyal subjects; the admirable maintenance of private rights made them that; but they were not intelligent patriots; and chiefly because they were not, the empire fell. That active interest in the service of the state, which makes patriotism in the better sense, can hardly arise while the individual's relation to the state is that of a passive recipient of protection in the exercise of his rights of person and property. While this is the case, he will give the state no thanks for the protection which he will come to take as a matter of course, and will only be conscious of it when it descends upon him with some unusual demand for service or payment, and then he will be conscious of it in the way of resentment. If he is to have a higher feeling of political duty, he must take part in the work of the state. He must have a share, direct or indirect, by himself acting as a member or by voting for the members of supreme or provincial assemblies, in making and maintaining the laws which he obeys. Only thus will he learn to regard the work of the state as a whole, and to transfer to the whole the interest which otherwise his particular experience would lead him to feel only in that part of its work that goes to the maintenance of his own and his neighbour's rights. (Green, 1895:130)

Between the Republic's expansion and the late Empire when citizenship was used to create bonds and hold society together, citizenship was essentially a status which conferred certain legal powers and benefits. It was also a moral demand that arose out of a historical and contemporary ethical belief and practice that defined a man's responsibilities toward his *patria*. It also came to represent a class culture which was the end result of a "class" education that was based on a curriculum common throughout the city-state world. A citizen knew who he was, and his rights and responsibilities were clear. All of this foreshadowed the medieval world. (Riesenberg, *op. cit.*:73)

Within a monarchy the concept of citizenship had no meaning; instead, there were subjects and the crown. With the disintegration of the Carolingian and Holy Roman Empires, there arose numerous counts, dukes, and barons that jealously protected their rights and privileges from the encroachments of the crown. One consequence of this stable but somewhat fluid dualistic power system was the rise of independent towns and trade centers. Royal power was limited by charter within town walls and patterns of self-government developed. Inhabitants of the city began to acquire fundamental rights and obligations and they developed attributes of the citizen as opposed to the subjects outside. It was in this environment that capitalism began to flourish. (Downing, 1988) In fact the early notion of citizen is simply the inhabitant of a city. (Turner, 1990) A certain level of economic activity may have been necessary for the institution of citizenship to develop, for it is only when there is a physical city of some size, the use of money and rudimentary banking that there was something to tax and defend. It is also under such conditions that there is some authority that makes citizenship valuable. (Riesenberg, *op. cit.*: 110)

If the social disruption resulting from of war and military occupation provide the social context which often has the unintended consequences of expanding citizenship rights (Turner, 1994:329), then it is not unusual that the modern conception of citizenship has its origins in the French Revolution. This cataclysmic event which lasted from 1789 to 1799 included internal conspiracy, rebellion and counter-rebellion, and warfare in response to external threats. The end result was the overthrow of the monarchy and the establishment of a republic. Citizenship was the central concept which embodied the claim of the whole population to inclusion. (Parsons, 1994) This claim was expressed in the catchwords of the Revolution: liberty, equality, fraternity. *The Declaration of the Rights of Man and the*

Citizen nullified the divine right of kings and enumerated the inalienable rights with which "all men" were endowed.

The controversy over taxation without representation was the main issue that led to the American Revolution. Up until this time the citizenship of the colonists was that of British subjects, but upon independence they became citizens of the respective states. The unquestioned achievement of the American Revolution was the ratification of the Constitution in its immediate aftermath. Citizenship is not defined in this document, but it is a requirement for election as a senator or representative. A representative must have been a citizen of the United States for seven years and an "inhabitant" of the state in which he is chosen. (Art. I, Sec. 2) The requirement for senator is nine years. (Art. I, Sec. 3) The President must be "a natural born citizen, or a citizen of the United States at the time of the adoption of this Constitution" (Art. II, Sec. 1) Article III extends the judicial power of the United States to controversies "between a state and citizens of another state, between citizens of different states, between citizens of the same state claiming lands under grants of different states, and between a state or the citizens thereof and foreign states, citizens or subjects". (Art. III, Sec. 2) Citizenship is made uniform in Article IV Sec. 2 which extends the privileges and immunities of citizens in the several states to the citizens of each state.

The first ten amendments enumerate rights which extend to persons and the people. Thus, these rights appear to be more basic than citizenship rights, but they obviously did not extend to slaves that were counted as three-fifths of a person for apportionment purposes. In the Dred Scott case (*Scott v. Sanford*, 60 U.S. 393) citizenship was defined as (1) white persons born in the United States as descendants of "persons, who were at the time of the adoption of the Constitution recognized as citizens in the several States and became also citizens of this new political body", and (2) those who, having been "born outside the dominions of the United

States", had migrated thereto and been naturalized therein. The states were able to confer state citizenship upon anyone residing therein, but they could not make such a person a citizen of the United States. The "Negro" or "African race" was ineligible to attain United States citizenship from a state or by virtue of birth in the United States, even as a free man descended from a Negro residing as a free man in one of the States at the date of ratification of the Constitution.

After the Civil War citizenship was extended to former slaves and the right to vote could not be denied citizens based on race or color. The Dred Scott decision was abrogated by the Civil Rights Act of 1866 and then in the Fourteenth Amendment. The Fourteenth Amendment preserved the distinction between national and state citizenship. (*Slaughter House Cases*, 83 U.S. 36) A child born in the United States of Chinese parents who were ineligible to be naturalized is a citizen nevertheless. However, citizenship does not extend to children born in the United States of diplomatic representatives of a foreign state, children born of alien enemies in hostile occupation, and children of members of Indian tribes subject to tribal laws. (*United States v. Wong Kim Ark*, 169 U.S. 94) The government of the United States, of any state, or any other governmental unit cannot shift, dilute, or cancel anyone's citizenship. Once acquired, citizenship is kept unless the holder voluntarily relinquishes it. (*Afroyim v. Rusk*, 387 U.S. 253) A corporate body is not a citizen of the United States. (*Paul v.* Virginia, 75 U.S. 168) Although women were citizens of the United States, it was not until 1920 that women were given the right to vote.[11]

---

[11] In a recent work Michael Schudson (1998) discusses four models of citizenship in the United States: (1) it has its origins in the politics of assent, (2) it passes through a democratic transition in the politics of parties, (3) it becomes impersonal with the politics of information, and finally (4) it is privatized by the politics of rights. The types of authority by which society is governed is seen as evolving from personal authority, to interpersonal authority, to impersonal authority. The

The idea of citizenship has had a very uneven development over the centuries. The reasons for this have to do with the fact that citizenship has been manipulated for political purposes to be inclusive or discriminatory depending upon which approach was expedient. Although the general trend since the French Revolution has been toward greater inclusiveness, the issues surrounding citizenship remain murky. There has also been a shift in emphasis over the centuries from citizenship obligations to citizenship rights with the trend toward inclusiveness focused primarily on citizenship rights. This trend involved a shift from a public (community) orientation to a private (individual) orientation. Aristotle's formulation of citizenship involved a rigid separation of polis from *oikios* - public from private. For Aristotle citizenship was available only to those who could rule themselves, and this was not possible unless they were able to rule over their household which included the persons and things therein. Aristotle made it quite clear that only a few adult males could achieve a fully developed humanity, and this could only be accomplished in the public realm where persons interacted with persons. (Peacok, 1994)

The focus of citizenship shifted from persons to things in Roman jurisprudence which was developed by the jurist Gaius. Gaius viewed the world as divisible into "persons, actions, and things", and citizenship became a legal status that denoted a member of a community defined by law. Citizenship carried with it rights to certain things (possessions), immunities, and expectations. Thus, there could be as many different definitions of "citizen" as there were kinds of law. It is here in Roman jurisprudence that we can locate the origins of possessive individualism, a development that would come to fruition with the rise and supremacy of the market.

---

ownership of the public sphere has also shifted from control by gentlemen, to control by organized parties, and finally to control by interest groups.

Citizenship became a practice of rights which involved pursuing one's own rights and assuming the rights of others in various communities (legal, political, social, and cultural) that were developed for purposes of this kind. One strength of this idea is that it enabled the definition of an indefinite series of interactions between persons and things which could be restated as rights. These rights opened the possibility of defining new persons as citizens and thus bringing them into the world of politics. However, the Aristotelian citizen ruled and was ruled in turn which meant that he determined the laws by which he was bound. The Roman citizen, and citizens since then, could only appeal to Caesar, but were not involved in the actual making of the laws or determining their content. Thus, the history of the concept of citizenship in Western thought can be thought of as an unfinished dialogue between the Aristotelian ideal and the Gain real - of persons interacting with persons and persons interacting with things. (*Ibid.*)

Some insight into where this dialog may be headed can be seen in the present state of citizenship. The current status of citizenship in the United States is that the citizen is an economic conception, not a political one. That is, the ideal of citizenship in its current manifestation is one of a fully functioning participant in the market, but not as a participant in the polity. The market citizen derives her citizenship from the private realm of the workplace, not the public realm of the political. A market citizen is much more closely identified with his place of employment and the interests of his employer than he is with the interests of his local community or the larger interests of the state or nation. A market citizen is much more closely identified with the problems encountered in her profession than she is with the problems created by political conflict. The archetype of the market citizen is the middle manager in a corporate entity.

The idea of market citizenship, as opposed to political citizenship, raises some serious problems regarding the public

19

sphere. A corporation is a creation of the state, but it is not a citizen. As such, it has no rights of citizenship. Although it is composed of individual employees who possess individual citizenship, the corporate entity assumes an identity and interests of its own which are market driven. Although it can sue and be sued and is subject to law, it does not possess ethical personality. It is neither moral nor immoral; it is simply amoral. It's whole reason for being is to create wealth and make a profit for its shareholders. It is the paragon of private interest. Any ethical attributes an individual corporation may exhibit derive from its individual members, not the corporate entity itself.

The problem of market citizenship is that individual citizens are preoccupied with their role in the market and have abdicated their role as participants in the political community. The definition of good citizenship is to be employed in the market. A good citizen is one who works and is not on welfare. A good citizen's value is measured in terms of wealth, not social utility. The abdication of the citizenship role on the part of the individual has created a vacuum in which the corporation and various interest groups, in all their various manifestations, have rushed in and coopted citizenship for particularistic ends, primarily private economic gain. The role of political citizenship has been assumed by the corporation and redefined in terms of corporate interests. The individual, under the guise of individualism, has surrendered her political identity and is left with a vacuous shell of citizenship restricted to the realm of commerce.[12]

The loss of individual political citizenship is particularly frightening in the current trend toward globalization. Globalization is privatization writ large. Just as corporations within the nation state

---

[12] Riesenberg (1992) discusses the skillful manipulation of Roman citizenship which left political control with patricians while allowing others to participate in commerce.

have managed to privatize much of the public sphere, globalization may supplant the nation state itself. If this happens, the consequences in terms of the worldwide degradation of the natural environment and the distribution of resources is frightening to imagine. Competition among the multi-nationals will reign supreme and the political identity of the individual will be a thing of the past. Under these conditions what will be the meaning of liberty, equality, and justice? This is one of the reasons that the citizenship dialog needs to be brought to center stage.

The idea of citizenship as an unfinished dialogue involves internal complexities along political, sociological, psychological, and philosophical dimensions. A rather extensive literature has been developed on this topic, and I shall draw upon this literature to develop a model of citizenship. The purpose of the model is to visualize the potential next stage of citizenship development, a development that could lead to the restoration of the citizen, not as a participant in the economic market, but as an active participant in the political marketplace of ideas. This development is a necessary precursor to the creation of a culture of democracy.

Models of Citizenship

Citizenship theory has developed along two lines that may be described as classical or political theories and more contemporary or sociological theories. The political theories may be characterized as those ideas which seek to explain and justify the process by which human beings create that institution known as government which regulates their affairs such that they can live with one another. Sociological theories seek to explain the more informal processes by which human beings form that aggregate known as society through which they define their identity and relations with their fellow beings. Obviously, there is no clear demarcation between these two

21

sets of ideas. The literature on citizenship involves elements of both and other areas such as psychology also enter in. At the root of all of this are various philosophical orientations dealing with questions of good and evil and their meaning in terms of how we behave and the institutions we create.

Alegandro (1993) has identified five historical views of the citizen: (1) a legal construction aimed at order (Montesquieu), (2) as a productive member who always obeys the law (Kant), (3) as an active participant in a constant search of communality (Rousseau), (4) a divided self caught between isolation and shared goals (Tocqueville), or (5) a self divided between abstract freedom and concrete oppression (Marx). There are five models of citizenship that correspond to these views: (1) citizenship as universality and as a legal construction (Ralph Dahrendorf, Peter H. Schuck, and Rogers M. Smith), (2) citizenship as neutrality (John Rawls), (3) citizenship as community and participation (Benjamin Barber, Michael Walzer), (4) citizenship as amelioration of class conflicts (T. H. Marshall), and (5) citizenship as self-sufficiency (Lawrence Mead, Robert Fullinwider) (*Ibid.*:13-14)

These models will not be reviewed here, but a few them will be referenced in the pages that follow. However, before presenting my own model of citizenship, I will review two others here. My reason for doing this is that the model I will develop lies between these two. The first is a model that attempts to account for how citizenship rights arose in different historical contexts in Europe. The second is an attempt at constructing a model of European citizenship that transcends the nation. Since the model I am going to present is a model of the next possible stage of citizenship development within a nation state, it can be said to lie between these two models.

Bryan Turner (1994a) has developed a heuristic typology of four political contexts within which the institutionalization of citizenship rights can occur. The typology is based on two dimensions. The first is whether citizenship rights are seen as being granted from above by a political authority or whether they are seen as being demanded from below by individuals and groups. The second dimension is a cultural tension between the private realm of the family and the public arena of political action. The general model is outlined in Figure I.

Figure I General Typology		
Below	Above	
A Revolutionary Contexts	B Passive democracy	Public Space
C Liberal Pluralism	D Plebiscitary authoritarianism	Private Space

Applying this model to specific cases, Turner found that the Revolutionary French Tradition corresponded to case A, the passive English case corresponded to B, American liberalism corresponded to C, and German fascism to D. The significance of this model lies in its usefulness in understanding the relationships in the cultural organization of public and private space.

The second model proposed by Gerald Delanty is a model of a future European citizenship. (Delanty, 1997). This is a model in which expanded inclusion and substantive citizenship participation will be based on residence, a multilevel European polity, a recognition of the idea of collective citizens, and a reflexive

European identity. Residence, instead of place of birth, as a basis of citizenship will reduce the exclusionary aspect of citizenship. The multilevel polity is one in which national governance will be supplemented by subnational and supranational entities. Collective citizens will be regions and social movements that currently only have lobbying power. Thus, citizenship will no longer be reduced to the individual actor. The reflexive identity is a self-critical identity that is not based on the dichotomy of Self and Other but occurs within the limits of 'constitutional patriotism.' These ideas of what could constitute a future European identity point one way toward a future world citizenship.

Before the idea of world citizenship can be addressed in any meaningful manner, citizenship needs to evolve within the context of the nation state into a secular ethic that can create a culture of democracy. The model I will present below is intended to outline how this next stage of citizenship can be constructed. Thus, it is a model that lies between the two models outlined above.

Citizenship as a Secular Ethic

In the model I will develop, citizenship is conceived as that secular ethic which defines the membership role in the political community as an inter-related nexus of rights and obligations which provides the cooperative context within which the competition of politics takes place. It is the homeostatic mechanism that maintains the dynamic equilibrium in the tension between the individual and the community. It is also a hermeneutic ethical filter through which the culture we inherit from past is interpreted and re-interpreted into the present on its evolutionary path toward the future. I am going to use this definition of citizenship to develop a model of citizenship. The model will be developed in two parts: citizenship at the level of the individual and citizenship as a collective enterprise. The purpose of this model is to conceptualize a potential next stage of citizenship development within a society that has achieved a highly articulated form of elective government. This stage is seen as a necessary development that must occur before any meaningful form of world citizenship can evolve. It is also a stage that must occur if a culture of democracy is to evolve. The term "citizenship" will be applied to both this next potential stage of development and to its current manifestation. Hopefully, the intended meaning will be clear from the context obviating the need for qualifiers. Figure II shows the general outline of citizenship as I have defined it.

Figure II
General Model

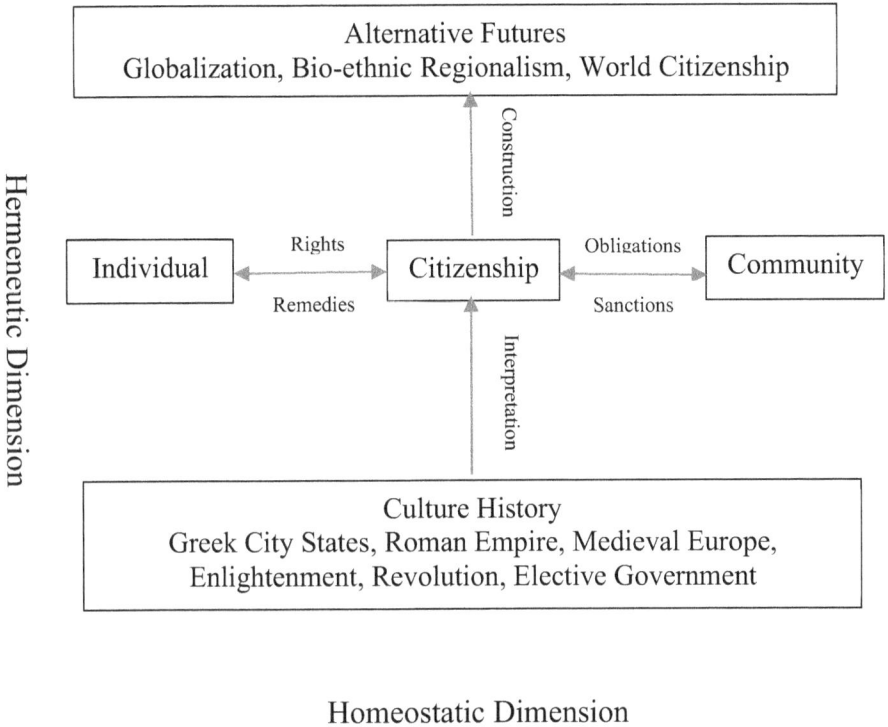

Homeostatic Dimension

The Homeostatic Dimension

The horizontal dimension occurs in the present represents the tension between individual and community. This tension is mediated by citizenship which is the manifestation of individual identity in the political community. A healthy citizenship creates political homeostasis by providing a context of cooperative competition. The idea of cooperative competition is a difficult idea to explain. It includes the sociological tension between individual and community and the philosophical tension between liberalism and civic republicanism - a tension that Habermas (1996) attempts to resolve through his theory of communicative action. The political ramifications of these dimensions will be explored in the pages that follow.

Politics has been defined various ways. Harold Laswell defined it as the art of who gets what, when, and how. (de Leon, 1993) Michael Shapiro defined it as the sanctioned control of what constitutes valued experience. (Bowers, 1987) Robert Bellah (1994) provides three definitions: (1) it is a matter of making operative the moral consensus of the community - the politics of community, (2) it is the pursuit of differing interests according to agreed upon neutral rules - the politics of interest, and (3) it is statesmanship in which the high affairs of national life transcend particular interests - the politics of the nation. It is about solving problems that affect, in common, people who may have little else in common people with all the imperfections to which humankind is prone. (Matthews, 1996) I shall define it as the art of goal directed public communication. This is a broad definition that includes all types of community. Politics occurs in any community and its complexity depends upon the type of community in which it occurs. Citizenship, however, does not refer to membership in any community, but in a particular type of community which is normally the nation state, but may be a subdivision thereof. The political community consists of citizens as individuals, and as such, it encompasses the other communities of which society is composed.

Goal direction initially arises out of self-interest, but, in a healthy society, it becomes transformed into community interest. Self-interest, sooner or later, finds itself in conflict with other self-interest. The regulation of self-interest such that it does not destroy the common interest is what the art of politics is all about. In

27

authoritarian regimes this regulation can occur through the dominance of a particular self-interest. In democratic regimes this regulation occurs through a blending of self-interest into the common interest. This is an extremely difficult balancing act which is precisely why citizenship is so important.

The ideas of homeostasis and community can be clarified by looking at ecosystems in general. An ecosystem is a community of organisms interacting in a given physical environment. Within this community various species may be in competition with one another, and within a given species, individuals may be in competition with one another. But this competition is occurring within a larger context that is cooperative. It is the cooperative context that allows the ecosystem to maintain itself. A political community consists of other communities that may be in competition with one another, and within each of these communities, individuals may be in competition with one another. To be in balance, however, the ethic of citizenship is required to provide the cooperative context for this competition.

Without the arena of citizenship, the art of politics cannot be presented. Like any good arena, the arena of citizenship needs easy access, comfortable seating, good lighting, high quality acoustics, and an ample stage for participation. The arena of citizenship is politically constructed on a floor of sound constitutional principles built upon a solid foundation of justice. Upon this floor the legislative auditorium with the executive stage and the judicial roof are erected.

The Hermeneutic Dimension

"We hold these truths to be self-evident, that all men are created equal, that they are endowed by their creator with certain inalienable rights, that among these are life, liberty, and the pursuit of happiness". If the history of the American republic, and western history in general, has made anything self-evident, it is that these

28

self-evident truths are anything but self-evident. The core values of equality, liberty, and justice have a fluid meaning. They are interrelated, they mean different things to different people, and they mean different things in different historical periods. Interpreting this fluid meaning is the task of hermeneutics. Philosophers have wrestled with these concepts over the centuries in the search for absolute ethical principles that are universal in their application. The assumption is that once discovered, these principles can form the basis for the creation of a just society.

The fact that concepts such as equality, liberty, and justice have been philosophically problematic for centuries is in part a result of the fact that language is not sufficiently precise to articulate the conceptual meaning of the value. At one level an individual experiences an intuitive "feeling" that a particular event or act violates one or more of these values. But when he or she attempts to generalize the sentiment into a comprehensive philosophical concept that is universalizable, the task of doing so becomes a virtual impossibility. The reason for this has to do with the concept of limit. The idea is similar to the idea of a limit in the calculus. Through infinitesimals a limit is approached every more closely, but it is never attained. In human affairs the idea of a limit is more complicated because in addition to the difficulty of approaching the limit at any one point in time, the limit may shift about through history. But looking at the limits of fundamental values from many points of view at various points in time may allow us to achieve a better understanding of their meaning. There is a tension inherent in looking at fundamental values from different points of view. The trick is to manage that tension such that the process is homeostatic. The individual and collective limitations to our knowledge become evident when a theory or doctrine held to be sacrosanct is displaced by a new theory or doctrine arising out of the discovery of new information. When it comes to the search for ethical truths, the fact that human beings are both individually and collectively inconsistent

29

places another roadblock in the path of the search for truth. However, this does not mean that the search is in vain, but it does mean that the value sought after is fluid - i.e., it is limited in its application and its contours change through time.

An analogy may help explain the problem. Imagine one of these values as bounded in an amoebae shaped space that moves through space and time. No one observer can get at the "truth" because what she sees from her vantage point is different than what an observer at a different vantage point at the same point in time sees. What she sees is only a portion of the surface manifestation of an internal value. In addition, the amoebae are moving, so what is seen changes in time. This is not to say that the value that is in there does not have universal significance, but it does imply that it has limits and that these limits may change with the passage of time. The value of liberty is an example. The 'paradox of freedom' is that if we are to have more freedom, we must limit its exercise. If complete freedom is allowed, the tyranny of the strong over the weak will eventually result in less freedom for all. It is taken for granted that there is an absolute liberty to reproduce. However, what will happen when the exercise of this liberty leads to overpopulation that will threaten the survival of the species? We are already witnessing the consequences of the exercise of this liberty in terms of urban sprawl, congestion and its attendant stress, and environmental degradation. Added to this is the fact that children are being born into environments in which they receive no support and have little chance of becoming citizens in the most minimal definition of the term.[13]

The task of hermeneutics is to interpret the historical meaning of values such as liberty, equality, and justice to construct their meaning in the present. It is a collective endeavor which

---

[13] The limits to liberty are about to be tested with respect to fetal alcohol syndrome. Legislation has been passed in several states that calls for restricting the liberty of an expectant mother who abuses alcohol to prevent damage to her fetus.

requires interpreters from different points of view. No one interpreter, no matter how acute her powers of observation and interpretation, is competent to grasp the whole. But when combined with the observations and interpretations of other reasonably competent interpreters, it becomes possible to construct a meaning that 'works' in the present.

The vertical dimension, then, represents citizenship as a temporal hermeneutic endeavor. It is this dimension that connects the individual citizen to his or her past through the process of interpretation and provides him or her with a worldview of the possible future of humanity through ethical evaluation of the past and present. In discussing this hermeneutic dimension, I shall draw upon the work of Roberto Alegandro (*op.cit.*,1993). In other models of citizenship, the citizen is the *object*, not the *subject*, of citizenship. (*Ibid.*:34) Alegandro conceptualizes citizenship as a hermeneutic construction in which citizenship should be viewed as a space of memories and struggles where collective identities are played out, and as a space where citizens decode languages and practices. In this perspective citizenship consists of (1) a hermeneutic horizon, (2) a practice, and (3) a textual reality. The hermeneutic horizon is a worldview nurtured by traditions, institutions, and practices with open boundaries for reflection. The practice is a way of life that assumes social, but not necessarily shared norms, and pursues certain, but not necessarily common, goals within a shared historical contest. The textual reality is a web of principles and practices addressed to a plurality of readers. (*Ibid.*:37)

Alegandro's conception of citizenship implies a public realm that ought to make room for the construction of meaning, not the quest for meaning. The political is not a place where citizens search for a meaning that is already given and longing to be discovered, but the political is a space where interpreters construct meanings thereby carrying out the interplay between themselves and their surrounding circumstances. (*Ibid.*:72) To become a citizen one must be engaged

31

in a fourfold dialog: a dialog with other citizens, a dialog with the past, a dialog with institutions and traditions, and a dialog with himself or herself. (*Ibid.*:76) Hermeneutic citizenship interprets traditions, dialogues with past generations, remembers atrocities, and constructs moral standards that deny legitimacy to other moral or political conceptions.

Alegandro's argument may be summarized as follows: there is a plurality of guiding principles founded in finite interpretation implied in the hermeneutic historical consciousness. Every generation seeks to discover its own truths, but each generation is not starting with a clean slate. It begins with an already given accumulation of facts and truths that the living cannot brush aside at will. Even though our principles are historical outcomes, a plurality of guiding principles can be ascribed to human history, and within these principles there will be malleable boundaries enclosing the analysis of moral values, but the *worth* of those values will be rendered immutable in the light of our principles. (*Ibid.*:113-19) Alegandro also points out that rights were not constructed to defend a universal cultural identity, but they were designed to defend different economic interests, different talents, and different moral outlooks. The principle of men as universal bearers of rights was not meant to protect a universal identity of interest or a universal culture, but the universality of different talents, levels of property, and religious perspectives. (*Ibid.*:124-5)

There are various apparitional alternatives beginning to appear on the hermeneutic horizon of the future, some of which are not particularly attractive. Although it is virtually impossible to predict the future, it may be useful to consider some of the alternatives that may be possible. The one that appears most likely given current conditions is globalization, and, as I have already mentioned, this prospect is not appealing. The trend toward globalization is marked by the increasing concentration of economic resources within the multi-national corporation. The trend is accelerated through the merger of these entities, and the concentration of economic power that results will eventually supplant the nation state. Citizenship, if there is to be such a thing under these conditions, will be defined by membership in the corporation rather than the state. The market will reign supreme unregulated by anything other than the profit motive of the multi-nationals. The consequences of institutionalized greed on such a scale for the global environment, the growth of poverty, and the deprivation of individual liberty are frightening. The history of the nation state is a history of the abuse of political power, but there have been institutional developments designed to contain political power and prevent its more overt abuse. These developments have resulted in the formal recognition of human and citizenship rights. What will happen to these in a world dominated by private corporations? The nation state, as ugly as its history has been, is still our best hope for the future.

A second alternative, although not particularly likely, is for the nation state to evolve into some sort of world federation based on bio-ethnic regionalism. Under this scenario the various regions of the earth that constitute identifiable ecosystems would become self-governing entities united in a world federation. In this scenario ethnic diversity would be included in the much broader conception of biodiversity, and the dependence of our species on other life forms would be formally recognized. Citizenship in this future would consist of a primary citizenship in the ecological region with a secondary citizenship in the world at large. This is a highly developed form of citizenship far removed from current practice.

Delanty's model of a future European citizenship discussed above is another alternative. In this case group citizenship replaces individual citizenship and it is the collective citizen that replaces the individual. This alternative is unattractive because, aside from the problems associated with the definition of collective citizens, the individual becomes submerged into the group. The fact that interests other than the interests of the market are recognized in this model makes the model more attractive than globalization. However, the individual is still reduced to the uni-dimensional identity of the group and individual liberty is supplanted by group identity.

Another possibility is a world citizenship that can be envisioned as arising out of the convergence of various regional citizenships each of which tends to cluster around a reference society unique to that region. The general idea is outlined in Figure III.

Figure III
Convergence Toward World Citizenship

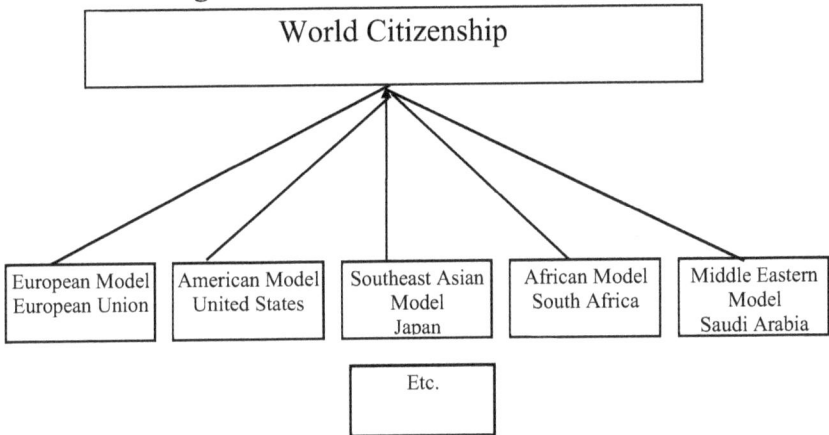

This possibility envisions citizenship taking different forms in various regions of the globe that gradually converge into some form of world citizenship. The form that citizenship takes in each region would be compatible with the indigenous culture of the region. For example, the type of citizenship that would develop in Southeast

Asia in which the bi-lateral extended family is a major social unit would take a different form than in the western cultures with their emphasis on individualism.

The hermeneutic dimension of citizenship points to the fact that whichever alternative emerges in the future is a direct result of what we do in the present, and what we do in the present is shaped by how we interpret our past. The future is not given, it is created, and how it is created will be determined, in no small part, by how we conceive of ourselves as citizens and how we act on that conception.

The homeostatic dimension occurs in the present and may be viewed as the expression of the role of citizen while the hermeneutic dimension may be viewed as the expression of a culture through time. This cultural expression, however, is filtered through the present. The homeostatic dimension requires linguistic fluency, the hermeneutic cultural fluency. It is important to remember that the conception of citizenship in Figure II is a schematic representation of a complex entity. In reality role and culture cannot be neatly separated into separate orthogonal dimensions. Nor can the individual be neatly extracted from the community within which he or she is embedded. With these caveats in mind, I shall proceed to discuss citizenship as an attribute of the individual and as a collective enterprise. But first, I must briefly mention what I mean by democracy.

Democracy

I am going to use a variant of Lincoln's definition of democracy as a government of citizens, by citizens, and for citizens. Lincoln's use of the word "people" is too broad, because it could be construed to include legal and illegal aliens. Since citizenship defines membership, it also defines inclusion which implies exclusion.[14] Even though the historical trend has been toward greater and greater inclusion, the fact that we belong to different cultures and nation states means that most of the the world's population is excluded from membership in any one particular nation state. A right of citizenship implies a right to membership in a nation state, but not necessarily a particular nation state.[15] Democracy, in this Lincolnesque variation, does not exist in any nation state. What does exist in those states that have come closest to the democratic ideal is some form of elected government which achieves the minimal level of citizen representation that is captured in the term "representative government". The development of citizenship is what will make the transformation to a democratic culture possible.

The essential element of democracy is it is a *process* of political choice which includes all citizens as equal participants. Political choice is decision making which organizes political space and regulates social space. Basically, it is choice about what kind of society we want to live in. The how of how this is done is what distinguishes democracy from other decision methods. The first characteristic of the process is that it is *collective*. Collective

---

[14] The problem of inclusion is in part a problem of appropriate exclusion–i.e.it is as much about filtering out the various moral toxins that threaten to contaminate public reason as it is about honoring differences we ought to honor. (Callan, 1997)
[15] Humanity cannot grant membership, but nation states can. Citizenship is permanent, exclusive, and direct - i.e. states cannot revoke membership acquired by birth, membership is possible only in one state, and no other loyalties can interfere with the state-citizen relationship. (Halfmann, 1997)

There are arguments for open borders on ethical grounds. Carens (1995), for example, argues that citizenship in Western liberal democracies is the modern equivalent of feudal privilege - an inherited status that greatly enhances one's life chances. Theories that postulate some kind of assumption about the equal moral worth of individuals which treat individuals as prior to community leave little basis for distinctions between citizens and non-citizens. None of the arguments for open admission adequately deal with the problem of numbers.

decision making means that it is the body of citizens that does the deciding. In ancient Greek city states and New England town meetings, the body of citizens as a whole made political decisions. In a polity of any size it is impractical for the body of citizens as a whole to make decisions, so various forms of *representation* have been developed as a substitute for direct citizen participation. This idea is explored in the next chapter, but here I want to distinguish between *representative, or elective, government* and *representative democracy*. Elective, or representative, government involves nominal citizen participation through various electoral devices. Representative democracy involves direct citizen representation based on random selection.

A second characteristic of the democratic process of political choice is that it is *public*. Publicity means not only that the decision making is conducted in a forum open to the inspection of all citizens; it also means that the informational resources upon which the decision is based are available to all citizens. This leads to the third characteristic of the democratic process of political choice. The decision that is reached must be *justifiable*. When a decision needs to be made, the information available may be incomplete, contradictory, and difficult to interpret. Thus, *reasons* are required to legitimate the decision that is reached.

It is the process of political choice that is institutionalized in government. Choice necessarily involves conflict. A solitary individual making a choice may experience conflict; collective choice is rife with conflict. So democracy also involves processes of resolving conflict. Conflict arises in two main areas - conflicts that are involved in the decision itself and conflicts that arise out of the interpretation of the decision. Policy conflicts are resolved by representatives in the legislative branch. Interpretative conflicts are resolved in the judicial branch. Interpretative conflict resolution in a democracy must meet the criteria of publicity, impartiality, and justifiability.

Democracy is distinguished from other forms of decision making in that each individual citizen participates equally in policy making and conflict resolution. Obviously, this statement appears to be nonsense when applied to a large modern society such as the Unites States. But it becomes possible when the idea of representation is defined in terms of giving each citizen an equal probability of participating. Equal probability coupled with the idea of absolute rotation in office will achieve the truest form of citizen representation in the long run. Thus, representation becomes the primary obligation of citizenship. I have not mentioned the executive and administrative functions of carrying out the decisions of the body of citizens because citizens are not directly involved in this activity. Citizens make policy, resolve conflicts, and monitor the execution of policy. The day-to-day management of government is left to the administrative branch.

These ideas, which sound so simple, have been, and are, extremely difficult to elucidate and even more difficult to achieve in practice. Democracy is more than a type of government; it is a culture–a way of behaving and a system of values–that represents the diffusion of the political into the social. It is created through the practice of citizenship which builds the social bonds that make democracy possible. A culture of democracy is a culture in which both the value of the individual and the community are preserved. The tension between individual and community are resolved through citizenship as a political endeavor. This means that the political must have primacy over the economic and social. (Negative reactions that may be invoked by this statement are a result of the fact that the political has been corrupted by the economic and social.) The first attribute of a culture of democracy, then, is the primacy of the political.

A culture of democracy does not simply appear as a result of random historical processes, it is created through human volition. It must be consciously initiated and constantly *practiced*. Democracy is a *learned* form of social behavior. It is the practice of the politics of democracy that results in the culture of democracy. What would a *culture* of democracy look like? A culture of democracy will grow out of political democracy which is the practice of citizenship. Without getting into details, a culture of democracy will have the following attributes. The first is *a reasonable distribution of wealth and resources* that achieves distributive justice to the extent that the basic needs of all citizens are met and provides enough discretionary income to allow them to develop their unique natural talents and interests. A second characteristic is a *reasonably high level of education* achieved by most citizens, a corollary of which is an informed citizenry, politically and culturally. A third characteristic is *civility* which involves a high degree of tolerance for diversity within the unity of a common citizenship. Civility implies respect for the *expression* of ideas with which we may not agree. A fourth characteristic is *ecological balance* with nature which implies a stable population and economic restraint. The final characteristic which is a result of these other characteristics is *adaptability*. This characteristic implies that the practice of democratic citizenship involves continuous learning and does not lapse into mere habit.

Even though I have not dealt with the problems of what is *reasonable*, it is not particularly difficult to at least imagine a culture which has these characteristics. These characteristics are idealistic, but not necessarily utopian. After all, the attributes of a better society must arise within the human imagination before there can be any hope of achieving a more just society in practice. The challenge before us in the next century is to develop the democratic imagination into a practical reality. The transition from government by ascription to government by election was a radical change in a society accustomed to habits instilled by monarchy. Compared to monarchy, election was a courageous step forward in the evolution toward democracy. It required a level of trust in one's fellow citizens that must have felt strange after centuries of dependency on the monarch for political decisions. It also required adjustment to the idea of regular changes in political leadership. Today these features are so routine that citizens take them for granted. From today's vantage point the institution of election is so firmly instilled in the public thought that the idea of the citizen-legislator is regarded as bizarre even though it has been around since ancient Athens. But to citizens born into a world in which citizenship means governing, the obligation to govern will already have been established as a cultural norm, and from the perspective of such citizens, the practice of election will be viewed in hindsight as a manifestation of democratic adolescence–a necessary, but turbulent, period of development that their society was fortunate enough to have survived.

Individual Citizenship

At the individual level citizenship may be seen as a progressive development of the role of citizen from status to internalized ethic. An individual is born into citizenship status, he or she then develops the citizenship role which results in the internalization of citizenship values. Individual citizenship involves the acquisition of rights and the discharge of obligations. Remedies and sanctions serve as corrective mechanisms when rights are violated and obligations are not fulfilled. These four elements constitute the framework within which the citizenship role develops. The development of the citizenship role can also be seen as a process of maturation in which the individual's social orientation shifts from a focus primarily upon him or herself to a focus upon the broader social community. The schematic for individual citizenship is presented in Figure III.

Figure III
Individual Citizenship

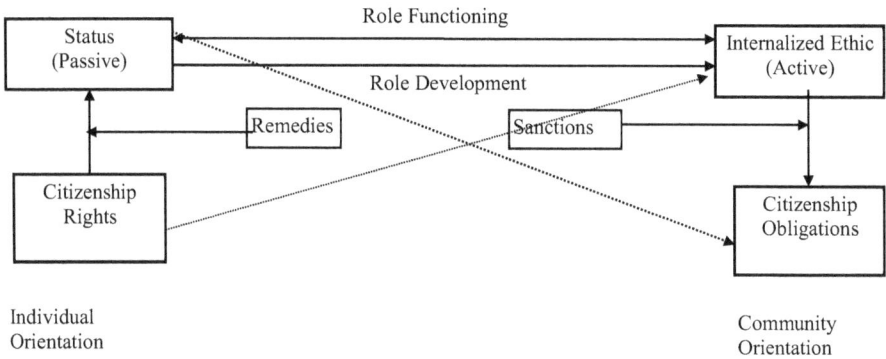

The schematic is intended to represent individual citizenship as a role in which there is tension between an orientation to the self and an orientation to the community. That tension is represented by the double headed arrow which represents the citizenship role functioning in a social environment. The development of the role, however, is represented by a one headed arrow that progresses from status to internalized ethic. This is intended to illustrate the fact that citizenship status is acquired at birth, but a process of socialization and education is required to transform the status of citizenship into an ethic of citizenship that is internalized. Rights are primarily acquired with the status of citizenship which is represented by the upward directed arrow. Obligations, on the other hand, arise out of some form of motivation from within the individual. This motivation may be as simple as a fear of the consequences of not performing the obligation, or it may arise out of a deep commitment to a salient value. The downward directed arrow represents the performance of

41

obligations as arising from motivation within the individual. The dotted arrow lines represent the fact that some obligations arise out of the status of citizenship (e.g. military service when there was a draft) and that some rights are acquired after the citizenship role has developed to some degree (e.g. the right to vote). Remedies are applied primarily to the enforcement of rights and sanctions are applied to the enforcement of obligations. These two items represent a coercive element in citizenship, and it is this element that requires justification so that it may be legitimated.

The status of citizen is acquired at birth or through the process of naturalization and is primarily a matter of legal definition.[16] Citizenship status confers membership in the political community and it is defined primarily in terms of rights. The concept of *rights* is fundamental to the idea of citizenship. T. H. Green defined a right "as a power of acting for his own ends, - for what he conceives to be his good, - secured to an individual by the community, on the supposition that its exercise contributes to the good of the community." (Green, 1895:207) "A right is a power claimed and recognized as contributory to a common good. A right against society, in distinction from a right to be treated as a member of society, is a contradiction in terms." (*Ibid.*: 110) Thus, "[N]o one therefore can have a right except (1) as a member of a society, and (2) of a society in which some common good is recognized by the members of the society as their own ideal good, as that which should be for each of them. The capacity for being determined by a good so recognized is what constitutes personality in the ethical sense; and for this reason there is truth in saying that only among persons, in the ethical sense, can there come to be rights;...."(*Ibid.*: 44) A right has three elements: it (1) is a power secured to an individual, (2) by the community as a result of membership in the community, and (3) its exercise contributes to a common good. Rights are created by being

---

[16] 8 USC §§1401, et seq. provides this definition.

exercised which generates the capacities associated with them. For those who accept them, rights define the essential limits of the social order beyond which social existence itself is under threat. (Barbelet, 1994)

Citizenship rights are that subset of rights which derive from membership in the political community. Membership in the political community implies a liaison between participation in government and subjection to it; citizenship does not exist when the separation between the governors and the governed is total and permanent. Thus, the citizenship of a person is defined by the degree to which he can control his own destiny within the political community. (Leca, 1994) The modern notion of citizenship in sociological terms has its origins in the work of T. H. Marshall who described citizenship in terms of the expansion of rights from civil rights in the 18th Century to political rights in the 19th to social rights in the 20th.[17] There is

---

[17] Marshall asked the question how social class which is based on inequality could be reconciled with citizenship which is based in equality. His answer was that the modern drive toward social equality as the latest phase in the evolution of citizenship allowed for the democratic legitimization of status differences provided they did not cut too deep, were not based on heredity or privilege, and occurred within a united population. The evolutionary phases of citizenship were the civil, political, and social, and each roughly corresponded to a separate century. The reconciliation with the capitalist class system was achieved in the social phase of the 20th Century through the combined effect of three factors: (1) compression at both ends of the scale of income distribution, (2) expansion of common culture and experience, and (3) enrichment of the universal status of citizenship. (Marshall, 1994) These trends no longer hold, particularly in the United States. By 1980 the average chief executive officer of a Fortune 500 company earned 72 times as much as the average teacher and 93 times as much as the average factory worker. In 1990 the CEO of United Airlines earned 1272 times as much as a starting flight attendant, and the chairman of Time-Warner took home more than $78 million. Although this amount could keep the average clerk on the payroll for 1500 years, the following year 600 of Time's employees were let go. Between 1978 and 1987 the number of people who worked full time and remained poor increased 57%. These facts fly in the face of the Founding Fathers' idea that there

43

also historical evidence that war and social dislocation have had the unintended consequences of extending citizenship rights because they erode conventional patterns of social interaction which provides the context within which this expansion can occur. (Turner, 1994:Vol. I,329)

Citizenship has, for the most part, been truncated at the status stage; citizens are spectators who vote. Between elections they are served, for good or ill, by the civil service. (Walzer, 1995:164) Citizens are disengaged and alienated from politics. Individuals and organizations are focused on making a living, profit maximization, and the mission statement. One source of this disengagement is the fact that our society is fractured by the division of labor and economic competition which is a direct consequence of liberalism. Liberalism in various variants is the predominant social philosophical doctrine in the West. In brief outline, it has the following features: (1) the notion that human beings are atomistic, rational agents whose existence and interests are ontologically prior to society, (2) the idea that society should ensure the freedom of all its members to realize their capabilities, (3) an emphasis on human equality, (4) the conception of the individual as the 'bearer of formal rights' designed to (a) protect him from interference from others and (b) to guarantee him the same opportunities or 'equal access' as others, and (5) the idea of the free individual as a competitor. Liberalism began in capitalist market societies and can only be understood in terms of the social and economic institutions that shaped it. (Dietz, 1994)

Citizenship under liberalism is more of an individual economic activity than a collective political endeavor. Individual worth is measured in terms of capital accumulation and profit maximization instead of attributes such as moral character. There is

---

should be enough income inequality to give people an incentive to work, but not enough to demoralize them. (Coontz, 1997)

44

an emphasis upon the obligations of citizenship, but these obligations are defined in economic instead of political terms. There may be passing reference to a citizen's duty to vote, but the primary focus is on developing one's capacity to participate in the economy so as not to be a drain upon the economy through the welfare system. The rights of citizenship are likewise focused upon economic as opposed to political participation[18]. At the individual level of citizenship, liberalism has resulted in possessive hedonism and at the collective level in the commercialization of the political. The end result of liberalism is aptly captured by Alegandro:

> With the principle of moral autonomy, the modern era invented the individual, endowed him with moral sovereignty and placed him in a specially designed realm, the private, where he could display all his unexplored potentialities, while following the dictates of his reason. The individual thus displaced the citizen as a central object of reflection, and the citizen became the public garb of the self. The citizen was no longer an all-encompassing category enjoining both the public and private. The individual came to be the new universal principle. (Alegandro, *op. cit.*:11)

While the concept of rights is primarily associated with citizenship as a status, the concept of *obligations* is involved in the idea of citizenship as an internalized ethic. Citizenship as internalized ethic results in a shift in focus from individualism to a community orientation. The difference between these two orientations is analogous to the liberal-individualist conception on the one hand and the civic-republican conception on the other

---

[18] The first amendment right to free speech was originally intended as a political right, but recent Supreme Court decisions in this area are emphasizing commercial as opposed to political speech. (cf. Buckley v Valeo, 424 US 1 (1976))

(Oldfield, 1994, Habermas, 1996). In liberal-individualism citizenship is considered a status. This private conception of citizenship gives rise to the language of needs and entitlements. In civic republicanism, which is Aristotelian in its origins, citizenship is considered a practice which gives rise to a language of duties, and individuals are considered free only when their duty and interests coincide. Individuals are not thought of as being prior to society in the civic-republican tradition, and they have no sovereign or overriding moral authority. Citizens must be empowered to act which means that they require many of the freedoms and entitlements that appear as "rights" in the liberal-individualist conception, but they also need access to a forum in which potentially everyone can take part. Although citizenship in its current manifestation is primarily a status, the purpose of this model is to visualize a more fully developed citizenship in which it becomes an internalized ethic and the citizenship role becomes a mediating mechanism that maintains homeostasis in the tension between the individual and the community. The challenge is to construct the role of active citizenship such that citizenship sits on top of all the other roles and integrates them all into the individual's identity.

When the citizenship role is fully developed, citizenship becomes an internalized ethic that has its source in a psychological dimension of role development that involves intangible emotional elements. It revolves around feelings of what is just or unjust, of belonging or not-belonging, of being in control of one's destiny, and of the feeling of being a good citizen.[19] This is akin to the notion of "conscience" which provides the internal motivation to behave in an ethical manner. Citizenship in this sense is a motivator that drives the individual to perform those behaviors that we call "responsible citizenship". These can be seen at a rudimentary level when individuals are motivated to perform voluntary public service on

---

[19] See for example John Sohtter (1993).

behalf of their communities. In a more fully developed citizenship, we will see citizens actively participating in the political arena in the pursuit of goals that "are in the public interest". The idea of citizenship as an internalized ethic is similar to what Leca calls "citizenship for itself" which has the following characteristics: (1) the belief that the intelligibility of the political world to each citizen is logically linked to the liaison between participation in government and subjection to it, (2) empathy, the ability to put oneself in the place of other citizens in order to understand, not their strategies and structures of preference, but their interests and justifications, (3) civility which allows for the management of the tension between social differentiation and common membership.(Leca, 1994:155-6) It is also dependent on what Habermas refers to as a *"forthcomingness* of a kindred background of motives and beliefs of citizenship geared toward the commonweal - motives and beliefs that cannot be enforced legally". (Habermas, 1994)

The development of the citizenship role as an internalized value is also analogous to Kohlberg's cognitive-developmental theory of moral reasoning. Moral reasoning, according to Kohlberg, develops through three levels consisting of six stages. Stage 1 morality is oriented toward punishment and obedience. Stage 2 is oriented toward instrumental relativism. These two stages constitute the preconventional level of moral reasoning. The conventional level consists of stage 3 which is an orientation toward interpersonal concordance and stage 4 which is oriented toward law and order. The highest level of moral reasoning is the postconventional level in which reasoning is autonomous and principle based. It consists of the fifth stage which is a legalistic orientation toward the social-contract. A sixth stage has been added in which moral reasoning is oriented toward universal ethical principles. (Kohlberg, 1985) It is important to stress that this theory is a theory of moral reasoning, not moral behavior. Although there is a strong correlation between the two, his

47

research suggests that there are factors other than moral reasoning that enter into moral behavior. (Kohlberg, 1987)

Moral behavior requires four processes: (1) interpreting the situation in terms of recognizing possible actions and how each action affects all the parties involved, (2) applying moral ideas to the situation to determine what one ought to do, (3) choosing among moral and non-moral values to decide what one actually intends to do, and (4) implementing what one intends to do. (Rest, 1985) Rest found that moral judgment is highly correlated with formal education, but what it is about formal education that produces the effect is unknown. This appears to be at odds with Kohlberg's (1987) finding that maturity of moral judgment is not highly correlated with IQ or verbal intelligence which implies distinguishing moral reasoning from logical reasoning. These findings have implications for the development of citizenship as an internalized value and the role of education in that development. Kohlberg makes an important point regarding education, namely that while other factors may affect moral behavior, moral judgment is the only *moral* factor in moral behavior. Change in moral judgment is irreversible - once attained, a higher stage is never lost, but moral behavior is situational and reversible in new situations. There is something in the process of education that promotes moral judgment, but whatever it is, it does not appear that standard measures of academic achievement will indicate its presence.

Citizenship as an internalized ethic is not to be confused with the sentiment of patriotism. Patriotism is defined as love for or devotion to one's country. It is an emotion that appeals to the symbols and rituals that represent one's national identity. It has often been hostile to moral criticism of the nation, and this hostility to criticism has often taken the form of hostility to criticism of the status quo. Patriotism, in its more negative forms, has found expression in chauvinism and xenophobia. However, it is rooted in the political community and its emotional appeal is a source of social solidarity. While the liberal moralist may conclude that patriotism is a source of moral danger because it places the nation beyond rational criticism, the patriot may conclude that liberal morality is a source of danger because it renders our social and moral ties open to dissolution by rational criticism. What has been confusing in the United States is that the nation has been identified both as an object of patriotic regard and as a source of liberal morality.(MacIntyre, 1995:226-8)

In his discussion of the acquisition of the sense of justice and the other moral sentiments, John Rawls provides some insight into how citizenship could become an internalized ethic. The sense of justice proceeds from love and trust being bestowed upon the individual as a child which leads to feelings of friendship and mutual obligation which in turn lead to the recognition that he or she and those he or she cares for are the beneficiaries of just institutions. This three step process results in the internalization of a sense of justice. (Rawls, 1971:458-474) Citizenship as an internalized ethic is less intuitive and emotive than the sense of justice and it develops later in life. While the rudiments of citizenship may begin to form within the family, a fully developed citizenship is dependent upon the system of education. The formation of citizenship starts with the moral values and sentiments that are acquired in childhood, but its development as an internalized ethic is a dialectical process that begins with the exposure to conflicting ideas in school and continues throughout life. It is in the school that citizenship as a collective endeavor is developed.

Collective Citizenship

Although citizenship is an attribute of the individual, it is basically a collective endeavor. At the most basic level it defines who is included and excluded from membership in the political community. However, it has the potential to do much more than merely define who is included in the political community. If it is developed into a secular ethic that provides the cooperative context for political competition, it will serve as the normative glue that holds the political community together. It will provide a common identity to our diversity. More importantly, it will provide the means through which we can begin to control our evolution. In this section I will develop a model of collective citizenship for the next stage of its development. The model is presented schematically in Figure IV.

Before I discuss the schematic, I need to explain the distinction between *public* and *private*. Any activity that occurs in a social setting is public in the sense that what occurs is visible to two or more persons.[20] A purely private activity is something that an individual conducts by himself in solitude. Private space therefore is non-social and it is mainly filled with matters pertaining to individual thought and conscience. Social space is the space of social activity which usually arises in the family and ranges from informal associations such as friendships up to highly formal associations such as one's position in a career or profession. Social space by definition is public; the degree of publicness depends upon the number of people involved and the relative position of the association in the social order. Any organization is a public entity; the term "private organization" is an oxymoron. Privacy is an attribute reserved to individuals. The use of the terms "public" and "private" is confusing because the idea of privacy is, in addition to matters of individual thought and conscience, associated with the idea of an area of social space within which relationships occur that is protected from the intrusion of any party outside the relationship. The ideas of the public and private become more confusing when the

---

[20] Another definition of public, as opposed to private, is that which has no immediate relation to any specified person or persons, but may directly concern any member or members of the community without distinction. Thus public law is distinguished from private law in that the former affects the whole community whereas the latter affects some definite person or persons. (Barry, 1965)

political dimension enters in. This confusion is partly the result of the application of the private - a property of individuals - to organizations, particularly corporate entities. Organizations are socially created and are therefore public. Some organizations, such as corporations, are not only created socially, but they are endowed with legal personality by governments and given some the characteristics of individuals and other unique characteristics of their own. The conflation of the attributes of individual citizens with corporate entities has radically distorted the notions of public and private.

The concepts of "positive" and "negative" liberty are often associated with public and private autonomy. Positive liberty is the liberty to be master of oneself, to be a subject and not an object, to realize goals of one's own conception as an actor, not one who is acted upon. Negative liberty pertains to the idea that there should be a certain area of individual freedom that must on no account be violated. Positive liberty pertains to the "freedom to" and negative liberty to "freedom from". As a set of rights negative liberty developed concurrently with capitalism and is more a property of modernity than democracy. The clashes between privatizers and political activists that result from these different conceptions of liberty represent not conflicts of style, but vastly different moral orders.[21](Tétreault, 1998)

I will use the term *pure private space* to refer to that area of social space involving matters of individual thought, conscience, and solitary activity. *Social private space* will refer to that are of social

---

[21] Tétreault discusses three scenarios–benign and malign capitalism, and the triumph of the saints–as cases that result in the shrinkage of the power of the nation-state. Her analysis of the sociology of Puritanism as an extreme example of positive liberty that forbids the private autonomy that was the defining quality of the ancient citizen is particularly interesting in terms of the potential impact of Islamic and other fundamentalist religious movements on the realm of the political.

space within which social actors engage in relationships and activities that are protected from the intrusion of others. *Political private space*, an unfortunately somewhat goofy term, will refer to that area of social space which impacts and is impacted by the political but is outside the political realm proper. Political private space occurs in political space and is public. The only reason I am calling it private is because it occurs outside the public sphere proper which is what I call *political public space*. The activities that occur in political public space are supposed to be visible and accessible to all citizens without restriction. It is within this space that citizens create the kind of society they want to live in. The activities in political private space may be of political concern but are not public in the sense of being politically public. These are conceptual distinctions; in reality there is no clear spatial demarcation between them. The variety and complexity of social relationships and the discourses that occur within and between them keep such boundaries in a constant state of flux.

I need to distinguish the difference between the terms *privacy* and *privatization*. Privacy has to do with the right of the individual to be left alone. It refers to those areas and activities within which the individual is to be free from state interference and the interference of other individuals. Privatization refers to the transfer of public activities to private organizations. It is a term with a heavy ideological loading that emphasizes a preference for the private market over public agencies and private goods over public goods. It is fair to say that in the current social environment in the United States, there is an increasing political preference for privatization and a decreasing political emphasis on the individual's right to privacy.

In the diagram citizenship is represented by two normative membranes. I shall use the term *normative membrane*[22] to mean that set of social norms, values, and beliefs that define a political culture. It is analogous to de Tocqueville's *mores*, but it is more limited in the sense that it applies to those customs, beliefs, habits, and standards of behavior that pertain to political activity as opposed to general social activity. The outer membrane, which I will call the *citizenship minimum*, defines membership in the political community. The inner membrane, which I will call the *citizenship frontier*, defines participation in the political community. It is important to remember that membranes are filters that regulate flow across them - i.e., these membranes are normative filters that serve a regulatory function.

The diagram also contains irregularly shaped objects that represent various organizations, associations, and institutions. Each of these is encased in a membrane which serves to define its membership. Those organizations that are inside the citizenship frontier are politically public entities and those outside are politically private. The area inside the citizenship frontier shall be referred to as *political public* space or the public sphere and the area outside as *political private* space or the private sphere. The total area shall be referred to as *political* space or the political sphere. Political activity may arise in political private space, but since this is a model of a democratic citizenship, it cannot produce a political result without its entering political public space. *Social* space is not represented in the schematic since this is a model of collective citizenship as a democratic institution instead of a social system. Social space may be viewed as including but extending beyond political space - i.e. political space is embedded in social space. The social, then, is both inside and outside the citizenship minimum and social forces from both locations impinge upon it. The model of citizenship is highly

---

[22] This term was coined by Bryan Turner, I believe.

differentiated which means its various components are clearly demarcated and arranged in an orderly manner - i.e. it represents the political aspect of a well ordered society. This implies that it takes quite a bit of moral effort to create and maintain a democratic citizenship - i.e. citizenship must be an active endeavor. When citizenship becomes passive, entropy results and the whole system tends toward disorder.

Figure IV
Ideal Collective Citizenship Model for a Nation State

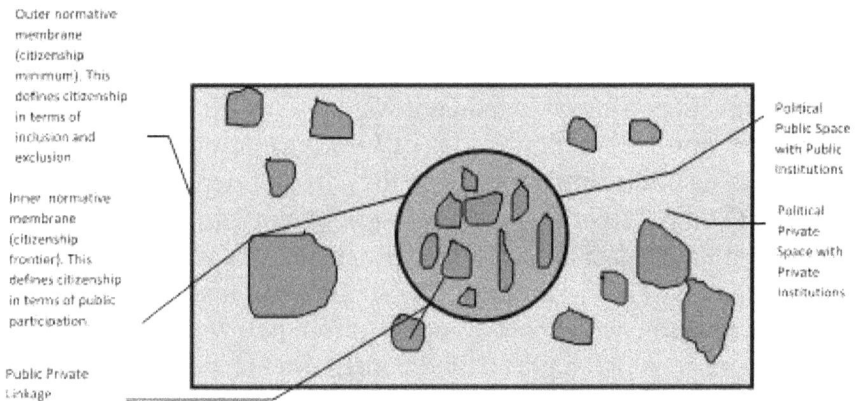

Outer normative membrane (citizenship minimum). This defines citizenship in terms of inclusion and exclusion

Inner normative membrane (citizenship frontier). This defines citizenship in terms of public participation.

Public Private Linkage

Political Public Space with Public Institutions

Political Private Space with Private Institutions

The Citizenship Minimum

The citizenship minimum defines membership in the political community and as such it specifies the minimum content of citizenship. For most citizens, membership is acquired at birth. In the

54

case of immigration, it is assumed that the naturalized citizen became a citizen to attain the benefits of citizenship and therefore accepts the requirements of citizenship.[23] The minimum content consists of moral, cultural, and social minima. It is based on the proposition that "every society is judged, and survives, according to the material and moral minima which it prescribes to its members". (Newman, 1928:80) The moral minima specify those ethical standards all citizens are expected to accept in their dealings with one another. These are usually formulated in terms of duty and obligation. The cultural minima specify what citizens are entitled to expect from one another in terms of behavior and conduct. These are specified in terms of common customs and modes of behavior that one can assume to expect from his fellow citizens. The social minima refer to basic goods (which may not always be material goods) that are regarded as necessary for citizenship. These are usually formulated in terms of rights.

To prevent confusion, we do not want to conflate the idea of the citizenship minimum with the idea of *human rights*. Human rights are outside of citizenship because they are not tied to the nation state. (Turner, 1994b) Nor do we wish to conflate it with the idea of natural law and/or natural duty. The model of citizenship that is proposed here will have to arise out of some form of social contract which can be envisioned as arising from below through citizen initiative in which a preexisting constitution is modified to construct a citizenship on this basis. A proposal for moving in such a

---

[23] In the United States the cases of African Americans and Native Americans are problematic because of historical circumstances. Although birth is not a voluntary act, it is assumed that acceptance of one's citizenship is. Likewise, immigration is assumed to be voluntary and the children of immigrants are assumed to be citizens on a voluntary basis. The fact that African Americans were brought here not only involuntarily, but under conditions of slavery and that Native Americans were conquered people present obvious difficulties, particularly in light of the continuing racism exhibited toward these two groups.

direction will be presented in Chapter IV. I do not mean to imply that the idea of human rights (or the idea of the rights of animals and nature generally) are unimportant. Quite the contrary, they are essential for human survival and evolution. My point is, however, that the question of human rights and the ecological crisis we are in cannot be effectively addressed until an ethic of citizenship is developed that will lead to the creation of a culture of democracy. The citizenship minimum includes human rights.

The Moral Minima

The moral aspect of the citizenship minimum has its origins in the notion of a social contract which is a device designed to deal with the precarious nature of human existence. The idea of a social contract provides a theoretical explanation for the formation of human cooperation. It requires that the parties that create it do so from a position of equal bargaining power. The source of this equality lies in the fact that each individual is born into a world of risk.[24] From the moment of birth each individual faces both the certainty and risk of death. Death is certain in that it will happen to everyone and the risk of death is the uncertainty of when it will occur. The fact that there is wide variability in the distribution of natural talents and abilities does not obviate the fact that we are all equal in the face of death. Another source of equality lies in the limitation of our individual and collective knowledge. Although our knowledge is increasing and it has enabled us to extend the limits of our natural abilities, it is still limited.[25] Since we all share in this

---

[24] Turner (1994b) defends the universality of the concept of rights through a sociology of the body which is derived from two related ideas–that human beings are ontologically frail, and that social arrangements or institutions are precarious.
[25] Callan (1997) points out that much of the pluralism that permeates our social world is not a consequence of evil or folly but is inherent in the limits of human reason. We must gain an appreciation of this fact and learn to imaginatively enter

limitation, it is another source of equality. The assertion of the equal moral worth of all individuals is based on the fact that all of us must make choices within the context of limited knowledge and scarce resources, and we are all subject to judgment for the choices we make. It is through these evaluative judgments that our ethics develops. It is this process which gives us moral personality. Rawls defines a moral personality as one which has a sense of justice and a conception of the good. When these moral powers are combined with the powers of reason, moral personality is transformed into citizenship. (Rawls, 1997)

The Rawlsian citizen is one that is both reasonable and rational. Rationality involves the pursuit of one's ends in an intelligent manner. The rational applies to how these ends are given priority as well as to the choice of means. It does not possess that particular form of moral sensibility that underlies the desire to engage in fair cooperation. This is where the reasonable enters in. The reasonable involves a willingness to propose and abide by fair terms of cooperation and it involves the willingness to recognize the burdens of judgment and to accept the consequences for the use of public reason in directing the legitimate exercise of political power in a constitutional regime. The burdens of judgment involve an account of the sources, or causes, of reasonable disagreement. The following are basic elements in the conception of the citizen: the citizen has moral personality (i.e. the two moral powers of the capacity for a sense of justice and a capacity for a conception of the good) and the intellectual powers of judgment, thought, and inference. The citizen is also assumed to have, at any given time, a reasonable comprehensive view that provides a determinate interpretation of the good and the capacity and ability to be a cooperating member of society over a complete life. Citizens display

---

ethical viewpoints in deep conflict with our own to accord them the respect they are due.

a readiness to propose fair terms of cooperation that others may be reasonably expected to endorse and are willing to abide by the terms agreed to. However, the burdens of judgment limit what can be justified to others which results in the affirmation of reasonable comprehensive doctrines only. Finally, citizens possess a "reasonable moral psychology".[26] Citizens are not assumed to have equal capacities, but they must possess, to at least an essential minimum degree, the moral, intellectual, and physical capacities that enable them to be fully cooperating members of society over a complete life.

Equal citizens for Rawls have the capacity to be cooperating members of society over a complete life, but they have different, incompatible, and irreconcilable conceptions of the good. Cooperation is secured through adherence to the principles of justice[27] which allows for the formation of an overlapping

---

[26] This moral psychology consists of the following elements: (1) citizens have a capacity for conceptions of the good and of justice as fairness and a desire to act as these conceptions require, (2) when the social practices or institutions are perceived as just, they are willing to participate in these practices provided they have reasonable assurance that others will do their part, (3) if other persons "with evident intention" strive to do their part, citizens develop trust and confidence in them, (4) this trust and confidence becomes stronger and more complete as the success of cooperative arrangements is sustained over a longer time, and (5) the same is true as the basic institutions framed to secure the basic rights and liberties are more firmly and willingly recognized. (1997:86)

[27] These principles were originally stated as follows in Theory of Justice:
First Principle
      Each person is to have an equal right to the most extensive total system of equal basic liberties compatible with a similar system of liberty for all.
Second Principle
      Social and economic inequalities are to be arranged so that they are both:
            (a) to the greatest benefit of the least advantaged, consistent with the just savings principle, and
            (b) attached to offices and positions open to all under conditions of fair equality of opportunity.

consensus. The Rawlsian view is one of neutrality toward
reasonable comprehensive doctrines. Even though these doctrines

---

First Priority Rule (The Priority of Liberty)
> The principles of justice are to be ranked in lexical order and therefore
> liberty can be restricted only for the sake of liberty.
> There are two cases:
>> (a) a less extensive liberty must strengthen the total system of
>> liberty shared by all
>> (b) a less than equal liberty must be acceptable to those with the
>> lesser liberty.

Second Priority Rule (The Priority of Justice over Efficiency and Welfare)
> The second principle of justice is lexically prior to the principle of
> efficiency and to that of maximizing the sum of advantages; and fair
> opportunity is prior to the difference principle. There are two cases:
>> (a) an inequality of opportunity must enhance the opportunities
>> of those with the lesser opportunity
>> (b) an excessive rate of saving must on balance mitigate the
>> burden of those bearing this hardship.

General Conception
> All social primary goods--liberty and opportunity, income and wealth,
> and the bases of self-respect--are to be distributed equally unless an
> unequal distribution of any or all of these goods is to the advantage of the
> least favored. (1976:302-3)

In Political Liberalism they are restated as follows:
> a. Each person has an equal claim to a fully adequate scheme of equal
> basic rights and liberties, which scheme is compatible with the same
> scheme for all; and in this scheme the equal political liberties, and only
> those liberties, are to be guaranteed their fair value.
> b. Social and economic inequalities are to satisfy two conditions: first,
> they are to be attached to positions and offices open to all under
> conditions of fair equality of opportunity; and second, they are to be to
> the greatest benefit of the least advantaged members of society. (1997:5-
> 6)

These principles are derived by representative citizens behind the veil of ignorance
in the original position. This means that the parties do not know their station in life
or what generation they belong to. It is assumed that they will choose justice as
fairness over various principles of utility. In Political Liberalism the
comprehensive theory of justice is limited to its political conception.

are irreconcilable and incompatible, the duty of public reason makes it possible for citizens to reach agreement over constitutional essentials which are derived from the background conception of political justice. The moral duty of citizenship - the duty of civility - is for citizens to explain to one another how the principles and policies they advocate that are derived from their comprehensive doctrines can be justified by the political value of public reason. Understanding how to conduct oneself as a democratic citizen requires an understanding of the ideal of public reason. (1997:217-8) For Rawls public reason is similar to the reason a judge must use in reaching a decision in the case that is before the court. When arguments are reasonably balanced on both sides, the citizen cannot resolve the question with appeals to his or her religious or philosophical views because to do so would be to violate the principle of reciprocity and thus violate the moral duty of the office of citizen. From the point of view of public reason citizens should vote for that ordering of political values that to them are sincerely reasonable. (1997: lv)

This notion of public reason is somewhat vague and it has limits. Rawls recognizes three limits to public reason: (1) there is more than one reasonable answer to a particular question, (2) there is a difficulty as to what is meant by a citizen voting his or her sincere opinion, and (3) it may be difficult to specify when a question is resolved by public reason. (1997:240-4) These limitations derive from the fact that our knowledge is limited and that no one philosophical, religious, or scientific doctrine or theory has a monopoly on the truth. Rather our conceptions of the truth are in constant flux. It is the recognition of this fact that may give us the humility to recognize the virtue of public reason as a collective endeavor. By bringing to the table our various individual perspectives and ideas on what constitutes the good in the context of public reason, it becomes possible to develop and promote a public interest that combines the preservation and protection of individual liberty and equality on the one hand and the ideal of social cooperation on the other. Thus, public reason is one aspect of the moral minima of citizenship and operates primarily on the homeostatic dimension.

Alegandro's hermeneutic conception of citizenship goes beyond the Rawlsian notion of neutrality in that it asserts the necessity for a minimalist conception of the good in addition to Rawls's freedom and equality. His ideal of public reason is directed toward the goal of understanding. For understanding to come about, "one does not go about identifying the weaknesses of what another person says in order to prove that one is always right, but one seeks instead as far as possible to strengthen the other's viewpoint so that what the other person has to say becomes illuminating." (Alegandro, *op. cit.*:89) The minimalist conception of the good life as a source of norms to guide both society and the individual's goals is implied in this hermeneutic understanding of interpretation and memory. (*Ibid.*:97)

What is sought here is an overlapping consensus on what constitutes the good. For starters the minimalist conception of the good ought to include freedom, equality, the value of peace, the value of moral excellence, and the value of justice. These principles are socially constituted. For example, the value of moral excellence does not mean that there is agreement on what constitutes moral excellence, but it does mean that there are some boundaries within which moral excellence is to be sought. In other words, this means that society as well as the diverse groups and communities of which it is composed are the source of the critical standards that may help individuals to define their own understanding of moral excellence. In addition to the above, the minimalist conception of the good ought to include: (1) autonomy: the right of each individual to challenge the conventional wisdom and the conventional beliefs in his or her community under (as far as possible) conditions of respect for other individuals, (2) understanding and interpretation: responsibilities that

61

are exercised recognizing the primacy of civil society as the locus of debate and deliberation, (3) social rights: each person should have equal opportunities to develop his or her character through education, sports, cultural activities and to be able to live under decent conditions of living, (4) ecology: each citizen should live in a community that seeks (as far as possible) a balance with nature, and (5) religious diversity: citizens will respect the religious sensibilities of other members of the community so long as the religious principles they hold are compatible with the moral sensibility of the community as expressed by other moral principles. (*Ibid.*:107-11) The minimalist conception of the good allows for the development of a citizenship where prescriptions must be the outcome of deliberation based on a recognition of both the prospect of shared goals and the reality of difference. Politics cannot exclude the possibility of agreement in advance, and citizenship becomes a space of difference and an arena to explore common goals. (*Ibid.*:157-61) The hermeneutic conception of citizenship recognizes that even if the reality of ideologies and dysfunctions between motives and actions is accepted, both political institutions and dialogue may prevent deception from becoming the fundamental trait of the public domain. (*Ibid.*:224)

The moral minima of citizenship, which arise out of the social contract, are the source of political obligation. Where there is no citizenship, the source of political obligation is derived solely from the coercive powers of the state. There may be claims against the state on human rights grounds, but the moral authority for these appeals is outside the nation state and hence outside citizenship. The idea of human rights implies a universal conception of decency that ought not be breached. In citizenship this notion of decency is expanded into notions of civility and reasonableness. Although Rawlsian reasonable comprehensive doctrines are incompatible and irreconcilable outside of politics, the fact of their reasonableness makes possible an overlapping consensus within politics. Thus,

Rawlsian political justice is one conception of the moral minimum of citizenship - a conception that is operative primarily on the homeostatic dimension. Alegandro's minimalist conception of the good relies on a dialog with history and looks toward future generations.[28] It is operative on the hermeneutic dimension. The minimalist conception of the good is arrived at through a dialogical process of interpretation, a process that requires civility and reasonableness.

Civility and reasonableness are not traits acquired at birth. They are instilled in citizens by other citizens. One is born into citizenship, but birth does not create the citizen. What one acquires at birth is the status of citizenship, but social support is necessary for that status to flourish into the role of citizen. Civility and reasonableness are the moral minima necessary to make that support possible and it is through that support that the developing citizen acquires civility and reasonableness and hence becomes a fully cooperating member of society over a complete life.

The Cultural Minima

In addition to the moral minima of citizenship, certain cultural minima are required. While not as important as the moral minima, they are needed to provide a common ground for citizenship and in some respects, they may overlap the moral minima. Since citizenship is a collective enterprise that requires communication, and politics has been defined as the art of goal directed public communication, a common language is a cultural requisite for citizenship. In order for the individual citizen to represent[29] himself in the political community, he or she must be able to do so through

---

[28] Rawlsian justice as fairness considers future generations in terms of the savings principle.
[29] The idea of representation is taken up in greater detail in the next chapter.

the medium of a common language. Collective citizenship is a dialogical endeavor which can only occur through a shared language.

In addition to a shared language, there are certain shared cultural modes of behavior that enable the process of communication. Etiquette is one class of these behaviors. Judith Martin (Martin, 1995) argues that in many everyday situations where there is a conflict between ethics and etiquette, giving preference to etiquette may be the more virtuous choice. She points out that the chance of producing a higher moral good by forcing a confrontation over moral issues is small, but that the chance that these morally righteous transgressions of etiquette will cause embarrassment and hurt feelings is great. She goes on to point out that the tendency to tolerate rudeness and other behavior not prohibited by law has led to the expansion of law to outlaw rudeness. Thus, insult leads to slander and libel and meanness to mental cruelty. The lack of etiquette training in the home has led to increased disciplinary problems in the schools - a problem that I will consider in Chapter III.

The Social Minima

The social minima of citizenship involve the socio-economic level of support necessary for a citizen to be a citizen and the minimum obligation to perform the role of citizen. The socio-economic level of support includes those things that have traditionally been included under the label of welfare. The minimum obligation to perform the role of citizen involves education. Education is both a right and an obligation. It is a right in that every citizen is entitled to it, and it is an obligation in that every citizen has the duty to become educated him or herself and to educate his or her children. Education is a necessary component of the social minima because it is through education that the citizen develops the ability to represent him or her self in the political community. Representation is an obligation of citizenship that will be burdensome. It will require the individual citizen to not only be governed, but to govern when called to do so.

Since the social minima includes both material support and social obligation, the idea of the social dividend proposed by Ronald Dore (1994) makes sense as an alternative to the current notions of welfare that are currently under attack. Dore has introduced the idea of the social dividend as a means to achieving a minimum level of dignity. The social dividend is (1) a monetary payment to all citizens as a citizenship right instead of a means-tested contingency fallback, and (2) all wage income is an extra supplement to this basic citizen wage. This idea would redefine the concept of a right to a job and the social significance of jobs. It destroys the idea that it is only through jobs that men and women have a right to a basic livelihood and that the community has an obligation to provide jobs regardless of economic conditions. One of the problems in capitalist societies is that the individual's search for meaning and self-worth is confined to what he does for a living, a problem which has its source in the Protestant ethic. The function of the citizenship minimum is to provide a source of dignity through the role of citizen independent of other roles and social locations. [30]

The reason that the idea of the social dividend or citizen wage has merit is that the conception of citizenship presented in this model is a political conception that involves political obligations that

---

[30] To work out all the implications of the idea of the citizen wage would involve an intellectual enterprise of Rawlsian proportions raised to a Habermasean order of magnitude, but it would well be worth the effort. Intuitively this idea seems possible if a stable population with a balanced age pyramid is assumed because it is not the abundance of wealth that is an issue, but its distribution. However, it would require an economics based on some other principle than the maximization of utility. Utility maximization cannot continue indefinitely because we are about to bump up against ecological limits. A serious investigation of the citizen wage idea could help us not only learn to live within ecological limits, but also restore the moral constraints on capital by taking seriously the ideas of human dignity and the balance of nature.

extend well beyond our current conception of citizenship obligation. The pinnacle of citizenship obligation is to participate in the legislative process based on random selection. This obligation imposes a significant burden in two ways. First, it is an obvious burden for those citizens chosen to serve. But it is also a burden in that there is the uncertain element as to if and when a particular individual citizen may be chosen. Citizens chosen to serve will be compensated directly for their service. But since there is a risk element that imposes a burden on all citizens, the idea of a social dividend or citizen wage can be partially justified on this basis. The potential duty to serve as a legislator also requires not only the acquisition of a basic education to make competent service possible, but the maintenance of that basic education through ongoing personal development and keeping informed on public issues. These obligations bring us to the citizenship frontier.

The idea of a basic guaranteed income has gained currency since this book was first published, and the persistent question about this idea is how to fund it. One possibility is to create a Citizens' Compensation Fund that would be funded by damages assessed for corporate crime. Corporate crime has never been adequately punished in this country and many of these financial and environmental crimes harm the citizenry at large. Once this fund has sufficient assets to serve as principal, the interest would help fund the citizen wage.

I have outlined the various components of the citizenship minimum. The minimum has its origins in the more basic concept of human rights which are universal and have been internationally sanctioned through the United Nations. They form the basis for citizenship rights. Citizenship is a more restricted concept because it is Western in its origins and it is tied to the nation state. It is also an evolving concept, and it is being examined here in terms of what it should look like *in the next stage of its evolution in the context of a reasonably well functioning elective government.* Thus, it is not being viewed as a universal concept that can be applied across cultures and across time. It is being viewed as the evolutionary vehicle to move from a system of nominal participation based on election to democracy. Human rights which are more basic than citizenship are the necessary foundation of the citizenship minimum. Upon this foundation other rights must be added. Dore's idea of a dignity minimum and a social dividend is a useful candidate for consideration. Other minima need to be considered with respect to education, health care, occupational safety, the protection of the natural environment, etc.

There are two problems that must be dealt with in defining the citizenship minimum: (1) the problem of individuals that lack moral personality, and (2) the problem of the underclass. The first problem relates to the moral minima of citizenship and involves various types of incapacity for citizenship which may result from mental illness, criminality, or other forms of anti-social behavior.[31] Since citizenship is a collective enterprise, the political community must have the right to temporarily or permanently revoke it from an individual when that individual's behavior threatens the citizenship of another.[32] The issue of under what conditions citizenship can

---

[31] Rawls distinguishes between the unjust, bad, and evil person. The unjust person seeks to dominate others for the sake of acquiring wealth or security which are legitimate aims under limited conditions. The bad person enjoys arbitrary power for the sake of social acclaim and the sense of mastery that it gives him. The evil person is motivated by a love of injustice; he delights in subjecting others to humiliation and a sense of impotence and relishes being recognized as the cause of their degradation. (Rawls, 1976:439)

[32] In terms of the model in Figure IV, penal and mental institutions are public institutions with a membrane of extremely limited permeability. Confinement to a penal or mental institution results in the loss of some citizenship rights, and in the case of capital offenses, the loss of citizenship is permanent. In theory these institutions are supposed to restore citizenship through rehabilitation; in practice, unfortunately, there are some individuals that simply lack moral personality and

legitimately be revoked will require clarification after the citizen legislature has been established as discussed below. The problem of the underclass relates to the material minima of citizenship and raises Dore's question of what happens to our concept of citizenship when a growing number of people find themselves relegated to permanent membership in a socially recognizable status of un or underemployment and a substantial number of children are born into that underclass with little chance of getting out of it. (Dore, 1994) The underclass has been described by Heisler as a category that is located outside the class structure whose members, while they "live in a politically defined territory and are thus bodily present, they are not included in ongoing economic, social, and political life. Ultimately the underclass is best conceptualized in terms of its superfluousness and uselessness." (Heisler, 1994:129) In the case of those who lack moral personality, citizenship is revoked *de jure*, but in the case of the underclass it is revoked *de facto*.

The Citizenship Frontier

The citizenship frontier controls participation in the political community. Since sovereignty in a democracy resides in the will of the people, the citizenship frontier provides the mechanisms through which that will is represented in public and political space. I am calling it a frontier because it represents the boundary between political private and political public space. It is the filter through which the private heterogeneous wills of individual citizens are represented in the public sphere. It represents a crossing into the unknown and uncertain. Political public space is a space of turmoil, unpredictability (i.e. risk), and potential conflict. It is also the space

---

cannot be rehabilitated. The whole area of criminal justice is problematic and will not be dealt with here.

where citizenship can achieve its highest expression. It is in this space that the hermeneutics of citizenship takes place, and it is the citizenship frontier that maintains the homeostatic balance between public and private.

The citizenship frontier encapsulates the political public sphere which includes public institutions which are represented by the irregular shapes in the schematic. Each of these institutions has its own membrane that defines its membership. Individual citizens may be visualized as diffusing through the citizenship frontier in both directions at various times in their lives. When citizens enter public space, they do so for the purpose of *representation* - the process of presenting one's self in public for a public purpose. It is the *individual citizen* who represents *him or herself* in the political public sphere[33]. The first time an individual crosses the citizenship frontier is for the purpose of public education. This is when the citizen learns the art of citizenship which involves learning how to present him or herself in public. A citizen may cross the citizenship frontier at other times for such things as jury duty, as a member of an interest group engaged in advocacy, or as an employee of a public entity. All of these instances involve various aspects of the citizen representing him or herself. However, the most important instance is when citizens enter public space to serve as legislators or electors. It is at this time that the citizenship frontier acts as a bridge between the individual and the community. The public will emerge through the ability of citizens to represent themselves as individuals in the legislative body.

It is important to emphasize that citizenship resides in individuals, and it is individuals that cross the citizenship frontier.

---

[33] For the remainder of this chapter the term "public" will refer to the political public sphere and the term "private" will refer to both political private and social space.

Collective entities are not citizens[34] and when they displace citizens, various disease conditions result. Citizenship does have an earned component that is necessary for crossing the citizenship frontier to serve in a legislative capacity. While the citizenship minimum defines membership and applies to all citizens, the citizenship frontier must select citizens that meet a certain level of competency. This level of competency is acquired through the process of public education the primary purpose of which is to enable the student to represent him or her self. A healthy citizenship frontier regulates the flow into public space at various levels, but at the legislative level representatives are selected randomly and can only be excluded if they fail to meet the required level of competence. I will refer to citizens that have met the required level of competence as *public citizens*.

The citizenship frontier has three characteristics: (1) it is highly permeable, (2) it maintains a healthy ratio between the volume of the public and private space, and (3) it provides a clear separation of public and private space. These characteristics are required if citizenship is to create and maintain a culture of democracy.

Permeability

Highly permeable means that there is a regulated free flow, as opposed to a restricted flow, of societal resources across the membrane. I have been using the term membrane to describe the citizenship frontier because it is both a boundary and a filter. It is a boundary which distinguishes public from private space and it is a filter which regulates the flow of resources into and out of public

---

[34] The idea of collective citizenship that Delanty advances in his conception of European citizenship is not appropriate here. The issue of group representation is discussed in the next chapter.

space. The term resource is being used in the generic definition as a source of supply and support. Thus, it is not only the flow of individual citizens that is regulated by this membrane, but other resources including tangible and intangible goods. Public space includes not only public institutions, but public goods. A public good is characterized by its indivisibility and publicness - i.e. there are many individuals who want to enjoy the good, but if they are to do so they must enjoy the same amount. The consequence of these characteristics is that public goods must be produced through the political process rather than the market.[35] There are various features of public goods that result from these characteristics. These include (1) the free rider problem, (2) externality - i.e. their production may cause benefits or losses to others that were not taken into account by those who decided to produce them, and (3) there is no necessary link between the ownership of the means of production and the proportion of social resources used to produce them. (Rawls, 1976:266-70) The classic example of a public good is defense.

The production of public goods requires resource flows into public space. The public goods produced flow back out. I said that the citizenship frontier is a homeostatic normative filter - i.e. it regulates both distributive of justice and retributive justice. It may be thought of as regulating the functions of allocation, stabilization, transfer, distribution, and exchange[36] which are performed by the institutions within public space. The purpose of allocation is to keep the price mechanism competitive and prevent the concentration of

---

[35] Boyte and Kari (1996) point out that public goods are produced by public work. This idea of public work could be tied to the idea of the citizen wage mentioned above, but this requires an examination of the meaning of work in all its nuances which is beyond the scope of the present work (no pun intended).
[36] The first four of these were originally described by Musgrave (1959) and the fifth as added by Rawls (1976:282). They were presented as branches of government, but I am presenting them as regulatory functions of the citizenship frontier.

market power. The purpose of stabilization is to bring about reasonably full employment in the sense that all who want employment are able to find it in their chosen occupation. The transfer function has the purpose of maintaining the social minimum. Finally, the distribution function maintains justice in distributive shares through taxation and adjustments in property rights. The exchange function comes into play when citizens decide to make further public expenditures in the case where the marginal benefit of public goods is greater than that of goods available through the market. In this case no public expenditures are to be made unless the means of covering them are also provided. (Rawls, 1976:275-85)

The citizenship frontier must be permeable in both directions. In the inward direction it is necessary so that citizens can gain access to public institutions and participate in the public sphere. In the outward direction it is necessary so that public outputs reach their intended destination in private space.

Optimum Balance

The second criterion of a healthy citizenship frontier is an optimum equilibrium between the volume of the public sphere in relation to the volume of the whole. The challenge for western societies striving toward democracy is to find this optimum balance. There is no specific rule that specifies what this balance should be because it depends upon circumstances. For example, during a war or other national emergency, public space will increase dramatically. Conversely, in times of peace and relative stability, it will decrease. What is important is that it is the citizenship frontier itself that maintains this ratio. When public space overwhelms the private, the result is totalitarianism. In this case there is no private space and all resources including citizens are regarded as public entities belonging to the state. There are also no private institutions; institutions are extensions of the state into what was formerly private space. The opposite condition is extreme libertarianism or anarchy in which public space is transformed into what Rawls refers to as a private society. The theory of competitive markets is the model of this type of society. No one takes account of the good of others or their property; rather everyone strives toward the most efficient scheme that gives him the largest share of assets. (Rawls, 1976:521-3)

The current tendency toward reducing the size of the Federal Government does not necessarily mean that there is a change in the ratio of public to private; it may only mean that various governmental functions are being shifted within the public sphere. The development of the welfare state in the Twentieth Century has led to an overall increase in the size of government in the Western societies. Within the United States this tendency has manifested itself in the rising tide of expectations in which the citizen has become a consumer of an increasing array of governmental services.[37] When the volume of the public space becomes too large relative to the surface area of the citizenship frontier, the citizenship frontier becomes stressed to the point where it can no longer manage the flow of resources across it. In this case citizens loose control of the public space.

On the other hand, if the volume of the public space is too restricted, the citizenship frontier shrinks to the point where it breaks down because there is inadequate public space to maintain it. It is too early to tell if the rise of the multi-national corporation and the trend toward globalization may lead to a condition like this. However, it is

---

[37] Daniel Bell argues that rising expectations is being turned into a revolution of rising entitlements the consequence of which is that we have no normative commitment to a public philosophy that would mediate private conflicts. The hope for the future lies in the reaffirmation of our past, for without it we cannot know our obligation to our posterity; a recognition of the fact that resources are limited which means a priority of needs over appetite and wants; and an agreement upon a conception of equity which gives all persons a sense of fairness and inclusion in society. (Bell, 1994)

73

possible to imagine parasitic private entities eviscerating the public sphere in such a manner. A multi-national corporation outside the control of any nation state could combine the effects of both internal and external parasitism (discussed below) to bring about this result. A healthy citizenship is the antidote to both a bloating and a collapse of the public sphere. Citizenship as a secular ethic is homeostatic and the citizenship frontier provides a balancing among competing ideologies and philosophies. The resolution of this competition into public policy is what government is all about, and in democratic government, citizenship is the mediator that facilitates this resolution.

Separation of Public and Private

The citizenship frontier must maintain a clear separation of public and private. This is necessary because of the very nature of the public. If the public becomes commingled with the private, it is no longer public. Public implies openness, common possession, and common interest. Openness is necessary for citizenship because without it the citizen cannot be informed. It is through openness that it becomes possible to articulate the public interest. Acts or policies are in the public interest when they either serve all members of a community or advance shared goals such as defense. (Etzioni, 1984:210) When the private invades the public, corruption results.

To clarify the importance of the citizenship frontier in the maintenance of a democratic culture, it will be instructive to consider parasitic pathologies of this vital membrane. These pathologies are located under the general label of corruption. The phenomenon is so deeply embedded in our political culture that the term corruption has lost its normative impact.[38] Privatization is a particular form of

---

[38] Corruption was important in the dispersal of Machiavelli's works. For Machiavelli the goal of the moral leader was to prevent the victory of private

parasitism which is defined as the appropriation of public space by private entities for private gain. In addition to parasitism, there are other conditions, real and imagined, that threaten public space. These include such things as espionage, conspiracy, organized criminal activity, etc. In the political history of the United States, notions of sedition and conspiracy have played a much more prominent role than corruption, and the political response to these perceptions has been a greater threat to our citizenship than any actual act of conspiracy or espionage.[39] My focus here, however, will be on generic parasitism, which is a far more pervasive and insidious, although a less salient, feature of the political culture. Its lack of saliency is one of the main reasons it is so insidious. One of the main reasons for this is the failure to recognize that the entities that benefit from parasitism have managed to legalize most of it. (Etzioni, 1984:18)

Internal and External Parasitism

In the ideal type of democratic citizenship, there will be a clear distinction between the public and private space. To gain an appreciation of what this means, we need to consider a pathological variant of our ideal type - a variant that corresponds to the United States today where special interest politics has distorted the

---

interest over public interest. In his age, when politics was not neatly separated from religion, the term corruption was easily understood with all its negative connotations. (Riesenberg, 1992:196-7)

[39] This fear of internal subversion was most prominent regarding the fear of Communist conspiracy that resulted in Macarthyism. The phenomenon was aptly labeled the "paranoid style of American politics" by Hofstadter. (Hofstadter, 1965) However, it goes back to the very founding of the Republic with the Alien and Sedition Acts of 1798. Talcott Parsons suggests that the fear of Communist conspiracy was a displaced effect that had its origins in the problem of including Catholics in citizenship. The link between them was based on a highly integrated internal political organization with an international orientation. (Parsons, 1994)

boundary between the public and private. Figure V illustrates this condition which I will label as internal parasitism.

Figure V
Internal Parasitism

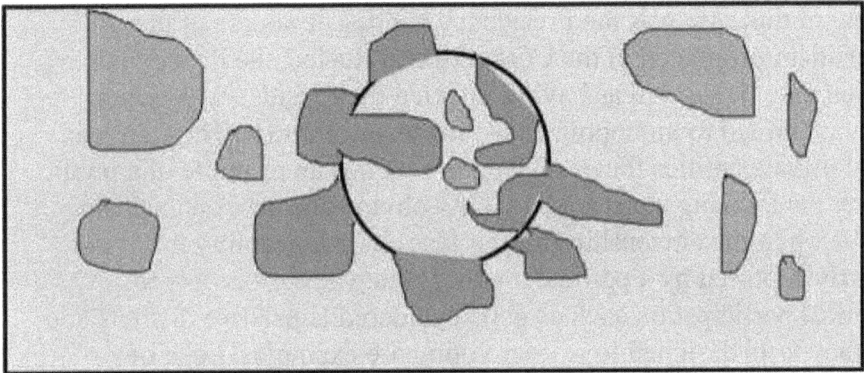

In this condition private organizations have become linked to public organizations in various configurations. The condition is pathological, because it represents an actual capture of a portion of the citizenship frontier which allows the private organization to control the resource flows across the membrane. The monopolization of the citizenship frontier in this manner prevents individual citizens from crossing the membrane and participating in the process of government. The private entity may not only block the citizenship frontier, but in all likelihood, it will capture control of one or more public agencies and direct its resources toward its own use. Under these conditions, the institutions within the public sphere will either become eviscerated or bureaucratically bloated, but the end result is that government is no longer capable of serving the public interest and common good.

Internal parasitism may also originate in public space and occurs when a public entity captures a private entity and monopolizes the citizenship frontier from within the public sphere. The Watergate affair was a particularly unique form of parasitism not only because it came perilously close to destroying our constitutional form of government and resulted in the resignation of a President in lieu of impeachment proceedings, but the parasitic entity in this case was the Presidency itself. The source of the parasitism originated in the Committee to Reelect the President which may be viewed as having infected the Presidency which in turn attempted to monopolize the citizenship frontier. The CIA has used private entities for its own ends which is an example of a public entity parasitizing a private one. Less obvious forms of parasitism occur when the citizenship frontier loses its permeability but is not overtly captured by a particular entity. The various barriers to political participation such as gerrymandered legislative districts and literacy tests designed to restrict voting are examples. Lack of permeability also arises out of more general disease conditions such as anomie and other social conditions that result in disengagement from politics.

Figure VI represents a condition that I call external parasitism. This is the case where a foreign entity manages to gain influence and control over a domestic public institution. It is this type of situation that the authors of the *Federalist Papers* were most concerned about.[40] In this situation the citizenship frontier is pierced, and the control of a public organization is directed from an alien agency rather than the citizens it is supposed to serve. If the objective of the alien entity is the destruction of the citizenship frontier, then we have an actual case of sedition and conspiracy. In

---

[40] See for example Alexander Hamilton's discussion of foreign corruption as being one of the weaknesses of republican governments in Federalist # 22.

the more common and less noticed cases, we have a foreign entity (which may or may not be associated with a foreign government) appropriating our public space to promote a particular interest it may have.

Figure VI
External Parasitism

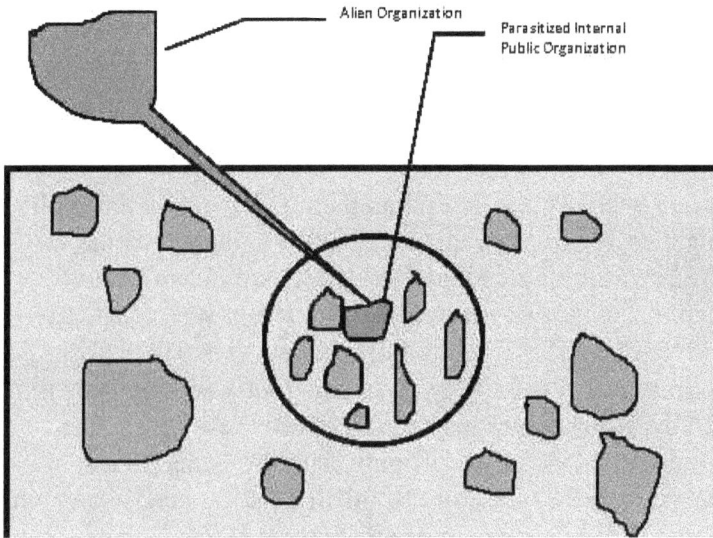

Both internal and external parasitism can and do occur simultaneously. Both result in compromising the citizenship frontier disrupting its ability to function. The objectives of both is private gain which may be economic, social, political, or ideological. (DeLeon, 1993:25) The dispersal of power among the federal branches was intended to prevent parasitism, but what has occurred instead is the colonization of different parts of government by various interest groups - e.g., labor, commerce, agriculture, etc.

(Mead, 1987:173) The fact that the public tends to focus on individuals rather than the political process itself allows parasitism to take place in the background, so to speak. One reason for this is that our society does not have a well-defined citizenship frontier to prevent it from happening. Without a citizenship frontier of any significance, there is no clear distinction between public and private, and nothing to prevent the market forces of the private sphere from seeping into the public sphere. The clearest example of this seepage is in the case of election for public office. I will consider this topic in the next chapter. Other examples of recent incidents of parasitism include the savings and loan scandal and the Iran-Contra affair. Although the incidents that receive the most attention occur at the Federal level, no level of government and no branch of government is immune from this disease.

It has been argued that parasitism, if viewed in a morally neutral manner, is useful in that it performs a "latent social function". The argument is that there are a number of desired governmental functions that are not sufficiently well attended to by authorized, legitimate offices and procedures (i.e., bottlenecks - a condition in which the delivery of public goods and services is obstructed by bureaucratic impediments). In these cases "the functional deficiencies of the official structure generate an alternative (unofficial) structure to fulfill existing needs somewhat more effectively". (deLeon, quoting Merton, 1993:27) This argument, when combined with the arguments that parasitism is a trivial sideshow of American politics and that a certain amount should be tolerated because its exorcism is not worth the expense, tends to trivialize the effect of parasitism on citizenship. The problem with this argument is that (1) corruption undercuts the ideals of equity upon which our government is based, and (2) it is extremely unlikely that society in general or even the specific users of government goods and services benefit from these illicit activities. (*Ibid.*:32-9)

While the functional argument is misleading in that it implies social utility in a social disease, it does make a point that is very important regarding the eradication of parasitism. That is "any attempt to eliminate an existing social structure without providing adequate alternative structures for fulfilling the functions previously fulfilled by the abolished organization is doomed to failure.... To seek social change, without due recognition of the manifest and latent functions performed by the social organization undergoing change, is to indulge in social ritual rather than social engineering." (deLeon, *Ibid.*:n 42 quoting Merton) In other words, we must replace those institutions that give rise to parasitism with other institutions that will fulfill the functions replaced. That is, in the case of citizenship, we must replace those institutions that have restricted access to the public sphere and limited citizenship participation therein with alternative institutions that provide for the full expression of citizenship. What needs to be established is a citizenship as an internalized ethic at the individual level and a viable citizenship frontier at the collective level. A viable citizenship frontier will begin to develop when the right to vote is transformed into the obligation to legislate. Intimately connected with legislation is the idea of representation, to which I now turn.

Chapter II

The 3R's of Representation, the Myth of Election, and the Idea of Random Selection

Giving civic and public voice legitimate civil articulation is a priority for all who want to invest that once sublime title citizen with renewed meaning.
Benjamin R. Barber

It is my thesis that citizenship is politically constructed. I have defined citizenship as that secular ethic that defines membership and participation in the political community which provides the cooperative context within which the competition of politics takes place. In the last chapter I developed an abstract model to illustrate a conception of democratic citizenship. The raw material for any political construction is ideas, and to continue the conceptual development of citizenship I need to consider four interrelated ideas–rights, responsibility, reason, and representation. Rights and responsibility interact with reason in a process that Habermas (1996) refers to as political opinion and will formation. Once it is formed, political opinion and will, or what I shall call political ideas, needs to be presented in political public space, and this is where the idea of representation enters in. These ideas are arranged as illustrated in Figure I. Figure I illustrates that these ideas are related; and that responsibility, rights, and reason come together within the concept of representation. They also form the ethical structure of citizenship. That is, they provide the ethical structural context within which the competition of politics takes place.

81

Figure I
Ethical Structure of Democratic Citizenship

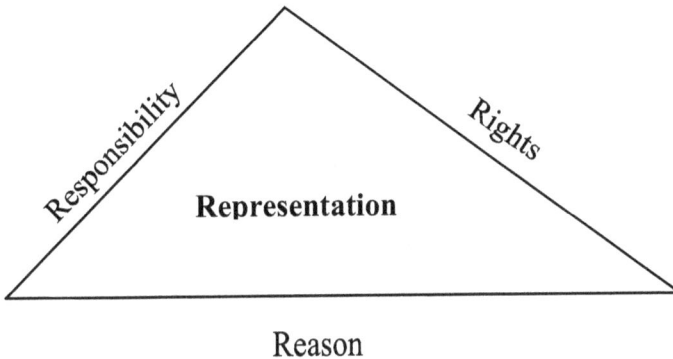

Reason

    Rights and responsibility are depicted in Figure I as being erected upon a base of reason. Rights and responsibility are in a sense opposite sides of the same coin. The exercise of a right creates responsibilities and responsibility involves the recognition of rights. Rights and responsibilities cannot be comprehended except through reason. Reason makes the recognition of rights and responsibility possible, and it mediates the tension between them. Political reason operates within the context of rights and responsibilities to generate political ideas that eventually become formalized in law and policy. It is within the framework of reason, rights, and responsibility that political representation occurs. Representation is simultaneously the greatest right and the greatest responsibility of democratic citizenship. It is a right in that it is the process through which citizens make their political ideas known; it is a responsibility in that

82

it requires citizens to respond to political ideas. Reason is required to express both the rights dimension and the responsibility dimension and to provide the link between the two. Representation involves elements of both making present and presentation. It expresses democratic citizenship by making present the presentation of political ideas.

      In what follows I shall examine the idea of representation to illustrate the complexity of the concept. Then I shall turn to an examination of election as the means of creating representative government. This is necessary to lay the foundation for re-introducing the idea of randomness as a necessary component in the political construction of democratic citizenship. I shall then examine jury duty as the only instance in which the idea of random selection has been institutionalized, an idea that I am arguing should be extended to legislative representation. Representation occurs primarily at the citizenship frontier because it is what regulates participation in the political community.

The Idea of Representation

      The idea of representation is intimately involved with citizenship in western democracies because it is the representative who acts as a surrogate for the citizen in conducting the affairs of state. The idea of representation is a multi-faceted concept that involves the idea of *mandate*, the idea of *representativeness*, and the idea of *responsibility*. The first idea pertains to the juristic interpretation, the second to the sociological interpretation, and the third to the political interpretation. (Sartori, 1962:465-473) The juristic interpretation pertains to the idea of agency where the agent represents the principal. An example of this is legal advocacy. A lawyer is said to represent his or her client, but the role performed is advocacy of the client's interest in the case at hand. The lawyer assumes the client's interest as his or her own and applies his or her knowledge of the law in presenting the client's case before the court. In this role the lawyer represents the client in the process of presenting the client's case to the court. But legal advocacy involves more than presentation; it occurs in an adversarial setting which requires protection of the interest at stake. Legal procedure regulates this adversarial process. Other examples of agency relationships are real estate and insurance agents where the agent is given a mandate to represent the principal in a particular type of transaction. There are three parties in this type of representation: the principal or party represented, the party to whom the principal is represented, and the agent or party performing the act of representation. The sociological interpretation is linked to the idea of resemblance. Representation occurs when the representatives resemble the represented. Statistical sampling is often used in social research and the sampling method is designed to produce a sample that resembles the population that is being studied. This same idea is applied to political representation when the test of an electoral system or a system of jury selection is its resemblance to the population from which legislators or jurors are extracted. In this case there are two entities: the population that is represented and the sample that represents the population. There is also the device that is used to extract the sample from the population.

Political representation is based on the idea of responsibility. The idea of responsibility entails the ability to respond which also involves responding to something.[41] This suggests that the sense of responsibility grows out of how we respond to our environment and how we are responded to. Responding to stimuli in the environment

---

[41] Etymologically the word responsibility has three distinct but closely connected elements of meaning: (1) to declare the presence of that which is present, (2) to declare oneself present, and (3) to declare a bond between oneself and that which is present to one. In common language it means to face the facts and stand up and be counted which means to respond to the facts and declare ourselves regarding them. (Denneny, 1979)

occurs at the moment of birth which implies that the rudiments of the sense of responsibility develop prior to the ability to reason. The ability to respond begins to develop when the self responds to itself in reaction to sensations such as hunger. These internal stimuli elicit responses from the self which in turn elicit responses from others which creates a dependency relationship for need satisfaction. It is in these dependency relationships within the family that social bonds are formed, and it is out of this bonding that obligations arise.

As the child continues to develop her ability to respond, she eventually runs into situations in which she finds that certain responses are inappropriate. Initially what is treated as an inappropriate response has to do with the child's own protection. But as development continues, the child learns that certain responses are inappropriate for other reasons. This is where the child begins to learn the normative structure of the society into which she was born. Social norms exist for the purpose of structuring our responses and creating behavioral expectations. As the child learns what these expectations are, her sense of responsibility develops further. The sense of responsibility at this stage of development is limited to a feeling or sensation as to what is appropriate in each situation. The child also learns that her reaction to certain stimuli results in predictable responses from others some of which are in the form of need satisfaction. This experience of having needs met is what will eventually develop into those types of expectation that are associated with the concept of rights. The ability to respond develops into the sense of obligation and the expectation of rights. The sense of obligation is prior to the expectation of rights because the former arises as a feeling whereas the latter requires a somewhat higher level of cognition. But it is not until language ability is acquired that these things take on meaning in a particular cultural context, and it is at this point that reason begins to emerge.

It is out of the feeling of what is appropriate within the normative structure that responsibility in the form of the ability to respond to right and wrong emerges, and it is by the introduction of these elements the term "responsible" takes on its everyday meaning. It is through responding to notions of right and wrong that moral personality begins to develop. Our notions of what is right and wrong are intimately related to our sense of justice the origins of which are the source of controversy.[42] With the development of moral responsibility and the increasing complexity of social relations, responsibility becomes differentiated into various categories such as social responsibility, political responsibility, legal responsibility, and financial responsibility. These classifications are based on the type of persons and things that are being responded to. No matter how it is classified, the defining characteristic of responsibility is action. A response is an act. Whether or not an act is considered responsible is based on how it is evaluated in terms of right and wrong, and it is because of this evaluative aspect that responsibility cannot be separated from reason.

Political Representation

Political representation is not isolated from the juristic or sociological interpretations, but it introduces the idea of the sovereign and its relationship to the citizen. Representation describes this relationship, but it is the nature of the sovereign that defines it. Representation takes a radically different form when sovereignty resides in the people than it does when sovereignty resides in the person of a monarch. The modern idea of representation reflects these changes in the idea of sovereignty. Political representation has

---

[42] This controversy involves whether there is a biological or genetic basis for the sense of justice.

its origins in Athenian democracy where the role of the citizen was more or less a full-time endeavor in which the citizen represented himself in the assembly. After the fall of the Roman Empire the idea of representation did not disappear, but it underwent a radical transformation. The theory of the divine right of kings was a theory of representation that arose out of the linkage between church and state. The king was God's representative on earth. Under a monarchy (and in Hobbes' theory of absolute representation) the state resides solely in the individual person of the king which is what makes the king sovereign. The king can be thought of as exercising a representative function in three ways. First, the king is a direct representative of God in that he acts as God's agent on earth. Second, the king is a symbolic representative in the sense that the realm is made visible or represented to the people in his person. Third, through his power he represents the whole in that the multiplicity can be made one only through the unity of his person. (Baker, 1994:411)

Since it was impossible for the king to rule the realm on his own, he needed advisors to help him with administrative tasks and to inform him as to what was going on in the kingdom. The institution of parliament arose out of these advisory councils. The idea of the representation of subjects had its origins in taxation. The major purpose of the Estates General was to give consent to royal taxation in France. In England the need to have the consent of the taxed was recognized as early as the Magna Carta. The type of representation that emerged was of a judicial rather than a legislative nature. In France, for example, the Estates General did not represent the nation as an entity that was separate from the king. The deputies were elected not to represent the nation, but to speak for the particularistic interests of the communities and corporate bodies that chose them for that purpose. This multiplicity of orders was made one only by and in the royal presence. The traditional juridical formula of the Old Regime was representation from above, deputation from below. The

Parliament of Paris throughout the eighteenth century reiterated the argument that as the highest judicial court in the realm, it "represented" the king to the nation, and the nation to the king. This is a complex double claim which took on different implications throughout the 18th century, but as the century advanced there was essentially a shift from the first to the second part of the claim. (Baker, *op. cit.*)

Hanna Pitkin (1967) has explored The Concept of Representation in depth in her book with that title which is an attempt to account for the various applications of a single, highly complex concept that has not changed much in its basic meaning since the seventeenth century. She begins her work with a consideration of the authorization view of representation which is exemplified in the work of Thomas Hobbes. The basic features of this view are that a representative is someone who has been authorized to act which means he has been given a right of action which he did not have before. The represented, however, has become responsible for the consequences of that action as if he had done it himself. The represented has given up rights and acquired responsibilities, while the representative has had his responsibilities diminished and his rights increased. Hobbes begins by distinguishing natural and artificial persons, a natural person being one whose words and actions are considered his own and an artificial person one whose words and actions are considered those of someone else. The person who performs an action is called the "actor" and the one by whose authority he acts is the "author". But a person who cannot be held responsible for his own acts cannot assume responsibility for the acts of another. Therefore, when these persons, and inanimate objects, are represented, authority must come from somewhere else. Representation does not merely mean acting on authority from another.

In addition to his well-known social contract, Hobbes also uses his concept of representation as a device to get men out of the state of nature. The commonwealth is created by men contracting with one another in such a way as to authorize one among them to represent them all. The sovereign is given complete power in perpetuity and obligation has been shifted to his subjects. This shift in power and obligation is a result of the fact that Hobbes was troubled by the people's inability to give their sovereign sufficient power to terrify them into conformity. The authorization view of representation is used to help solve this formal problem, but behind the formal problem there are the additional problems of how to enlist the capacities of citizens for positive political action, how to provide for participation, how to create motives for obedience and cooperation with a government. "We read the *Leviathan* and feel that somehow we have been tricked." (*Ibid.*:34-5)

In the authorization view there is no reason why unlimited authority cannot be granted at the outset and nothing that requires regular acts of authorization such as frequent elections. These theories tend to confuse: (1) attributing one's actions to another; (2) attributing the normative consequences of one's actions to another, (3) giving the right to act to another, and (4) having authority over another. (*Ibid.*:51) In this view authority has been conflated with representation and the formality of this view may be demonstrated by considering another view of representation that is diametrically opposed to authorization–the accountability view. In this view the representative is held to account after he acts to make him act in a certain way such as looking after his constituents and doing what they want. "One is held responsible in order that he may *become* responsible, that is, responsive to the needs and claims of others, to the obligations implicit in his position." (*Ibid.*:57) The accountability theorists fail to achieve this intention, because the definition they give is just as formal as the one they reject and it is still impossible to speak of the "obligations implicit in the position" of a representative. The authorization theorists focus on how representation is initiated; the accountability theorists focus on how it is terminated. Both views fail to come to grips with what goes on in the process of representing.

The next view of representation is the idea of descriptive representation or the resemblance theory. In this view there is a direct correspondence between the composition of the representative body and the population that is represented. What makes this view vulnerable to attack is that it neglects political action and the importance of the legislature's governing activities. In the descriptive view the purpose of representation is to supply information which must be distinguished in three ways when applied to politics: (1) the legislature is a passive object like a map or mirror that allows a spectator to gather information about the people, (2) the legislature represents by its activity rather than its composition like a painter or a "maker of representations to someone else", and (3) the idea that if the legislature is a sufficiently accurate copy, then it is justified to allow it to substitute for the whole people, to act in place of the nation. (*Ibid.*:81-2) This third idea views the legislature as a substitute for a democratic assemblage of the whole people. This notion goes back to the Roman law doctrine that parties who have legal rights at stake are entitled to be present or consulted in the decision. Since everyone is presumed present when Parliament meets, ignorance of the law is no excuse. (*Ibid.*:85)

Descriptive representation does not provide for representation as an activity except in the narrow sense of "making representations" or giving information. It also raises the question of which characteristics are politically relevant–a question that has been continually raised throughout the history of representative government as the suffrage has been expanded. Another way in which one thing can be substituted for another is through symbolization. Unlike descriptive representation, a symbol is not a source of information about what it represents, and accuracy of

90

correspondence is not an issue. The function of a symbol is to evoke feeling or emotion about the thing it represents. When the President of the United States performs ceremonial functions like receiving other heads of state, he is serving as a symbol of the nation.[43] In political representation the concept of a passive political leader must be supplemented by the view that the leader is a symbol maker that makes himself into an accepted symbol through effective leadership. The extreme form of symbolic representation is found in the fascist theory of representation by a *Führer*. In this case the idea of representation is turned on its head because both the party and the people represent the leader. (*Ibid.*:97-109)

Authorization theorists argue that the representative has no special obligation, activity, or role to perform as representative. He is free to do as he pleases without binding consequences for others. Accountability theorists seek to show that true representation entails responsiveness to the represented, but they defeat their own purposes by making it impossible for the idea of representation to serve as a guide for action. Descriptive or symbolic representation views the representative as an inanimate object with no particular concern for any activity. (*Ibid.*:113) All of these theories view representation as "standing for" rather than "acting for". From the latter perspective, there are five classes of rival terms: (1) terms which emphasize the element of action–e.g., "agent", (2) terms which center on the idea of taking care of another–e.g., "trustee", (3) terms involving the idea of acting in another's stead–e.g., "deputy", (4) terms involving the idea of being sent–e.g. "ambassador", and (5) terms involving the idea of

---

[43] The recent scandals involving the sexual activities of President Clinton are perceived as offensive because they "brought dishonor on the Office of President". The "representativeness" of the President's behavior depends on how much it deviates from sexual practices common in the population at large. But the President's behavior is perceived as offensive because it is seen as doing violence to the office he holds which is a symbol for the country. Flag burning is similarly perceived as offensive because it violates a national symbol.

specialist as representer. (*Ibid.:*121) These terms capture something that was missing in the other views of representation by emphasizing that representation as acting for others must be defined in terms of what the representative does and how he does it, but their usefulness is limited in defining it further.

The term representation means to make present in some sense, even though the represented is not present in fact. It is this paradoxical meaning of the term that gives rise to what is known as the mandate-independence controversy–is the representative bound to do what his constituents want or is he free to act independently in pursuit of what he perceives to be in their best interest. This is a continuing controversy for which there is no clear solution despite the effort of many astute thinkers, and empirical investigation has failed to produce any results that are clearer than the traditional "normative" controversy. Writers from both sides of the issue claim that the concept of representation supports their view. Although the meaning of representation supplies a consistent position about a representative's duties, the way the dispute is framed makes a consistent answer impossible. However, the consistent position regarding duties only sets outer limits within which there is a wide range for different views on how a representative should act. (*Ibid.:*145-6)

One of the distinguishing differences between an agent and representative comes to light when considering the agent or representative of a corporation. An agent of a corporation is more like a part of the whole whereas the representative embodies the whole in its entirety. In a similar way if the entire constituency is thought of as being present in the action of its representative two consequences follow: (1) why can it not change its mind here and now? and (2) how can the action it takes conflict with its express wishes? What is valid in the independence theory is derived from the first consequence. The representative must be permitted to have some discretion to act if the constituency is wholly present in him, otherwise he is more of a tool or puppet whose motivating power comes from elsewhere. What is valid in the mandate theory is derived from the second consequence. If the representative is consistently at odds with the desires of his constituency, it is also impossible to conceive the constituency present in him. The representative must act independently and the represented must in some way act through him–a paradox resulting from the fact of the represented being both present and not-present. (*Ibid.*:153-4)

This paradox was particularly evident in the events leading up to and surrounding the French Revolution which provides an illustration of the complexity of the idea of representation. First, there is the idea that deputies represent the entire nation. But when the revolutionaries accepted Rousseau's political theory as the basis of legitimating their conception of national political identity, they had to come to terms with Rousseau's abhorrence of the idea of representation. Rousseau argued that a multiplicity of individuals is made one by absolute and irrevocable submission to a single, unitary person. However, that person was not to be found in the person of the monarch, but in the collective person of the body of citizens as a whole. The independence of each individual can only be accomplished by the dependence of each on all. In giving oneself to all, one gives oneself to nobody which eliminates subjection to particular wills through subjection to the general will. This act creates an artificial, sovereign public person. As a result sovereignty can neither be transferred to a monarch nor can it be represented. (Baker, *op. cit.*) For Rousseau the chief business of the citizens was the public business, and once citizens would rather serve with their money instead of their persons, the state was not far from its fall. "When it is necessary to march out to war, they pay troops and stay home: when it is necessary to meet in council, they name deputies and stay at home. By reason of idleness and money, they end by having soldiers to enslave their country and representatives to sell it." (Rousseau, 1993:265) The deputies of the people cannot be representatives because they cannot legislate. Law is a declaration of the general will and the people cannot be represented in the exercise of their legislative power. The executive power, however, can be represented since it is only the force applied to give law its effect. Rousseau regarded the people of England as free only during the election of the members of Parliament; at every other time they were without liberty. Rousseau's doctrine led to the dilemma of choosing between unity without representation or representation without unity. To put this idea into practice, Rousseau required a binding mandate under strict conditions which would prevent deputies from assuming the powers of representation of the nation. (Barker, *op. cit.*)

The idea of social interest was introduced in place of principles of political sovereignty as one way to resolve the dilemma. The preservation of society depends upon the institution of property because it is the only source of a permanent common interest. Society is understood to be an association of individuals engaged in the common production and enjoyment of economic and social values. Social interests are the articulation of these values and they derive from the existence and ownership of property. Therefore, the entity to be represented is society in the form of property owners. Social theories of representation envision a form of representative local government based on property rather than privilege, and the representative assemblies are not intended to voice the political will of the nation. Each of these theories is marked by a distrust of any form of representation that involves restrictions on the representative to act freely and independently according to his own judgment. It is remarkable, therefore, that much of this distrust was shed in the revolutionary theory that took shape in the political debates of 1788 and 1789. During the subsequent debates, the initial idea that every deputy represented the entire nation in addition to his particular constituents evolved into the idea that each deputy represented the nation *rather than* his constituents. (Baker, *op. cit.*) The substitution of the nation for the people has far reaching implications. If sovereignty resides in the people, then there are two wills - the will of the people and the will of the representatives - and the will of the representatives is secondary to the will of the people. But if sovereignty resides in the nation then there is only one will and the will of the nation is the same as those who are entitled to speak for the nation. (Sartori, 1962)

Rousseauian theory either excluded the idea of representation altogether or it required a binding mandate that was better suited to a defense of particularism and privilege than an indivisible nation of equal citizens before the law. Since direct democracy was impossible in a nation as populous as France, an appeal to the people had to take the form of an appeal to an aggregate of particular communities rather than to a common body of citizens. It was in the interests of most men to confer active exercise of the right to participate in legislation upon those who had greater education, leisure, and enlightenment because most people were occupied with their daily labor. This idea of enlightenment made the binding mandate redundant. (Barker, *op. cit.*)

This development of representation reflects a fundamental historical change. Prior to the Glorious Revolution in England, the American Revolution, and the French Revolution, representation was not associated with government. Representative bodies were intermediaries between their mandatories and the sovereign: they represented *somebody* to *somebody else.* But the more parliament became located at the very center of the state, the more it took on a second function - that of ruling over the citizens in addition to representing them. Thus, present day parliamentary bodies are Janus-faced: they represent the citizens to the state and the state to the citizens. Having been inserted *into* the state, they must be allowed the discretion of acting *for* the state. A point may have been reached where the representative body represents an entity (the people or the nation) to itself. The third party - the one to whom the second party was to represent the first - has disappeared, and the principal of the representative relationship is hard to identify. With the emphasis on the representation of the *nation*, the representative cannot, and should not, represent those who elected him. But this makes it unclear as to what creates the representative. (Sartori, *op. cit.*)

Political representation focuses upon the representation of interests. The concept of interest involves a duality in that it may refer in one sense to what an individual finds interesting, and in another to having something at stake. At one pole there are what are referred to as unattached interests in which there are no relevant wishes to consult; at the other extreme there is interest in the sense of what an individual finds interesting which is surely up to him. In between these poles is a wide range in which interest *means* what a person has objectively at stake in fact, and yet he must also have some say in defining what his interest is. It is often assumed that welfare and wishes coincide and that an individual will want what is objectively in his interest. Representation enters precisely at this point where the person acted for is conceived as capable of acting and judging for himself and such a person is assumed to want what is in his interest. The concept of representation implies that the constituent's interest and the representative's judgment will normally coincide, and that if they fail to do so, there must be a reason to provide justification for the difference. The conceptual puzzle embodied in the mandate-independence controversy is what sets the outer limits to political representation. Within these limits the view a political theorist takes depends upon such things as his view of human nature, his image of politics, what he considers the relative intelligence and ability of the rulers and ruled, whether his model is one of representing abstractions like unattached interests, attached interests, or people. (Pitkin, *op. cit.*:156-167)

The major ideas involved in the representation of unattached interests are found in the writings of Edmund Burke. The ideal state for Burke is one which breeds and trains a true natural aristocracy and allows it to rule. In Burke's view reasoning is not a purely intellectual matter, but it is intimately bound to morality and the function of political reasoning is to discover the laws of God and nature, not in the abstract, but in practical wisdom. The superiority of the natural elite and the desirable qualities of the representative lie in his judgment, virtue, and wisdom derived from experience. There are two major concepts in Burke's theory of representation. The first is that the representative has no special relation to his constituency and does not represent those who elected him. Instead, the relationship of each member is to the nation as a whole and elections are merely a means of finding the members of the natural aristocracy to serve as representatives of the nation. But this idea is not sufficient because Burke also introduces the representation of interests through his second concept–virtual representation. Here he is not talking about the representation of the whole nation by every member of Parliament, but about the representation of disenfranchised groups and localities. Although the city of Birmingham elects no members to Parliament, it can still be virtually represented because Bristol sends members that represent trading interests in which Birmingham shares. Interests are discovered through parliamentary deliberation, but their discovery assumes the representation of every interest so that all come to light. Deliberation is at the heart of a complex representative function for Burke which also includes his ideas of elite representation of the nation and actual and virtual representation of particular constituencies. (*Ibid.*:169-189)

Whereas Burke was concerned primarily with the representation of unattached interests, liberals are concerned with the representation of persons. Burkean representation is a device for arriving at the right solution and acting upon it. In contrast, Madisonian representation is a means of forestalling action in the legislature until wisdom prevails among the people. Madison was concerned with the construction of a republic which differs from a democracy in two important ways: in a republic there is representation where government is delegated to a few men by the rest, and, as a result, a republic can include a greater geographic territory and a larger number of citizens than a democracy. Madison's primary concern is controlling the evils of "faction". Since election is likely to turn into a distorting mechanism that filters out desirable instead of undesirable materials, he relies upon the large size of the republic as the best hope of producing a diversity of special interests which reduces the possibility that they can combine for effective factious action. Property qualifications for voting are introduced because property is seen as the best index of stability and capacity in the individual. Persons who are without property are conceived as having no will of their own. (*Ibid.*:190-6)

The idea of the representation of attached interests is extended further by the utilitarians who conceive individuals as pursuing what is in their interest unfettered except by the "unseen hand" of the market. When interest is seen this way as purely subjective, then no individual can act for or represent another. However, this laissez-faire view of economic interest is modified in the legislative context through the introduction of the idea that each person has both a public and private interest. It is the public interest that is compatible with the idea of a universal interest which is seen as the aggregate of the public or social interest of each of the members. The individual may be the final judge of whether something is in his interest, but this is not equivalent to saying that only he can know what is likely to be in his interest. Men can know what is in others' interest, and the more intelligent, rational man is likely to know it best. As liberalism sees it, the theoretical advantage of representation is that it makes it possible for each citizen to be the final judge but allows the rulers to use their wisdom and information to further the citizens' true interest while keeping it in the ruler's interest to act in the citizens' true interest. (*Ibid.*:199-205)

The evolution from monarchy to democracy may be viewed as an evolution of sovereignty from the person of the king to the body of the people. Essentially this is an evolution from representation based on privilege to representation based on citizenship. It is an evolutionary process that is incomplete and that is mediated by the institution of property as illustrated in Figure II. The incompleteness of the process is partly the result of the changes that have occurred within the institution of property which are also illustrated in Figure II.

Figure II

Evolution of Representation

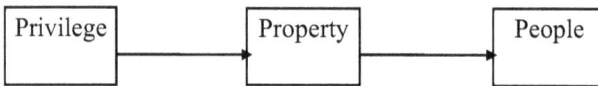

| Privilege | | Property | | People |

Evolution of Property

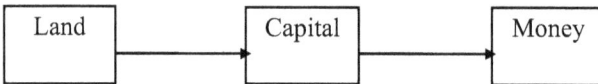

| Land | | Capital | | Money |

T. H. Marshall defines a property right not as a right to possess property, but a right to acquire property if you can and to protect it if you can get it. (Marshall, 1994:20) The institution of property arose out of land ownership. As land was made useful through labor, the individual acquired rights to the land by virtue of his appropriating it for his own use. Property and property rights initially were confined to real property. With the development of towns and the expansion of trade and commerce, the concept of property was broadened to include the implements of trade, and with the rise of manufacturing, the means of production. The expanded use of money as a means of exchange has equated the right to property to the right to acquire money. Thus, anything that can be used to produce wealth in the form of money is considered property. This includes intangibles, such as ideas, and most recently, the information contained within the human genome.[44]

Political representation has also evolved along with the evolution of the institution of property. Initially representation was confined to the person of the king who ruled by divine right and represented God on earth. This was the extreme form of privilege which could only be acquired by birth. Land ownership and the right of inheritance led to a secondary form of privilege in the form of the landed aristocracy, some of whom became the king's representatives to his subjects. The expansion of the institution of property and the rise of cities and towns resulted in a gradual expansion of the idea of representation. It was now necessary to not only represent the king in a downward direction, but also to represent the various fiefdoms and the cities and towns to the king.

---

[44] The idea that information that occurs naturally within the human genome can be patented as a property right by virtue of its discovery is frightening. This is another example of the types of problems that are arising because of the bifurcated nature of human evolution. Our ability to use technology is so advanced relative to our ability to create and use social mechanisms to control its use that we may literally end up creating monsters that we cannot control. The assumption that market mechanisms will provide the necessary regulation is a prime example of political responsibility avoidance.

When the American colonies were formed and the republic created, the idea of representation was still confined to property owners primarily in the form of land ownership. But the generation of wealth in the form of capital and then in the form of money has had the effect of expanding the idea of political representation, in terms of the suffrage, to include more and more people. Although the suffrage has become nearly universal, representation is still more or less confined to property holders who are defined by their ability to generate money. Thus, political representation may be viewed as evolving coterminously with the evolution of the institution of property, and, as a result, it is also an unfinished process marked by a tension between representation of people in terms of their wealth and representation of people in terms of their citizenship. The transformation from representation based on wealth to representation based on citizenship is what I will examine next.

Representation and the Citizenship Frontier

General Model

Democratic sovereignty is expressed at the citizenship frontier in the form of representation. The key element in the idea of representation is "present" in two separate senses: pres.ent and pre.sent. The first involves presence - being in a physical place or space. In this sense representation means to make present–i.e.rep-resent. The representative is someone who stands in for the constituent in a particular place at a particular point in time and thereby makes the constituent's presence known. This can be accomplished by resemblance. If the representative resembles the constituent, by that fact alone he can make the constituent's presence known. The second involves presentation–i.e., it implies the communication of something. In this sense representation means re-present, and the representative is someone who takes the constituent's ideas and interests and re-presents them. The representative need not resemble the constituent, but she must be able to present his values and interests and defend them against competing values and interests. This act of presenting the constituent's values and interests is obviously complicated by the fact that the representative - constituent relationship is a one-to-many relationship. This raises the question of what exactly does the representative represent? The general idea is shown schematically in Figure II. [45]

---

[45] One of the more interesting theories of representation in current political philosophy is John Rawl's original position. The original position is a device of representation that is inhabited by artificial persons who are merely rational. The parties in the original position are there as representatives of members of society, but it is unclear exactly whom or what they represent. Since they are located behind the veil of ignorance, they have no interest of their own to represent. They do not know their own interests, what class they belong to, what generation they belong to, or what their future will be. Since they are presumably ignorant of the

Figure II
The Citizenship Frontier as Representational Interface

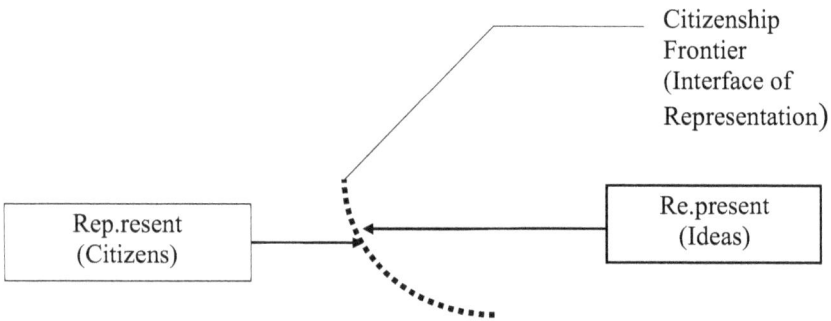

Citizenship
Frontier
(Interface of
Representation)

Rep.resent
(Citizens)

Re.present
(Ideas)

---

relative position of their constituents regarding all of this, they also could not represent the interest of their constituents. It is precisely this environment which is unpolluted by private interest that makes the selection of justice as fairness as the preferred principle for a well-ordered society possible. As the veil of ignorance is gradually lifted, other constitutional principles are developed through the four stage sequence. It remains unclear, however, exactly who or what is represented by this Rawlsian device of representation. In dealing with the question whether persons in the original position have duties to third parties, Rawls says the parties are thought of as representing continuing lines of claims. They are thought of as deputies for a kind of everlasting moral agent or institution. In terms of the model in the prior chapter, the Rawlsian original position must be some sort of extraction from society that is pure public political space encapsulated by a normative membrane that represents the veil of ignorance. As the veil of ignorance is lifted, we can envision the formation of the citizenship minimum, the introduction of political private space, and the transformation of the veil of ignorance into the citizenship frontier as the interface of representation. Rather than being seen as representatives of members of society, the parties in the original position may be thought of as representing their future citizenship.

103

As I pointed out in the last chapter, one of the properties of a healthy citizenship frontier is that it is highly permeable. In terms of democratic citizenship, permeability means that political ideas will flow freely across the citizenship frontier. The citizenship frontier can be conceptualized as a highly porous membrane, the pores of which are numerous with very small diameters. This property allows for the free flow of citizens into and out of political public space while at the same time preventing the entry of larger entities that would overwhelm the public realm. One of the main properties of citizens in this model is that they are bearers of political ideas. It is in this capacity that the citizenship frontier serves to facilitate their access to political public space. Citizens are physically located in political private space where they are engaged in all sorts of activities, some of which may be political. When they are represented politically, they are made present by crossing the citizenship frontier into political public space. Within this space their activities are solely political. It is in this space that they present political ideas which become the raw material for deliberation. Deliberation is essentially a competitive ideational process of presenting and re-presenting political ideas which eventually results in the formation of law and policy. The deliberative framework–e.g. consensus, majority-rule, or some other agreed upon procedure–is what determines how law is formed, but it is the political ideas that determine its substance. Representation, then, involves the rep-resentation of citizens in the sense of making present and the representation of political ideas in the sense of re-presentation.

A permeable citizenship frontier facilitates the representation of *individual citizens*, not groups and other associational entities. As a representational interface, the citizenship frontier defines and facilitates participation in the political community, and, by so doing, mediates the tension between the individual and community. It both preserves the identity of the individual citizen and promotes her

104

integration into the political community. It does this by preserving the representation of the individual within the political community. The individual, in her representative capacity, is liberated from group identification and integrated into the political community of ideas, and within this community she participates, with other citizens in their representational capacity, in the determination of the kind of society within which they collectively wish to live. In crossing the citizenship frontier the private individual becomes a public citizen.

Individualism and diversity are terms that describe the same phenomenon - i.e., individualism is the extreme form of diversity. The term diversity is used in reference to group categories, but if these are removed, we are left with individual differences. Group categories represent a unidimensional ordering of individuals according to one characteristic out of a multitude of possible characteristics. But at the genetic level variation is infinite which makes every individual unique. Rousseau envisioned the general will in the form of an artificial public person and abhorred the idea of representation, but for practical purposes he accepted the idea of the binding mandate. When individuals represent themselves but are constantly replaced with new representatives at regular intervals, a Rousseauian type of general will will gradually emerge. It will emerge through the expression of plural individualism which is bounded by the citizenship frontier. Representation is achieved by individuals presenting themselves–i.e. their interests, ideas, values– to other individual representatives and the public at large in the legislative forum. Their purpose is not to represent the nation, a legislative district (even though they may be selected on the basis of a geographic district), or any group with which they may be affiliated. Their purpose is to give public expression to those individual values and ideas that are salient in forming the public interest. It is individuals, not groups, that are represented.

The idea that representation occurs through individuals raises the issue that those individuals that belong to advantaged groups will be more effective in representing themselves than members of disadvantaged groups and that this will perpetuate the advantages of the privileged groups. Iris Marion Young (1994) argues that group representation is a way to solve the "paradox of democracy" in which social power makes some citizens more equal than others and equal citizenship makes some people more powerful citizens. This occurs in participatory settings because the more privileged and articulate groups are more able to articulate and promote their interests than other less advantaged groups. When some groups are privileged and others oppressed, the bias is in favor of the privileged groups which implicitly sets the norm which in turn becomes expressed in public policy and law. As an antidote some groups may deserve special rights at various times.

Young's group representation is not the same thing as interest group representation of which she is critical. Rather her groups are comprehensive identities and ways of life whose social location gives them distinctive understandings of all aspects of society and unique perspectives on social issues. The representation of such groups requires institutional arrangements and public resources that support (1) the self-organization of group members so that they gain a sense of collective empowerment and a reflective understanding of their group experience and interests in the context of society as a whole, (2) articulation of the group's analysis of how social policy affects them and the formulation of its own policy proposals, and (3) provision of a veto power regarding specific policies that affect the group directly. The purpose of group representation is not to compensate for an inferiority, but to allow the positive assertion of different ways of life.

Young argues that group representation is the best antidote to self-interest masked as an impartial or general interest. She states that in a democratically structured public, individuals and groups

106

cannot simply assert that they want something. Instead, they must show that justice requires or allows them to have it. Group representation provides the opportunity for some to express their needs and interests that would not be possible without that representation. The test of the justice of such claims occurs when the persons making the claims must confront others who have explicitly different, though not necessarily conflicting, claims. Group representation also maximizes knowledge expressed in discussion which leads to increased wisdom because members of different social groups are likely to know different things about the structure of social relations and the potential effects of social policies. These arguments are even more applicable in the case of individual representation based on random selection.

An individual's membership in a group is only one dimension, although perhaps very important dimension, of that individual's identity. Group representation cannot achieve the expression of the general will in public policy because its emphasis is on the differences among groups and the relative merits of competing group claims. While the arguments supporting these claims are asserted in public so that the justice of the claims is visible to all, this does not mean that the resulting policy will be in the public interest. Because of the emphasis on group difference, important policy issues may never come up for consideration. It is true that in the current system of representation privatized special interest has been promoted under the guise of the public interest, and group representation does offer a reasonable alternative. But those arguments that make group representation appear attractive are even more forceful when applied to true individual representation.

The permeability of the citizenship frontier is still restricted under group representation. Individual representation on a random basis will allow for the representation of all the various components of identity over time. The individual representative, while embedded in and influenced by the groups to which he or she belongs, is not obligated by these attachments in his or her representative capacity. This lack of specific obligation to specific groups expands the individual's representative horizon and frees him or her to raise issues that would not likely be raised where the focus is on competing group interests.

The restrictions placed on the permeability of the citizenship frontier by group representation become even more evident with multiculturalism, or what Salinas calls ethnic federalism (Salinas, 1997) The chief characteristic of ethnic federalism is that it is antiassimilationist to the core. Salinas is writing about immigration which is initially a matter of the citizenship minimum. However, the idea of assimilation is directly linked to a permeable citizenship frontier. The purpose of assimilation is to integrate immigrants into the society and promote their citizenship. Multiculturalism is directly opposed to this because it is essentially an ideology of grievances and inevitably leads to and justifies ethnic conflict. According to this ideology, ethnic Americans have the right to: (1) function in their "native" language not only at home, but in the public realm, (2) proportional representation in matters of power and privilege, and (3) demand that their "native" culture and their putative ethnic ancestors be accorded recognition and respect. Virtually every nation that has ever embraced it, from Yugoslavia to Lebanon, from Belgium to Canada, has had to live with perpetual ethnic conflict. (*Ibid.*: 11) Salinas argues that assimilation must be voluntary both on the part of the assimilated and the populace into which they are assimilated and that it is more akin to a religious conversion than anything else. The ultimate objective of assimilation is to incorporate the immigrant into a functioning citizenship. This is only possible when the native born make it work. Assimilation occurs when: (1) natives and immigrants accord each other *legitimacy*, (2) immigrants develop a *competence* to function effectively in American workplaces and in all the normal American social settings, (3) immigrants are encouraged to exercise *civic responsibility*, minimally by being law-abiding members of American society, respectful of their fellow citizens, and optimally as active participants in the political process, and (4) immigrants *identify themselves as Americans*, placing that identification ahead of any associated with their birthplace or ethnic homeland, and their willingness to do so is reciprocated by the warm embrace of native Americans. (*Ibid.*:49-50) For the immigrant, assimilation makes citizenship possible, and the hallmark of citizenship is representation.

In any group there will be an uneven distribution of abilities that will result in some members assuming a more dominant role. This is an unavoidable fact of life. However, where the members of the group are randomly selected, this dominance is not necessarily linked to the dominant economic and social interests in the society at large, and if it is so linked, it will be in terms of the numerical size of the interest group as opposed to its economic power. Those groups that are in a more favored social position will still tend to achieve more representation because of their greater social skills, but their dominance of the legislative process is by no means guaranteed. Individuals, when let loose from their group affiliations, are much more likely to express their own true interest. Since most individuals are neither totally good nor totally bad but probably more good than bad, and since most individuals possess a sense of right and wrong, a sense of justice, and a desire to promote the public good in most cases, individual representation is most likely to achieve the most justice in the long run. This is an obvious assumption that has its basis more in intuition than hard scientific fact because individual representation has never been tried.[46] The only model we have for this type of representation is jury duty.

---

[46] However, there is some experimental evidence to support this assumption. Experimental studies on voting and majority rule had results that did not precisely follow from the theory precisely because the "citizens" were more generous than

In the United States and most western democracies the idea of representation is further complicated by the tripartite structure of government. I will now examine legislative, executive, and judicial representation.

Legislative Representation

The idea of legislative representation in the United States is linked to physical territory. The States as individual entities are equally represented in the Senate, but in the House they are represented on the basis of size. Representatives are chosen from a Congressional District and are supposed to represent that district. The franchise has been made more inclusive over the years, but the entity that is supposedly represented is still a geographical territory. Each district, however, is supposed to consist of an equal number of citizens which is the main purpose of the census that occurs every ten years. But what is supposed to be represented and in what sense? Is it the district as a community of citizens that are somehow bonded to one another by the fact that they live in the district? Is it the district itself as an artificially defined socio-political entity? If so, for what purpose, and why was the district defined the way it was? Or is it individual citizens that are represented, and if so, how? How is the district represented: is it by the mere physical presence of the representative or are other elements involved?

---

predicted. They were not smarter or less ignorant than assumed, but morally superior. In contexts that resemble markets, non-cooperation predominates. But in non-market contexts, there is a significant residual of cooperation under virtually all laboratory conditions. (Frohlich and Oppenheimer, 1999)

These questions raise the who, what, and how of representation. In a democratic culture, the who that should be represented is the individual citizen, the what that should be represented is political ideas, and the how is by random selection. The forum of representation is the legislature. It is here that citizen representatives come together and present political ideas to one another with the aim of molding those ideas into legislation. The legislature is a forum of choice. It is in the legislature that citizens address the question of what kind of society they would like to live in and how they can go about creating it. Political ideas are the ideas that attempt to answer this question. Political ideas originate in the minds of individual citizens. No one citizen or group of citizens has a monopoly on the answer to the question of the desirable society because the answer to that question must be a collective answer. However, it is the ideas of individuals that are the building blocks that will create the answer. It is also an answer that is not only created, but continually re-created as historical, cultural, economic, and political conditions change. The legislature, then, is the forum where the homeostatic and hermeneutic dimensions of collective citizenship intersect.

The legislature is a public forum. It is homeostatic in that it mediates the tension between the individual and the community. The expression of political individuality that occurs here does not occur in isolation. It is a place where the ideas expressed by representatives are tested against the ideas expressed by other representatives. It is not a place that samples public opinion; it is a place where individual citizens take responsibility for their political ideas. This collective expression of individual political ideas is a process that results in law - the rules which define the type of society the citizen representatives want to live in. It is a continuing process with a constant change of membership, and the fact that it is stochastic is the best guarantee that the will expressed is in fact general and adaptable to changing circumstances through time.

Representation is the highest obligation of citizenship. The idea of representation advanced here is that of the citizen participating in the political community as a representative of him or herself. A representative is a public citizen who serves in the legislative assembly on a one-time basis for a set term and presents his or her political ideas and values to his or her fellow representatives. Although representatives may be selected from a geographical entity, they do not represent that entity. They do not represent their community, their employer or place of employment, a political or religious group, or any association or group of which they may be a member. Representatives represent themselves by presenting their individual political ideas and values directly to their fellow legislators and indirectly to their fellow citizens. They may consider their geographic locale, their community, and other groups to which they belong, but they are under no obligation to represent these entities. Their sole responsibility is to represent themselves. The presentation of individual political ideas and values in the public forum of the legislature is the highest expression of citizenship.

Hannah Arendt described the thought process of the ideal representative in her conception of representative thinking.

> Political thought is representative. I form an opinion by considering a given issue from different viewpoints, by making present to my mind the standpoints of those who are absent; that is, I represent them. This process of representation does not blindly adopt the actual views of those who stand somewhere else, and hence look upon the world from a different perspective; this is a question neither of empathy, as though I tried to be or to feel like somebody else, nor of counting noses and joining a majority but of being and thinking in my own identity where actually I am not. The more people's standpoints I have present in my mind while I am pondering a given issue, and the better I can

imagine how I would feel and think if I were in their place, the stronger will be my capacity for representative thinking and the more valid my final conclusions, my opinion. (It is this capacity for an "enlarged mentality" that enables men to judge; as such, it was discovered by Kant in the first part of his *Critique of Judgment*, though he did not recognize the political and moral implications of his discovery.) The very process of opinion formation is determined by those in whose places somebody thinks and uses his own mind, and the only condition for this exertion of the imagination is disinterestedness, the liberation from one's own private interests. Hence, even if I shun all company or am completely isolated while forming an opinion, I am not simply together only with myself in the solitude of philosophical thought; I remain in this world of universal interdependence, where I can make myself the representative of everybody else. Of course, I can refuse to do this and form an opinion that takes only my own interests, or the interests of the group to which I belong, into account; nothing, indeed, is more common, even among highly sophisticated people, than the blind obstinacy that becomes manifest in lack of imagination and failure to judge. But the very quality of an opinion, as of a judgment, depends upon the degree of its impartiality. (Arendt, 1968, 243-4)

She illustrates this type of thinking with this example:

Suppose I look at a specific slum dwelling and I perceive in this particular building the general notion which it does not exhibit directly, the notion of poverty and misery. I arrive at this notion by representing to myself how I could feel if I had to live there, that is, I try to think in the place of the slum-dweller. The judgment I shall come up with will by no means necessarily be the same as that of the inhabitants, whom time and hopelessness may have dulled to the outrage of their condition, but it will become for my further judging of these matters an outstanding example to which I refer....Furthermore, while I take into account others when judging, this does not mean that I conform in my judgment to those of others, I still speak with my own voice and I do not count noses in order to arrive at what I think is right. But my judgment is no longer subjective either. (Arendt, 1982:107-8)

This type of thinking is what would occur in the mind of the ideal legislator. However, most mortals are unable to think this way, and even if they are, they cannot apply it to all the diverse matters that may become before the legislature. The experience of a particular individual is not that broad. However, it may be possible to approximate this type of thinking in a legislative body of diverse membership where the individual members represent themselves and in which the membership is renewed on a regular basis.

The legislature achieves political homeostasis through its consideration of political ideas that arise out of all sectors of society. Each individual occupies his or her own social location that provides him or her with a unique perspective on what constitutes the desirable society. Through the presentation of individual perspectives in the legislature, the possibility of a comprehensive collective perspective emerges. It is this comprehensiveness that is missing when the legislature is not representative. Representation in this scheme is defined as original presentation. The citizen legislator presents his or her political ideas in original form. They are not filtered through a selection process and re-presented in some other form. However, though the process of confronting other political ideas in original form, they are tested, reshaped, and recreated. In other words, political ideas are presented and re-presented. Eventually collective political ideas will emerge, and it is these that

114

will find their expression in legislation. This homeostatic process is what takes individual wills and molds them into something akin to Rousseau's general will.

The legislature is also a forum of hermeneutics because the individuals that come to it are embedded in their culture and its history. Participation in the legislature is their opportunity to express their interpretation of their culture and history and listen to other interpretations of that culture and history and the interpretation of other cultures and histories. The purpose of this process is to use the interpretation of the past in creating a vision of the future. The legislature is the forum where that vision is played out. The fact that its membership is continually renewed prevents the stasis that could block this hermeneutic process. Even though its membership constantly changes does not mean that every session starts anew. The institution has a life of its own that is independent of its members, but it is the continual renewal of membership that will keep the institution vibrant. The work of the session just past will carry over into the new session and institutional norms will develop that will outlast any particular session. However, should these norms become dysfunctional, they are more likely to be changed because of the renewal of membership.

Although the obligation of representatives is to represent themselves, this representation takes place within constitutional constraints that define and limit the legislative power and the constraints of *responsibility* and *reasonableness*. The constitutional constraints are defined in the U. S. Constitution and the various state constitutions. Representatives are under oath to uphold the principles embodied in these documents as interpreted by the courts. Citizen representatives may seek to change these principles, but they may only be changed by a vote of the entire body of citizens.

Executive Representation

The executive in a representative democracy also represents. In this section I shall examine how executive representation arises out of the nexus of rights, responsibility, and reason. There are two broad forms of executive representation which, for lack of better terms, I shall label the passive and active form. The passive form is involved in the enforcement of the law and the refinement of law within the administrative structure. The active form involves policy formation and executive response to the political environment. The passive form is associated with what we call bureaucracy. The active form is associated with what we call executive leadership.

The result of legislative representation is the institutionalization of political ideas in law and policy. These embodiments may be visualized as being located on the citizenship frontier where they regulate both political private space on the outside of the membrane and political public space on the inside. In political private space their function is to maintain the social normative structure. This is accomplished through the body of the civil and criminal law which are re-presentations of political ideas in legal form. In political public space these legislative embodiments serve the function of providing the overall policy guidance to the administrative structure within the executive branch. In this case they are re-presentations of political ideas in the form of policy guidance to the administrative structure. Within the administrative structure this legislative policy is re-presented again through the actions and rulings of various administrative bodies and eventually may become codified within the body of administrative law. Many of these codifications may be visualized as making their way to the citizenship frontier where they serve to regulate political private space. Others serve an internal regulatory function within political public space. This re-presentation of policy within the administrative structure is the first type of executive representation–the representation of legislative policy within the administrative structure through which the will of the citizens is made present. A permeable citizenship frontier is required if this type of representation is to occur.

Executive representation also occurs in a more active form in which the executive herself proposes political ideas to the legislature in the form of her legislative program. This is one type of representation that results from executive leadership and it primarily relies on the use of public reason to take political ideas and formulate them into concrete policy proposals. In this type of representation, it is the executive that is proposing ideas to the legislature in the form of an original presentation which the legislature may re-present either in the form of alternative proposals or in the form of actual law. This is a type of opinion and will formation that originates *sui generis* within political public space, and it is the ability of the executive to justify her proposal using public reason that leads to its acceptance by the legislature and the public at large. In this type of representation, it is political ideas that are represented, but they are the executive's political ideas. The citizens, however, are made present when the legislature responds to the executive's proposals.

A second form of executive leadership concerns the use of the police and military powers. This form of representation involves a heavy dose of responsibility because the executive must respond to a constantly changing political environment in which unforeseen events may require her immediate attention. These types of events require the executive to decide what action to take, some of which may involve the use of the police or military power. It is in these instances that the coercive powers of the state become most obvious and it is in such instances that the executive is a representative of the state in the sense that the state itself is made present by her action.

While legislative representation occurs at the citizenship frontier, executive representation occurs within political public space and is bounded by the citizenship frontier. The maintenance of this boundary is extremely important in keeping the executive power in check so that representation may be preserved. As I pointed out in the previous chapter, it is possible for the executive to capture part or all of the citizenship frontier, a condition that is most likely to occur when the executive is acting in the role of representative of the state itself. This can become an extremely dangerous condition given the fact that the executive has control over the police and military power. Totalitarianism is the most extreme form of executive representation. In this case the citizenship frontier is overwhelmed and destroyed resulting in the invasion of the private by the public. Sovereignty is transferred from the body of citizens to the executive, the citizen becomes a subject, and representation is transformed from citizens being made present through the presentation of political ideas to the person of the executive being made present within his subjects. Thus, a culture of democracy requires that the sovereignty of the people be preserved through the citizenship frontier as a medium of representation.

Judicial Representation

Judicial representation also arises out of the nexus of rights, responsibility, and reason. Whereas legislative representation is primarily prospective and executive representation occurs in the present, judicial representation is retrospective. A court cannot act until a controversy is presented to it. The court will interpret the controversy in terms of the law as defined by the legislature within the constraints of the constitution and prior judicial decisions. Since the law may represent the public interest of past generations, the court may be said to represent them. This type of representation

118

occurs through the principle of *stare decisis* and is manifested in the frequent reference to the intent of the "Founding Fathers".

The use of public reason is most prominent in judicial representation. It is here that the political ideas embodied in law are re-presented through their interpretation and use in justifying the court's decision. In this process the authors of those ideas are made present not in the spatial sense that occurs in legislative representation, but in a temporal sense. This link to the past which is preserved in judicial representation provides stability in the political environment such that the preservation of the citizenship frontier is possible. Without judicial representation and the high standards imposed upon it by the requirement that its decisions be justified by reason, the citizenship frontier could easily become overwhelmed by the executive power or private interest or both acting in concert.

Judicial representation also occurs in the present and provides the one institution in which direct citizen representation currently occurs. The institution of the jury is the source of the only obligation of citizenship, other than conscription, that has a random component. Juries are not retrospective in their representation except in the very narrow sense that the case under consideration is in the past tense. Instead, their job as fact finders is to represent "justice" in the present. Although jurors are only concerned with the facts of the case, what is being represented is the political idea of justice–an idea that is both made present and re-presented in terms of these facts. Achieving justice, in the case of the jury, requires the element of randomness. Since jury duty, and this random component in particular, is the prototype for the political construction of legislative representation, it is treated more fully below.

The primary device for achieving political representation is election. This device has been used for millennia and is so well established that its use is virtually the sole criterion used to label a regime "democratic", even when a regime is abhorrent in every aspect and is the antithesis of democracy. Since election is such a prominent feature of the political landscape, I shall review its role in the development of representative government.

Election and Representative Government

A lucid explication of the role of election in representative government can be found in the recent work of Bernard Manin in *The Principles of Representative Government*. This work is particularly relevant for my purposes here because he explicitly discusses lot as a method of representation and concludes that

> Scarcely one generation after the *Spirit of the Laws* and the *Social Contract*, however, the idea of attributing public functions by lot had vanished almost without trace. Never was it seriously considered during the American and French revolutions. At the same time that the founding fathers were declaring the equality of all citizens, they decided without the slightest hesitation to establish, on both sides of the Atlantic, the unqualified dominion of a method of selection long deemed to be aristocratic. Our close study of republican history and theory, then, reveals the sudden but silent disappearance of an old idea and a paradox that has hitherto gone unnoticed. (Manin, 1997:79)

Democracy, as a government by the people, is based on three fundamental values: (1) the principle of rotation in office, (2) a deep distrust of professionalism, and (3) equality. These ideas have their origin in ancient Athens and need to be contrasted with the principles of representative government. Manin's analysis led to the development of four principles that are present in any representative government: (1) those who govern are appointed by election at regular intervals, (2) the decision-making of those who govern retains a degree of independence from the wishes of the electorate,

120

(3) those who are governed may give expression to their opinions and political wishes without these being subject to the control of those who govern, and (4) public decisions undergo the trial of debate. The central institution of representative government is election. The distinction between democracy and representative government is clarified by contrasting selection by lot with selection by election.

Manin examines lot and election historically and theoretically. His analysis seeks to resolve the paradox of representative government, namely, that when this form of government was developed it was explicitly aristocratic, yet today it is perceived as democratic. The resolution of the paradox is found in the combination of democratic and undemocratic elements. Manin's exhaustive analysis can only be summarized here. Although the political use of lot is considered a bizarre custom and is hardly thought about today, it was used historically and considered about the time of the French and American revolutions. Aristotle's conception of citizenship was based on the idea that a citizen was one who ruled and was ruled in turn. For Aristotle participation in politics was among the highest forms of excellence, and this could only be achieved by rotation in office. Selection by lot was consistent with this principle. Selection by lot was also consistent with the Greek distrust of professionalism which was seen as conflicting with democracy. They recognized that knowledge and skills were a source of power and were reticent to allow those who possessed these to have advantage over those who did not. Democracy consisted in placing decisive power in the hands of amateurs. Selection by lot was also consistent with the Greek idea of equality in that what was distributed equally was not power, but the probability of achieving power.

It was Aristotle's belief that a better constitution was obtained when democratic and oligarchic elements were used together. Lot was never used exclusively in Athenian politics and when it was used, it's use was restricted in certain ways. Lot was primarily used to fill the Council (*boule*) and administrative posts, and a citizen could occupy a given post only once in a lifetime. Only those who volunteered were considered and there were risks associated with volunteering in that a magistrate was subject to constant monitoring by the assembly. If he lost a no confidence vote, he would have to render account and could face the possibility of punishment. He also had to render account upon leaving office. Prior to taking office, those who were selected had to undergo an examination to check their legal qualifications and whether they had performed certain obligations. Some magistracies were filled by election and in this case magistrates could succeed themselves in office. Thus in Greek direct democracy the assembled people did not exercise all powers and selection by lot was not a peripheral institution.

The political use of lot found a limited use in Rome where election predominated and a to a greater extent in the Italian city states of the Middle Ages and Renaissance. In Rome lot was used to determine who should vote first in the centuriate assemblies and which vote should be counted first in the tribal assemblies. In the Italian cities, the crucial property of lot appears to have been that it shifted the allocation of offices to a procedure that was not subject to human influence. Because of its conspicuous impartiality, lot produced an outcome that was more acceptable to conflicting factions. By placing the decision beyond reach it prevented the divisive effects of open competition among factions. In Florence lot was used in combination with scrutiny. Those citizens who received more than a certain number of favorable votes were selected at random for the various magistracies. Rotation in office was also guaranteed by preventing the same office from being assigned to the same person or members of his family several times in succession during a given period. By the end of the fifteenth century, however, there was a clear shift in favor of election which was captured in a speech given by Francisco Guicciardini. Equality before the law and equal access to public office were the core values of Florentine republicanism. The first must be realized without restriction, but the second had to be limited for the fate of the city must not be left in the hands of those who are merely adequate. It is here that election is seen as superior to lot because election ensures that magistrates are as select as possible. In an elective system, eminence is conferred by others, not by oneself and the voters are able to distinguish the truly great from those who affect greatness. A recurring theme in Guicciardini's thought is the notion that the people is capable of judging what is put to it, whether persons or decisions, but is incapable of governing itself. Election will select the best while still leaving it up to the people to discern who are best.

Lot was also considered in the writings of Montesquieu and Rousseau. Both were fully aware that lot could select incompetents, but it had other properties or merits that at least made it an alternative worthy of serious consideration. Montesquieu established a close link between lot and democracy on the one hand and election and aristocracy on the other. The characteristics of lot that are necessary for democracy are that it neither humiliates or brings disgrace upon those who are not selected, and it obviates envy and jealousy toward those who are. Even though lot is the democratic selection procedure *par excellence*, it was no longer seriously considered after this point. The reason for its eclipse, according to Manin, is that by the seventeenth and eighteenth centuries it was manifestly unsuitable given the objectives that the political actors sought to achieve and the dominant beliefs about political legitimacy. Where lot and election are manifestly different and unequal centers around the notions of consent and political obligation. All legitimate authority must derive from the consent of those over whom it is exercised.

However, lot is interpreted, whatever its other properties, it cannot possibly be perceived as an expression of consent. One can establish, to be sure, a system in which the people consent to have their leaders designated by lot. Under such an arrangement, the power of those selected for office at a particular in time would be ultimately founded on the consent of the governed. But in this case, legitimation by consent would only be indirect: the legitimacy of any particular outcome would derive exclusively from the consent to the procedure of selection. In a system based on lot, even one in which the people have once agreed to use this method, the persons that happen to be selected are not put in power through the will of those over whom they will exercise their authority; they are not put in power by anyone. Under an elective system, by contrast, the consent of the people is constantly reiterated. Not only do the people agree to the selection method - when they decide to use elections - but they also consent to each particular outcome - when they elect. If the goal is to found power and political obligation on consent, then obviously elections are a much safer method than lot. They select the persons who shall hold office (just as lot would), but at the same time they legitimize their power and create in voters a feeling of obligation and commitment towards those whom they have appointed. There is every reason to believe that it is this view of the foundation of political legitimacy and obligation that led to the eclipse of lot and the triumph of election. (*Ibid.*: 85-6)

The idea of the consent of the governed as the sole source of political obligation and legitimacy arose out of the convergence of the medieval tradition and modern natural right theories. This convergence relegated the idea of distributive justice in the allocation of political functions to the background. However, when compared to the differences between election and heredity, the distributive effects of lot and election in the allocation of offices appeared negligible. There was a paradox here in that this was a time when equality among citizens was being declared, while a method known for distributing offices in an unequal manner prevailed without debate or qualification. The paradox was resolved through an idea of equality not based on the equal chance to hold office, but the equal right to consent to power. This idea of equality gave rise to a new conception of citizenship: citizens were not viewed as persons who might desire to hold political office, but as the primary source of political legitimacy.

Manin goes on to show that the founders of representative government were not only not concerned that elections would result in an inegalitarian distribution of offices, but they also deliberately introduced another inegalitarian feature of representative government, namely, that the chosen representatives be socially superior to those whom they represent. He calls this feature the principle of distinction - that aspect of election in which electors naturally choose their betters resulting in a "natural aristocracy" from which representatives are selected. In England this principle was a direct result of the cost of electioneering and deference as a cultural characteristic. In France it arose out of the distinction between a right and a function. Voting was considered a right but holding office a function. A function was to be performed on behalf of society and therefore society was entitled to keep it out of unqualified hands. The issue was not who could vote, but who could be voted for.

In the United States, the issue of who could vote was left to the various state *constitutions* because federal electors were to have the same qualifications as state electors for the most numerous branch of the state legislature. There was some debate over property qualifications for electors - e.g., Gouverneur Morris asked for a property qualification on the grounds that restricting the franchise to freeholders would prevent the corruption of propertyless people by the wealthy (*Ibid.*:103) - but in the end using state qualifications avoided restricting or extending the right to suffrage. The qualifications of representatives is much more interesting because there is no hint of the principle of distinction in constitutional requirements. Manin's analysis of the constitutional debates shows that the lack of a property qualification was an unintended result of the failure of the delegates to agree on a qualification that would work in all states and regions. Even though no property qualification ended up in the constitution, the majority of delegates favored one (1) to guarantee that representatives had economic independence to be immune to corruptive influences, and (2) to protect the right of property which was a principle object of government.

The debate over the ratification of the constitution involved two conceptions of representation which involved the issues of the size of the House of Representatives and the size of electoral districts. The Anti-Federalists were unanimous in their demand that representatives *resemble* those whom they represent. This is a "descriptive" conception of representation in which the aim of the assembly is to act as the people would have acted. In this sense, it is the same as the mandate theory, but it occurs spontaneously rather than being enforced through formal legal provisions. The Anti-Federalists were concerned that representation in the proposed Constitution was skewed toward the "natural aristocracy" - social superiority conferred by wealth, status, or even talent. The Federalist reply to this argument was that there was nothing wrong with a natural aristocracy and they stressed how it differed from aristocracy proper. In the end both sides to the debate shared the intuition that large electoral districts would result in the selection of a "natural aristocracy", but neither side could account for it. It was less of a problem for the Federalists since they didn't present it as one of the main merits of the Constitution. There is not a strict equivalence between large electoral districts and formal property qualifications

126

for two reasons. First, a formal property qualification will always result in the selection of an aristocracy, but the relationship between large electoral districts and the election of the natural aristocracy occurs most, but not all, of the time. Second, if the advantage of certain classes is written into law, abolishing it, or granting it to different classes, requires the consent of the advantaged. However, if the advantage of certain classes is the result of electoral behavior of the citizens, a change in the electorate will change the composition of the elite. The American constitutional debate made very clear that representative government was not to be based on resemblance between representatives and the represented.

The trend toward universal suffrage and the elimination of wealth requirements for representatives during the nineteenth and twentieth centuries gave the impression that the trend was toward democratic government. Manin argues that despite these trends, inegalitarian aristocratic effects still remained. The aristocracy that resulted from election had nothing to do with heredity or legal definition, but election nevertheless elevates those who enjoy superior status in society. This is due to four factors: (1) the unequal treatment of candidates by voters, (2) the distinction of candidates required by a situation of choice, (3) the cognitive advantage conferred by salience, and (4) the cost of disseminating information. The essence of the argument is that a quality that is favorably judged in a given culture that is rare and not possessed by others constitutes a superiority. If this quality is salient, the candidate who possesses it will stand out by virtue of its positive value. Combined with the fact that there is nothing that requires voters to be fair in their evaluation of candidates and the fact that the cost of conducting an election campaign is expensive, election by its very nature selects those who are superior. There are groups distinguished by wealth or some other favorably judged trait not possessed by other groups, and these elites generally exercise influence disproportionate to their numbers in any society. The establishment and stability of institutions is particularly dependent upon their support. They are particularly likely to support representative government once they realize that the elective method tends *de facto* to reserve representative functions for such elites. Popular self-government (democracy) and absolute representation (Hobbes) abolish the gap that exists between the governed and those who govern because in the first case it turns the governed into governors and in the second it substitutes representatives for the represented. This gap is preserved by representative government.

Manin concludes his book with a comparison of three ideal types of representative government using the four principles of representative government as a guide. These ideal types are parliamentarianism, party democracy, and what he calls "audience" democracy. All three meet the criteria of representative government, but representative government itself has been transformed. Today the reactive dimension of voting predominates, and the electorate appears to be an *audience* which responds to what appears on the political stage. Cleavages within the electorate are identified by representatives and brought upon the stage to be played out before the voters.[47] Manin concludes that what appears today as a crisis in political representation appears in a different light if it is remembered that representative government was conceived in explicit opposition to government by the people. Since its central institutions have remained unchanged, what we are witnessing today is nothing more than the rise of a new elite and the decline of another. The paradox we are left with is that without appearing to have evolved in any way, representative government today is

---

[47] Schudson's (1998) "monitorial" citizen is a similar conception. Since the wealth of information and complexity make an "informed" citizen a virtual impossibility, she is replaced by the monitorial citizen who scans the informational environment in such a way that she is alerted on issues and may be mobilized for a variety of ends. Neither of these conceptions address representation as an attribute of citizenship.

perceived as democratic whereas it was originally seen as undemocratic.

> The designation of representatives by election, with universal suffrage and without qualifications for representatives, combines the democratic and undemocratic elements even more closely. If citizens are regarded as potential candidates for public office, election appears to be an inegalitarian method, since, unlike lot, it does not provide every individual seeking such office with an equal chance. Election is even an aristocratic or oligarchic procedure in that it reserves public office for eminent individuals whom their fellow citizens deem superior to others. Furthermore, the elective procedure impedes the democratic desire that those in government should be ordinary persons, close to those they govern in character, way of life, and concerns. However, if citizens are no longer regarded as potential objects of electoral choice, but as those who choose, election appears in a different light. It then shows its democratic face, all citizens having an equal power to designate and dismiss their rulers. Election inevitably selects elites, but it is for ordinary citizens to define what constitutes an elite and who belongs to it. In the elective designation of those who govern, then, the democratic and undemocratic dimensions are not even associated with analytically distinct elements (though always mixed in practice), such as the prospective and retrospective motivations of voting. Election merely presents two different faces, depending on the observer's viewpoint. (*Ibid.*:237-8)

The Myth of Election

The association of election with democracy implies that it is through election that the permeability of the citizenship frontier is created and maintained. To find out why this is not the case it is necessary to examine the institution of election. We have already seen that the designers of representative government did not intend this form of government to be democratic. Election is undemocratic because it restricts the permeability of the citizenship frontier. The first restriction that results from election was already elucidated above: citizens are merely regarded as those who choose who may cross the citizenship frontier and are not considered capable of crossing it themselves. The effect of this restriction is to make the citizenship frontier selectively permeable. The condition of selective permeability is not, when taken by itself, necessarily a disease condition, and it can be plausibly argued that this condition is preferable to complete permeability. However, the effects of election upon the citizenship frontier extend well beyond restricting its permeability to a natural aristocracy. I shall examine these effects below.

Most of the factors to be examined here are well known to the average citizen. Taken in isolation they are not only perceived by many as not particularly serious, but as a natural unavoidable cost of representative government. Taken together, however, they combine and magnify their individual effects such that the citizenship frontier becomes, not a boundary that defines participation in the political community, but a barrier that prevents it. Election, when compared to monarchy and other forms of authoritarian government, must be regarded as a major political advance. It is necessary in initiating the evolution toward democratic government. The extension of the elective franchise is one of the major factors that leads to the rudimentary development of a citizenship frontier. But, election, by its very nature, guarantees the impermeability of the citizenship frontier. At some point, if a permeable citizenship frontier and a culture of democracy are to be created, election must give way to a selection method that achieves representation. I hope that the brief examination of the factors below will help make it clear why election prevents representation and is a bar to democratic government.

The Ecological Synergy of Electoral Pathology

These effects are all interrelated and at times difficult to isolate from one another. They all feed into a process that I will call the "ecological synergy of electoral pathology". This phenomenon is a result of the fact that an elaborate ecology of institutions has been created that lives in the internal environment of the electoral process. These institutions may be symbiotic among themselves, but they are parasitic upon the citizenship frontier and election enables them to thrive. While some could survive without election by adapting to other environments–e.g., the media–others would most likely become extinct without the electoral environment–e.g., the political party. This is one of the main reasons that the institution of election will be so difficult to replace, and one of the distinguishing features of a culture democracy will not only be the absence of election, but this entire set of institutions that have arisen around it. These institutions range the gamut from political parties to polling organizations to lobbyists and other sectors of the influence industry to advertising agencies to political science departments in our colleges and universities. They include a host of existing professions and some new ones have been created that are specific to the election process.[48] This phenomenon is so pervasive in our society that it is

---

[48] One of the latest additions to this array of organizations that make their living off election is the private eye. The insatiable demand for negative information in

virtually accepted without question, and the only reason it is noticed at all is that it is in an exponential growth phase. However, it is insidious, and the reason it is insidious is that it makes the citizenship frontier impermeable.

The institution most closely tied to election is the political party. Its purpose is to provide a filtering mechanism through which candidates are selected for public office. The traditional characteristic feature of the political party is its ideological orientation that is reflected in the party platform. In recent years, however, as the ecology of election has become increasingly complex, the political party has become more of a fund-raising organization that is more concerned with winning elections than it is with a particular political ideology or program. Political candidates have also become increasingly independent in the management of their campaigns. These trends have had the anomalous result that the parties are somewhat indistinguishable from one another and are yet dominated by extreme vocal minorities whose positions are very clear. The dominant characteristic of the political party is its role in raising vast sums of money.

The media and polling organizations make a substantial part of their living from the institution of election. Most opinion polls are conducted either to forecast election results or to influence the campaigns of those seeking office. The media thrives on the institution of election, and as soon as one is completed, it begins focusing on the next one. While, in theory, all this attention to election is supposed to help produce an informed electorate, much of it is presented in the form of entertainment geared toward the generation of advertising revenue. Thus, not only the media, but their sponsors are involved in using election as a means of making part of

---

political campaigns has created a fertile environment for private investigators. See Frantz (1999).

their living. And, of course, the study of election is what supports a large part of the discipline of political science.

The sector that has achieved the greatest amount of growth as a result of election in recent years is the influence industry, an industry that invested $1.2 billion in 1997 in various forms of rent seeking. (*New York Times,* 1998a) While lobbyists are found wherever government agencies are located, the one place where they exist in heavy concentration and have achieved the most explosive growth is on K St. in Washington, D.C. The purpose of these organizations is to influence specific legislative outcomes, and achieving a favorable outcome depends upon a favorable electoral result. What is particularly characteristic of the ecological relationship between lobbying organizations and government offices is the fluidity of the niches. There is virtual unrestricted movement between the public and private in this case, and anyone with political connections is highly marketable on K St. This includes the family members and former aids of lawmakers in addition to government bureaucrats. This parasitism not only restricts the permeability of the citizenship frontier, but it corrupts its ability to maintain a clear separation of public and private political space.

The Inherent Corruptibility of Election

Because of the synergy that drives the complex ecology of the election process and the vast sums of money required, the institution of election is wide open to manipulation in many overt and covert ways and is thus inherently corruptible. It is this attribute of election that creates the parasitic disease conditions of the citizenship frontier, and it is this attribute of election that causes it to defeat representation. De Tocqueville observed that intrigue and corruption are natural vices of elective governments and was particularly concerned that this disease could become serious if the head of state were reelectable. (de Tocqueville, 1969:136) The framers of the US Constitution were concerned about corruption from domestic and foreign sources. They were particularly concerned about foreign corruption because they feared the potential corruptive influences of monarchy. As a result, they designed an elaborate system of checks and balances to mitigate the effects of corruption on the institutions of government. They also gave serious consideration to property qualifications for both representatives and the voters because property owners would be less susceptible to corruption from outside influences. Since the franchise was limited in scope, less attention was paid to the potential corruption of the electoral process itself.

Since corruption is an integral part of elective government, it has come to be accepted as a necessary evil that is inherent in these types of political systems. Consequently, its corrosive impact on society has been de-emphasized. Corruption is defined as moral perversion, depravity or perversion of integrity. One of the definitions of integrity is the state of being whole, entire, or undiminished. It also means a sound, perfect, or unimpaired condition. (*Webster's Encyclopedic Unabridged Dictionary*) Privatization is a particular form of corruption and is defined as the appropriation of political public space for private ends. It results in the transformation of public into private law. The opposite condition, totalitarianism in its extreme form, is the appropriation of all private space, not for public ends, but for the ends of the ideological state. Under these conditions there is no private law, and public law is transformed into an instrument of ideological control.

When it comes to elections, the vehicle most often used to corrupt someone or something is money. In discussing money in this context, the aqueous metaphor is quite appropriate. Money, like water, is necessary for human life. But money, like water, can also be destructive. Lack of money is like a drought, an overabundance like a flood. Like water, it can cause violent storms. Like water, it can cause erosion and corrosion. It is this erosive and corrosive property of money that is of interest to us here in terms of politics. Water seeks its lowest level. If there is the slightest crack or hole in a structure designed to keep water out, water will still seep in. If the structure is not repaired, it will eventually become impaired and crumble. When it comes to politics, political structures are full of holes and repair is virtually impossible. This is particularly true of elective systems because elections cost money.

An ideal election would be conducted entirely within the free marketplace of ideas in which the selection of candidates is based solely upon their policy proposals, their proposed means of implementation, and the general perception on the part of the voters of the candidate's ability to carry them out. It is not necessarily the concrete policy proposals that are important in the selection of candidates, but the quality of the thinking and the ethical context behind the specific proposals. As Manin correctly points out, representatives should not be bound by mandates. Conditions may change which warrant changes in or even abandonment of their promised policy proposals. However, all policy proposals must undergo trial by debate, and it is this fact that makes it possible to hold representatives accountable at election time. An ideal election, however, could only be carried out in small scale situations where the candidates are known and minimal resources are required to disseminate information. Once the scale increases, various filtering mechanisms are required to initially select candidates and the cost of disseminating information increases drastically. The performance of these functions is the purpose of political parties and the various modes of candidate selection that have been introduced - party caucuses, primary elections, etc.

Because electoral systems are inherently corruptible, we need to examine the general effects of electoral corruption. In one way or another, corruption de-legitimizes representative government. The core of Manin's justification for representative government is that it derives its legitimacy from consent. It is the consent of the governed expressed through electoral choice that is the source of political obligation. This idea of consent is tied to a conception of equality not based on the equal chance to hold office, but on the *equal right to consent to power*. It is this conception of equality that changes the meaning of citizenship: citizens are the source of political legitimacy rather than potential office holders. But what is meant by the equal right to consent to power? If we do in fact have an equal right to consent to power, why is there a feeling of malaise, even disgust, with representative government? Manin argues that the source of this malaise lies in the fact that despite other democratic trends, the social gap between the represented and the representers has not narrowed. "While one can certainly say that democracy has broadened, one cannot say with the same certainty that it has deepened." (Manin, *op cit.*:234)

What has caused the gap between the representer and the represented to widen? Manin's insightful analysis ignores the impact of interest groups on the electoral process. The question we need to ask is what are the implications of the role of interest groups in representative government on the equal consent to power? In other words, what is the impact of interest group politics on citizenship? It is human nature to look out for individual self-interest and to unite with others who share that same interest. This is particularly true in a social environment in which competition and the acquisition of material wealth are the primary values. Forming an interest group allows for the pooling of resources and the division of labor to promote that interest in an efficient manner. Interest groups provide a forum for participation thereby helping to subject issues to trial by discussion. In a complex society, interest groups serve the filtering function of helping to select candidates for office. After all, political parties originated as interest groups writ large. Why, then, would interest group politics be perceived as a source of malaise?

136

The answer to this question lies in the fact that the unequal distribution of resources among interest groups has a direct bearing on both the distinction between the public and the private and the equal consent to power. The term "special interest" is used to express the current malaise with representative government. The implicit assumption has been that competition among special interests would, through the processes of debate, coalition formation, compromise, etc., lead to the emergence of policies that "are in the public interest". However, as the current dissatisfaction with representative government attests, this is not the case. Instead, we have the conditions of internal and external parasitism in which private interests have gained control over a public agency or part of the public realm to use to its advantage. Remember that when this occurs the citizenship frontier is monopolized so that a portion of it becomes blocked which impedes its ability to maintain homeostasis through permeability, to maintain the proper ratio of public to private space, and to keep the public and private separate. We need to examine how the corruptibility of elections leads to parasitism.

Amitai Etzioni (1984) has examined the corrosive effects of money on elections in the context of Marshall's theory of citizenship. The movement toward enfranchisement in terms of one-person-one vote is seen as part of the development of democratic citizenship as conceptualized by Marshall. In Marshall's analysis the separation of public and private became possible because of status separation. Civil, political, and social statuses were fused during the feudal period, but gradually people became equal in the civil area while remaining unequal in the others. The trend was toward civil, then political, and finally social equality. The trend was so slow and uneven, however, that Marshall linked each phase to a separate century. The principle of equality of citizens to set against the inequality of classes is what made possible the separation of public and private space. However, in the United States this separation is limited as the result of what Etzioni calls interlocking elites. He

137

argues that the preservation of both democracy and the free market requires the downsizing of large power concentrations.

The current version of electoral corruption is in the form of the political action committee. In terms of the citizenship model, PAC's may be envisioned as parasitic entities arising in political private space that latch onto the citizenship frontier and appropriate public resources for private gain. It is not only the appropriation of public resources that makes electoral corruption insidious, but the fact that it also blocks the citizenship frontier by thwarting equal citizenship in terms of the one-man-one-vote criterion. The important point to remember here is that *it is an entity that is not a citizen at all that is blocking the citizenship frontier by manipulating the electoral outcome.*[49] Insult is added to injury when businesses reduce their profits and the taxes they pay by adding their lobbying expense to their regular business expense.

Etzioni provides insight into the parasitic strategies that are employed by PAC's. He points out that corruption exists in both retail and wholesale varieties; the former applying to a single piece of legislation and the latter applying across the board. The general public tends to contribute more or less equally to both winners and losers, but PAC's contribute much more to winners than losers (and more to the more powerful committee chairmen) thus achieving a

---

[49] The term "corporate citizen" is often used in the context of a corporate entity attempting to justify its behavior in terms of good citizenship. Viewed in light of parasitism, however, the term is far more dangerous than a mere justification for something a corporation does. There is no such thing as corporate citizenship, and the very notion is a threat not only to citizenship per se, but also to individual liberty. The trend toward globalization may be seen as an extension of the individual-community dichotomy in which the multi-national corporation replaces the individual and some form of as yet unformed global conglomeration of corporate entities replaces the political community. The multilateral agreement on investment (MAI) is the latest development in this trend toward globalization in which the nation state is becoming an instrument of the multi-national corporation rather than the arena of democratic citizenship.

greater return on their investment. But PAC's will also contribute to opposing members. This apparent contradiction is explained by the fact that a member can serve PAC interests even though he or she may vote against the PAC when it comes to the final count. A member can oppose a bill in earlier rounds when it is less visible to his or her constituents and can amend it in ways that serve the PAC interest. The member can even go so far as to help the bill progress all the way through the legislative process but vote against it in the final count.

The consequences of behavior such as this are: (1) numerous bills that a majority of the public favor, the classic case being gun control, are never passed, (2) numerous bills the public does not favor, such as various subsidies, are passed, (3) PAC interests dilute legislation that is passed such that it contains loopholes that make it more or less ineffective, (4) competing special interests may make it impossible to pass any legislation, (5) special interests engage in bidding wars through which they neutralize the political parties by playing then off against each other, (6) the competition of special interests prevents the formation of coherent public policy, (7) special interest groups exact a cumulative cost on public policy until the cost becomes prohibitive, and (8) PACs have become a means by which foreign interests can influence the Congress. In these ways PAC's and special interests make government unrepresentative. But they also make it impossible for government to serve common goals such as national security, advance common interests such as economic growth with low inflation and work out compromises among private parties. The final consequence of corruption is that it contributes to inflation by shifting allocative decisions from the market to the polity. In the market an increase in the allotment to one community must be accompanied by a decrease to another, but no such automatic adjustments are built into the polity. Instead, more can be allotted by printing more money.

The fact that interest groups tend to become parasitic does not mean they serve no useful purpose. Etzioni points out several useful functions that they serve beyond the general ones mentioned above. They provide a form of representation before executive branch agencies. Because of the difficulty of executive branch agencies consulting with individual citizens, interest groups are consulted instead. They provide a bridge between the administrative and executive branches of government and they contribute to political socialization. But most importantly they provide a mechanism for political representation above and beyond the electoral process.

Although interest groups serve some useful functions, their overall influence in the political process is corrosive. It is in the electoral aspect of the political process where this corruption most seriously threatens citizenship. Ideological or economic interests that are national in scope parasitize the electoral process in a particular locality by contributing money in the local campaign. The attempt to influence the outcome of elections within congressional districts clearly thwarts the wishes of the electorate in that district. These corruptive influences by national groups are now being extended down to minor local elections such as school board positions. The effects of this corruption are three: (1) it increases the costs of running for even a minor office, and (2) it breeds cynicism and apathy, and (3) it limits running for office to those who have the means to raise large sums of money. From 1972 to 1982 the amounts raised for the primary and general election campaigns for the House increased 450% and 512% respectively - three times the consumer price index. (Etzioni, 1984:12) The trend has increased even more since then.

Campaign finance reforms have been repeatedly suggested, but few have been enacted. Even those that are enacted may end up having unintended consequences. PAC's were supposed to be a reform that resulted from the Watergate scandal, but the result has been a new vehicle for corruption. What is established here is the fact that it is the process of election itself that invites corruption. The standard argument has been that direct democracy is only possible in an entity of small scale such as a township and that once that scale is exceeded, election becomes necessary. In theory election is more appropriate in small scale entities where the members of the community know each other on a personal basis. Unfortunately, we no longer have communities in the traditional sense anymore, so this theory does not apply. When the scale increases, we need to look at random selection as an alternative to election.

The repeated suggestions for campaign finance reform have another effect–they breed cynicism and voter alienation. The current manifestation of this is the repeated calls for reform on the part of the Clinton administration while at the same time engaging in an array of fundraising practices, many of which have been called into question, that are used to raise an ever-increasing amount of money. Since these practices are synergistic with complex feedback loops, the direction of parasitism has become unclear. The initial parasitic act may have originated in either political public or political private space, but the resulting interlocking web of parasitism has become so entangled that private and public entities are parasitizing each other and for any particular act, it is unclear as to who is parasitizing whom. It is precisely because these processes are so deeply embedded in the electoral environment that it is so difficult to break the chain of corruption.[50] The net result of this pervasive corruption is cynicism which is fueling the preexisting underlying culture of possessive hedonism and excessive individualism.

---

[50] Decisions regarding limiting one's use of certain campaign practices if the opponent will do likewise is a "prisoners dilemma" type of situation in game theory. The candidate justifies her use of particular practices on the grounds that everyone else is doing it and not to do it will surely result in electoral defeat. The cycle of corrupt practices grows exponentially as more and more money enters in.

The effects of corruption on citizenship extend beyond election to the phenomenon known as *rent seeking*. In economics a rent is a return on a factor of production more than the minimum required for its service. Rent seeking[51] is the political activity of individuals and groups who devote scarce resources to induce governments to grant them monopoly rights. The term comes from the concept of "monopoly rent" in economics which is income earned because of the ability to charge a monopoly price. I will adapt Gunning's[52] (Gunning, 1998) definition of rent seeking as consisting of "non-voting actions that are intended to change laws or administration of laws such that one individual or group gains at the greater expense of another individual or group". Gunning defined rent seeking as a legitimate activity, but I am dropping this qualifier because of the point made earlier regarding the fact that the beneficiaries of this type of activity have managed to legalize most of it which blurs the distinction between what is a legitimate and illegitimate form of rent seeking. Rents are created through various policy instruments that are designed to conceal the gains. Examples of rent seeking include the sales of subsidies, tax privileges, price supports, tariffs, quotas, or licenses to the highest bidders, with the proceeds going to officials in the form of higher salaries and perquisites. While the legislature cannot be legally sanctioned for

---

[51] "The expenditure of resources to bring about an uncompensated transfer of goods or services from another person or persons to one's self as the result of a 'favorable' decision on some public policy. The term seems to have been coined (or at least popularized in contemporary political economy) by the economist Gordon Tullock. Examples of rent-seeking behavior would include all of the various ways by which individuals or groups lobby government for taxing, spending and regulatory policies that confer financial benefits or other special advantages upon them at the expense of the taxpayers or of consumers or of other groups or individuals with which the beneficiaries may be in economic competition." (Felkins, 1997)

[52] Gunning's chapter on rent seeking is an excellent introductory discussion of the topic.

failure to adhere to its agreement with an interest group, it will do so because (1) the procedures for the enactment of legislation arising out of such agreements increase the cost of repealing it, and (2) the independent judiciary tends to enforce legislation in accordance with the legislative intent. The basic propositions of rent seeking theory are (1) that there is a social cost in the expenditure of resources to secure a transfer of a monopoly right, and (2) there is a welfare loss to consumers and taxpayers that result from the market privileges. (Parker, 1996).

A parasitic attack on the citizenship frontier usually results in the monopolization of one or more government agencies or branches of government. The legislative branch is particularly vulnerable to this type of parasitism because it is not only open to direct rent seeking from various interest groups, but also indirectly because of its attractiveness to candidates who may be motivated by rent seeking opportunities. The latter is a result of the facts that members of legislative bodies have considerable influence over the distribution of rents, they have broad discretionary freedom, and their activities are virtually invisible since there is no effective monitoring of legislative activity. (Parker, *op. cit.*: 57-8) A legislature inhabited by rent seekers inhibits the permeability of the citizenship frontier because it has become closed off to all except other rent seekers. The average citizen is then stuck in private space with no effective means to cross the citizenship frontier to represent his or her interests.

The corruption of political public space eventually seeps out into political private and social space. In the case of a public institution being parasitized by a private organization we find that the public institution's source of legitimacy has been displaced by the parasitizing entity and the institution can no longer command respect from its 'stakeholders'. The initial act of corruption is initiated by the private organization, but once the public institution starts to succumb to the corruption, mutual feedback loops escalate the process which eventually spreads beyond the original dyad throughout political space. If the process continues, it will eventually result in the complete disintegration of the citizenship frontier. As I mentioned earlier, an act of corruption may also be initiated by a public institution, but the result is the same. Although corruption has become accepted as a routine fact of political life because of much of it having been made legal, it nevertheless creates a condition in which citizens no longer accord respect to public institutions because institutional goals have been deflected from their original purpose. Once corruption has become endemic in the environment, social decline and decay are well under way.

Responsibility Avoidance

Election is a device of responsibility avoidance. The reason for this is that in an elective system, the citizen has a duty to vote, but that is virtually the end of the matter. The citizen, for all practical purposes, has no political responsibility. She may voluntarily assume political responsibility, but it is not an integral part of her citizenship. The elected legislator also avoids the personal political responsibility of the citizen. This may seem anomalous, but it results from the fact that the elected legislator does not have the responsibility of representing himself. Instead, he represents his constituents. If he creates legislation that is unjust, he can avoid responsibility for his actions by claiming that he was acting on behalf of his constituents. Politicians, in the words of Walter Lipmann,

> ...are in effect perpetual office seekers, always on trial for their political lives, always required to court their restless constituents. They are deprived of their independence. Democratic politicians rarely feel they can afford the luxury of telling the whole truth to the people. And since not telling it, though prudent, is uncomfortable, they find it easier if they

themselves do not have to hear too often too much of the sour truth....

     With exceptions so rare that they are regarded as miracles and freaks of nature, successful democratic politicians are insecure and intimidated men. They advance politically only as they placate, appease, bribe, seduce, bamboozle, or otherwise manage to manipulate the demanding and threatening elements in their constituencies. The decisive consideration is not whether the proposition is good but whether it is popular - not whether it will work well and prove itself but whether the active talking constituents will like it immediately. Politicians rationalize this servitude by saying that in a democracy, public men are the servants of the people. This devitalization of the governing power is the malady of democratic states. (Glazer and Wattenberg, 1996:40 quoting Lipmann)

In addition, representatives are in the legislature as members of a political party which allows them to hide behind the party platform, the party caucus, or the party leadership. In an elective system, then, political responsibility ends up in some never-never land located somewhere between the ballot box and the halls of the legislative assembly.

This situation is precisely what modern writers mean when they refer to a regime as democratic. For example, Walzer reiterates Manin's theme when he writes:

The truth about political activity in the modern state is that it does require hard work, that the citizens by and large do not do that work and probably cannot, and that the authorities can and do. As Hegel suggests in *The Philosophy of Right*, it is only the bureaucrats (we can add, the professional politicians) whose chief business is the public business and who "find their satisfaction in ... the dutiful discharge of their public functions." They are citizens in lieu of the rest of us; the common good is, so to speak, their specialty. What does "ruling and being ruled" mean, then, in the modern state? ... If the authorities can be empowered, they can also (sometimes) be removed from power, and that important possibility is what contemporary writers have in mind when they call one or another state democratic. (Walzer, 1970:215-6)

Citizenship, in this view, is passive and citizens are alienated. However, as Walzer points out, citizenship may be used ideologically in which case the claim is being made that citizens do exercise power, but this is done on the cheap with little expense of spirit. When this occurs, citizens are being told they make decisions and are implicated in the decisions made, but they do not in fact decide. Walzer, like Habermas, Rawls, and others, concludes that requiring people to attend meetings and join discussions is not possible in a free society, and since citizens will not govern themselves, "they will, willy-nilly, be governed by their activist fellows." (*Ibid.*:235) However, "we show a government to be representative not by demonstrating its control over its subjects but just the reverse, by demonstrating that its subjects have control over what it does. Every government's actions are attributed to its subjects formally, legally. But in a representative government this attribution has substantive content: the people really do act through their government and are not merely passive recipients of its actions." (Pitkin, *op. cit.*:232) To achieve representative government in this latter sense requires a substantive evolution in our conception of citizenship such that the citizen assumes some responsibility for his governing and what his government does.

There is another facet to this idea of responsibility avoidance which is the tendency to pass legislation in response to social ills that in fact is not responsive to the underlying problem. This phenomenon is most common in criminal law in which the severity of sentences is jerked up every time a horrific crime is committed. The area of drug enforcement is an obvious example. The political response to the problem is to increase sentences which has the effect of creating an artificial scarcity that increases demand. The resulting distortions in the sentencing structure are laughable except for the fact that they have real life unjust results. Simplifying a complex social and economic problem by reducing it to a matter of criminal law is responsive to electoral imperatives but is utterly unresponsive in terms of the underlying conditions that give rise to the problem. It may be that some of these problems cannot be solved, but their manipulation for electoral advantage is not the way to find out.

Election Places Demands on Legislators Unrelated to Governing

An elective system of representation also places a burden on the individual legislator that is impossible for most people to meet. The process of election itself forces the legislator to respond to competing demands in such a way that allows him to appeal to each. Responding to competing demands creates schizoid responsibility, and when responsibility becomes schizoid, the legislator's moral compass becomes disoriented. But this is just the beginning. While the legislator must perpetually run for office, he must also attempt to do the job for which he was elected, and this is not the easiest of jobs. The job of congressman, for instance, is frantic and becoming increasingly more onerous. Congressmen have duties both in Washington and in their districts, which require long hours and little time with their families. They are often confronted with the need to vote on issues which they know little about, frustrated by conflicts in committee meetings and overlapping jurisdictions, and debilitated by the need to run from committee meetings to floor votes. They encounter considerable internal conflict between their desire to work

147

on substantive policy issues and the need to respond to constituent requests. They have little time left for practicing the politician's art of compromise and in today's contentious political environment, they find this activity increasingly difficult. On top of this they must still electioneer. (Parker, 1996) Within Congress itself, the congressman must deal with five separate forums to formulate policy: the "Floor" where legislation is introduced, committees where legislation is referred after it is introduced and which are dominated by seniority rules, budget and appropriations committees which deal with money matters, interest groups and lobbyists which may affect the congressman's reelection, and the casework setting where the congressman must respond to constituent demands. (Zweig, 1981)

A non-elected, randomly selected legislature will avoid many of these onerous aspects which are found in the current job description of the legislator. Many become unnecessary immediately because electioneering is no longer a part of the job which allows much more time to practice the art of compromise. In this case, however, compromise is not being sought between competing interests within the legislator's constituency in which those compromises must then be negootiated into compromises reached with the legislator's fellow legislators. Instead, compromises must be negotiated solely among the legislators themselves. What this means is that the legislative process will become more deliberative. Deliberation is not the absence of contention and competition, but it is a result of a legislative environment that is freed from outside influences and pressures which gives the legislative process the potential of taking a much broader and future oriented view of the political landscape.

Election Results in the Professionalization of Politics

At the level of the individual, the citizenship role serves the purpose of providing a unity to the individual's other diverse roles. At the collective level, the practice of citizenship serves a similar unifying function which provides a generalist's perspective to counterbalance specialization and the division of labor. Modern society is becoming increasingly fractured by the division of labor which is one source of complexity in government. This is the type of complexity that can lead to government by "experts" in which the bureaucracy becomes a mirror of various economic or professional specializations and the legislature assumes a similar structure with career legislators specializing in a particular area on a long-term basis. What is lost here is the generalist perspective that looks at the whole and seeks to find a common purpose. One symptom of this type of complexity is a simple lack of common sense.

The notion of common sense may shed some light on the problem of professionalization in politics. Common sense in terms of the individual means using all the senses in common to achieve the most accurate perception of the environment. Collectively common sense means using our unique individual talents and abilities in common to achieve the most accurate perception of social reality. "Common sense is a great repository of culturally developed resources, not a 'marketplace' of possibilities put forward by already ontologically well-developed individuals in competition with one another for personal profit, but a great 'carnival' of different ways of socially constituted being in which everyone can have a 'voice' - in which they can play a part in the shaping and reshaping of their lives." (Shotter, 1993:131) Representation is the means through which collective common sense is exercised.

Perhaps the main function of representation is to achieve unity through diversity. This cannot occur when politics is a specialty reserved to the select few or relegated to a so called "expertocracy". Just as the role of citizen is to serve an integrating function for the individual's other diverse roles, so at the collective level, the function of representation is the principal means through which the tension between the individual and community is mediated. Just as the role of citizen performs a synthesizing function for the individual, the office of representative performs a generalist function for society. It is as a collective body of generalists, not as a college of specialists, that the legislature achieves representation. When politics becomes a career, it becomes just another specialty among a host of specialties. It loses its ability to connect and unify society's disparate professions and occupations and other divisions together in the context of citizenship.[53]

Politics is not strictly speaking a profession because it does not require a particular type of professional training, it has no formal admission procedures, and it has no professional canon of ethics. In theory it is open to anyone. As the result of election, however, it has taken on the qualities of a pseudo-profession, restricted to those few who can gain admission through their ability to raise large sums of money and skills in electioneering. When combined with the inherent advantages of incumbency, politics has become career in which the same legislators are returned to office term after term. One consequence of this is that the individual legislator tends to develop expertise in a particular area and may end up becoming an advocate for a particular industry or interest losing the perspective of the

---

[53] A phenomenon that has been widely observed is the tendency for voters to continuously re-elect their representative even though they claim to support the idea of term limits. One explanation for this phenomenon is that voters have a free rider problem. The tenure of the representative tends to be increased over time because longer tenure imply greater government transfers. In addition, when government wealth transfers are low, the opportunity cost of removing a politician who has acquired skills in creating transfers is low, but as the level of transfers increases, so do the opportunity costs of removing a relatively experienced representative. (Dick and Lott, 1966)

generalist. In addition, when representation becomes a career, it becomes routine and legislators simply get "used to it"–a problem that occurs in the other branches of government as well.

> Now, it is a terrible business to mark a man out for the vengeance of men. But it is a thing to which a man can grow accustomed, as he can to other terrible things; he can even grow accustomed to the sun. And the horrible thing about all legal officials, even the best, about all judges, magistrates, barristers, detective, and policemen, is not that they are wicked (some of them are good), not that they are stupid (several of them are quite intelligent), it is simply that they have got used to it.

> Strictly they do not see the prisoner in the dock: all they see is the usual men in the usual place. They do not see the awful court of judgment; they see only their own workshop....Our civilization has decided, and very justly decided, that determining the guilt or innocence of men is a thing too important to be trusted to trained men....When it wants a library catalogued, or the solar system discovered, or any trifle of that kind, it uses up its specialists. But when it wishes anything done which is really serious, it collects twelve of the ordinary men standing around. (Kennebeck in Simon,1955:239 quoting C.K. Chesterton essay "Twelve Men" in *Tremendous Trifles*.)

The solution suggested in this passage is examined below in the discussion on the idea of random selection.

Election is Noisy

Public discussion of issues is a basic element of democracy which requires that information be available and disseminated widely. Information is the raw material out of which policy positions on various public issues is developed. When a policy position is formed, it is justified by the giving of reasons for the preferability of the position taken. This process of justification is a form of persuasion. Election, however, involves much more than the mere dissemination of information about a candidate so that the voter may justify to himself his choice of a particular candidate; it involves elaborate forms of persuasion that go way beyond reasoned justifications for choosing a particular candidate. Instead of persuasion based on reason, the techniques of commercial advertising and propagandizing are employed to influence voter choice. These techniques result in an extremely high "noise level" which drowns out reasoned justification and blocks the citizenship frontier.

A political campaign is nothing more than an extremely noisy sales pitch in which the candidate is commodified into a product and given different features depending upon which particular interest group it is being sold to.[54] The product is manipulated by various "handlers" that package and re-package it to fit the occasion. The main vehicle for selling the product is television advertising which has increasingly taken the form of emphasizing the defects of the competing product rather than the virtues of the product being sold. Since entertainment is the principle tool used by advertisers to sell their product, entertainment values have replaced political values in

---

[54] This packaging of the candidate is an example of "framing" which is common in opinion research. Frohlich and Oppenheimer (1999) cite the example of two identical policy choices that were phrased differently. Opposite choices were made by experimental subjects based on how the choices were framed. Reframing the candidate for different audiences is just one example of how framing can be used to manipulate electoral outcomes.

campaigns and reduced them to nothing more than noisy marketing strategies. Entertainment, by its nature, tends to be noisy.

The effect of this noise level is to diminish the permeability of the citizenship frontier to the free flow of political ideas which results in an impoverished and corrupted public space. Most political ideas remain unheard, trapped in political private space. Political public space degenerates into an arena for a shouting match of charges and counter charges orchestrated by advertising techniques designed to entertain rather than inform. When the campaign is over, what remains of political public space is an arena of incivility where the animosities generated during the campaign are left to play themselves out. This closure of the citizenship frontier creates an ideal environment for the breeding of corruption which thrives in the secrecy of a public sphere that has lost its publicness. The citizen, in his disdain for the political, is left with the option of either becoming a member of an extremist group that attempts to recapture the citizenship frontier or retreating into economic pursuits focusing on utility maximization. The first option serves to maintain the noise level between elections; the second promotes further corruption through the subordination of the political to the economic. What is lost in all this noise is democratic citizenship.

Election by shouting enhances the ecological synergy of electoral pathology by adding noise making as an additional parasitic technique. This is a condition in which advertisers and marketers have joined with special interest advocacy groups in successfully taking over the campaign process as a means of making their living. This condition is not only one of the main drivers in pushing up the costs of political campaigns, but it is also a means of diverting attention from substantive issues the outcome of which the special interest advocacy groups are seeking to control. Random selection, on the other hand, will be noise free. It can be argued that this freedom from noise means that the process is not public. This is true in the sense that selection is not the result of a public contest. But the

153

publicity surrounding an election is not the same as public deliberation on a policy issue. It is imperative that the mechanics of the random selection process and the selection process itself be conducted in full public view with complete public understanding of the procedure and its results. While there is no "trial by debate" when legislators are randomly selected, the fact is that there is no meaningful discussion of public policy issues during elections. What has developed in place of actual debate are rather sophisticated techniques in obfuscation and the art of making unrealizable promises to the electorate.

Election Results in Unfulfilled Promises

Manin has rightfully argued that legislators should not necessarily be held to the policy positions they advocated during the campaign. It is entirely possible, if not probable, that once in office legislators will obtain additional information or conditions will change such that changing their position is the prudent thing to do. In addition, the art of politics–when politics is practiced properly– is compromise which requires a great deal of skill. The ability to compromise requires that the legislator not be locked into an ideological position such that she loses her flexibility. Election promises have three deleterious results. The first is that the candidate locks herself into an ideological position–usually extreme–to appease an interest group. The second is that she makes promises she knows cannot be actualized. The third is that she makes conflicting promises. Extreme ideological positions taken publicly make compromise impossible and result in legislative gridlock. Unfulfilled promises result in cynicism and amplify the malaise that has already developed out of the ecological synergy of electoral pathology. Contradictory promises obscure the candidate's position on the issue and may limit her ability to compromise.

Randomly selected legislators come to the legislature free of the baggage that would have been accumulated during the campaign. While their political ideas are unknown at the start, they will emerge into political public space during the process of legislative deliberation. It is here, in political public space, that these ideas, not the legislators themselves, will undergo trial by debate. It is not the personality of the legislator that is on trial, but his ideas, and it is through this process that political ideas will be re-presented iteratively until a policy is formulated. The practice of representation occurs in the forum of the legislature in the form of deliberation open to public view. But these representations also stimulate the formation of opinion in political private space which then flows across the citizenship frontier into political public space and becomes public opinion. Public opinion creates a dialogic environment which continues to stimulate legislative deliberation. Eventually this process of opinion formation and legislative deliberation results in the expression of the public will in legislation.

Skill in Electioneering Does Not Equate to Skill in Governing

The skills required to conduct an election campaign are not the same skills required to legislate. An election is an adversarial contest in which candidates compete for votes; legislating is a collective enterprise in which the relative merit of political ideas are tested against the merits of other political ideas with reference to the background public opinion. A campaign requires the marketing and propagandizing skills alluded to above. Legislating requires the ability to formulate and present one's political ideas, evaluate the political ideas of other legislators from diverse backgrounds, and the use ideational competition as a means of reaching a common result. Legislative bodies are by nature adversarial because of the range of opinion on any given issue that comes before them. However this natural contentiousness will not be distorted and magnified as a

155

result of the animosity generated during the campaign being carried over into the legislature and the application of campaign techniques to the process of governing.

Election Creates a Tendency for Representation to Become Advocacy

The dominance of special interest groups and the influence industry in the electoral process has transformed representation into advocacy. In addition to the effect of private money on electoral campaigns, an additional element is the fact that lawyers tend to be overrepresented in legislative bodies[55] and lawyers by trade are advocates for the interests they represent. They are specifically

---

[55] Miller (1995:64-68) offers several theories as to why lawyers are so predominant in American politics: (1) The "high status" argument. Based largely on the observations of Tocqueville, some scholars argue that because attorneys are in a high-status occupation, American voters tend naturally to choose them for political office. (2) The so-called American legal culture argument. Some scholars argue that the American political culture prefers to judge political results by legal standards, thus viewing the legal profession as the legitimate source of public leadership. (3) The expansive historical development of the legal profession. Some commentators argue that lawyers as a profession were the natural group to mold a distinctly American political culture because the swiftly expanding and decentralized society of the late eighteenth century demanded laws and rules to prevent chaos and disorder. (4) The "special skills" argument. Various scholars have argued that attorneys bring special skills and training to politics, which give them major advantages over nonlawyers. (5) The flexible time requirements of the practice of law in the U.S. Lawyers could serve in state legislatures on a part time basis and enter and leave politics without damaging their legal careers. (6) The lawyer advertising argument. Some scholars argue that lawyers were and are attracted to political office as a way to advertise and gain name recognition in order to attract more clients for their law practices. (7) "Lawyers as free agent" theory. American voters tend to prefer to send lawyers to the legislatures because lawyers are seen as independent, neutral parties, not naturally beholden to any special interests.

trained in advocacy and tend to focus on rights and procedures. What they do not have is the generalist's skill of representation.[56] The fact that lawyers are predominant both within legislative bodies and lobbying organizations creates and maintains a symbiotic relationship that is parasitic upon the citizenship frontier. Lawyers are trained to operate in an adversarial arena that is focused primarily on the client's rights. In a legislative environment, special interest campaign contributions become "retainers" for the advocacy of the contributor's rights. The fact that this rights focus may be generalized to some extent obscures the special interest nature of the advocacy.

Election Emphasizes Accountability, not Political Responsibility and Representation

The idea of accountability is significant in a culture where the primary feature is money. The idea of accountability is associated with money and the idea of responsibility in the fiduciary sense of the term. The accounting function is prominent in both government and business–a prominence derived in no small part from the fact that money has the attribute of measurability. The fact that money and things that can be converted to monetary terms (i.e. various conceptions of utility) is measurable has led to a whole movement that can be captured under the term "performance measurement", and the principle technique of justification has become the cost-benefit analysis. Within both private and public

---

[56] "Law school seems to change people's behavior; lawyer-legislators have a superiority complex. On technical issues, clearly, they know more than you do. But generally, they are so vague and abstract. Some of the lawyer-legislators here are very narrow and not very bright. They use their legal training to see the world in a very restricted way, but they can't generalize to make the kind of quality decisions that legislators must make every day. They all have tunnel vision." (Miller,1965:80 quoting a non-lawyer member of the Massachusetts legislature.)

bureaucracies there is a whole host of professionals who job it is to provide justification for various programs and activities.

The root of the word "accountability" is "count" and accountability involves the counting of money. This is not an insignificant area of responsibility, and it is obviously intimately linked with government because government collects its revenue through taxation. After all, the battle cry in the American Revolution was "No taxation without representation". If government is going to place the burden of taxation upon its citizens, it should be held to account to them as to how the money is spent. As a result, a very large segment of the bureaucracy is devoted to various budgeting and accounting functions. However, this accountability is the accountability of the executive branch to the legislature. In theory, since the legislature is supposed to represent the citizens, this is the most expeditious way of holding the executive accountable to the citizens. It is the legislature, and its more representative house, that has the power of raising revenue. This power is vested there precisely because it provides the most direct representation of the citizenry. And it is the institution of election that is supposed to hold the representatives directly accountable to the citizens.

However, the accountability of legislators for the wise allocation of monetary resources has been distorted by the process of election. Legislators should be accountable to their constituents in two ways. In the first instance, legislators should be accountable to the citizens who as taxpayers pay their salaries, but the fact that a significant portion of their income may come from elsewhere has disrupted this fiduciary relationship. In many instances the legislative salary is not the primary source of monetary remuneration for legislators. As an example, Etzioni cites a study which shows that members of Congress used surplus campaign funds for every conceivable item from country club dues to safaris to gifts for wives and children. He also points to other extra sources of income such as the lecture circuit. (Etzioni, *op.cit.,*1984) Further disruption is

158

provided by the availability of rent-seeking opportunities and the ability to obtain lucrative private sector employment either for themselves after leaving office or for members of their families. This latter item is of no small significance because what it means is that although a legislator may be removed from office through election, the benefits of having held that office continue to accrue to him for a long time afterward, often for the rest of his working life. This is hardly the type of accountability (such as that mentioned by Manin above with respect to officeholders in ancient Greece) where an actual count is made, and if the legislator were found to have been using his office for his own benefit, he would have to do something to make restitution to his constituents.

In the second instance, legislators should be accountable to the citizens as taxpayers through the wise allocation of the monetary resources collected. Pork barrel legislation is the traditional way legislators attempt to demonstrate accountability to their districts, and the waste that has resulted from this practice is well known. This has not only resulted in the inefficient allocation of resources, but oftentimes in complete waste such as in the case of keeping a military base open that is no longer necessary. The classic example of the practice is the numerous water projects that have occurred, particularly in the west. The fact that in many, if not most, cases they fail to make economic and environmental sense does not matter.[57] They provide a prime opportunity for a legislator to demonstrate his "accountability" to his district.

The cost of election campaigns has disrupted the fiduciary link of the legislator to his district. The fact that legislators must raise large sums of money to conduct their campaigns displaces the citizen and replaces him with the contributor. We have already seen that in many instances the contributor is an entity that is not even a

---

[57] See Reisner (1986) for an account of the manipulation of water in the American west.

citizen. The fact that many legislators receive contributions from contributors outside their districts disrupts the fiduciary chain even further. Now there need not be even token accountability to the district. The break in the fiduciary link to the district is often masked by the fact that the legislator in question has developed an area of expertise of national importance.[58]

The idea of accountability should not be confused with the idea of responsibility. Representation entails responding to in a more fundamental sense than accounting. It involves justification which is both broader and deeper than accounting for how resources are used. Accounting is essentially uni-dimensional and empirical in that it focuses on what can be measured. Responsibility is multi-dimensional and normative; it requires justification that goes beyond the empirically measurable.[59] It is linked to notions of justice and fairness that include elements that are not always amenable to measurement in terms of money and utility. But these elements are often ignored because election tends to reduce representation to

---

[58] In Minnesota Representative Oberstar of the 8th Congressional district is a classic example of this. He has developed an area of expertise in transportation and was instrumental in getting the State of Minnesota to bail out Northwest Airlines when that company was in financial trouble. The payoff was to get a ticketing center and an aircraft maintenance base located in his district. This demonstrates "accountability" both in terms of pork and accountability to entities other than citizens.

[59] Hannah Arendt's critique of the social sciences arises in this context. The development of the social sciences is an effort to amplify the "rational" administration of mass society, where men have learned to "behave" instead of acting. The quest for abstract laws in the social sciences that render human behavior predictable coincides with the administrator's goal of controlling men. If human affairs can be reduced to questions of causality and probability by the social sciences, then calculation can replace the need for judgment as the goal and method of those in positions of authority which effectively relieves them of the responsibility that goes with judgment. This provides an additional fictional element in the social scientist's belief that not men, but the "laws of mankind" govern. (Hill, 1979)

accountability, and the idea of accountability has been corrupted by the process of election itself.

Election Does Not Select the Best

Although the theory of election presumes it will choose the best because it inevitably results in the selection of a "natural aristocracy", this is not the case. As Frederick Grimke of South Carolina explained in 1848 regarding the idea of rotation in office:

> It has been supposed that where these changes are frequent the persons elected must for the most part be inexperienced and incompetent. The fear lest this should be the case is wisely implanted in our nature. It holds us back when we are about to run into an extreme. ...But public office itself creates to a great extent the very ability which is required for the performance of its duties. And it is not at all uncommon when individuals have been snatched up from the walks of private life to fill responsible stations to find that the affairs of society are conducted pretty much upon the same principles and with as much skill and intelligence as before. Habits of order and method are soon imparted to the incumbent, and they constitute the moving spring of all effective exertion, either mental or physical. (Quoted in Petracca, 1966))

In addition, it is well known that many well qualified candidates will not subject themselves to the demands of electoral campaigns. Proponents of election argue that this deselection is a natural part of selecting the true aristocracy. The assumption is that anyone who cannot withstand the rigors of an electoral campaign is unfit for office which implies that there is some sort of direct correspondence between the ability to conduct an electoral campaign and the ability to legislate or govern. I have already discussed the fact that the skills required to conduct a campaign are not the same skills that are required in governing. In addition to the lack of correspondence between campaigning and governing is the fact that an individual who seeks public office through election must sacrifice her personal privacy (discussed below) in order to do so. Most normal people will not do this and for good reason which reduces the field of candidates further.

Election often Produces Misrepresentation, not Representation

When a candidate runs for office, she is supposed to represent herself in the descriptive sense of giving information about herself. This information about herself includes not only information about who she is, but information about her political ideas–her vision of the good society and the policies she believes are necessary to help attain it. This type of representation is different than the type of representation she will provide if elected. In the latter instance, her function is to make her constituents present, to represent them. In the campaign her function is to represent herself–to present and re-present her ideas to her potential constituents so that they may choose from among the competing candidates which one will represent them. That is how election is supposed to work, in theory. In theory, that his how the "natural aristocracy" arises out of election.

Practice is far different than theory, and one of the main reasons it is different is that it does not involve candidate representation, but *misrepresentation*. Since election is a contested event, what is "natural" is the presentation of the candidate in the most favorable light, and this presentation often has little to do with the rational presentation of political ideas but includes whatever persuasive techniques will ensure a victory at the polls. In most cases this involves the use of various forms of entertainment and

162

advertising techniques that have little to do with concrete political ideas. It also involves the candidate not only in the misrepresentation of herself, but the misrepresentation of her opponents. It is much easier to misrepresent the opposition by taking things out of context and turning it to one's advantage than it is to present one's own ideas in a manner that demonstrates consistency such that the voter knows what he is voting for. The point is that misrepresentation is a natural result of election, and it is one additional factor that enhances the ecological synergy of electoral pathology.

Election Results in the Loss of Privacy

One reaction to the corruptibility of election has been an outright assault on the right to privacy. The assumption that a candidate is entering the campaign on a voluntary basis has come to mean that he has also voluntarily surrendered his right to privacy which has created a highly corrupted meaning of the term "public". To be a candidate for public office has come to mean not only opening one's financial affairs to public view (where there might be a conflict of interest), but the entire gamut of one's activities ranging from one's medical records to one's sexual habits. This is another area where entertainment values have overwhelmed the political with two direct results. The first is that it deselects many, if not most or perhaps all, qualified candidates simply because a normal person would not subject himself to the media circus that surrounds political campaigns. No matter how highly motivated an individual may be to serve in public office, she would also have to have an element of psychological pathology in her personality to allow her personal habits and behaviors to become the subject of public entertainment. This is one factor that is involved in the reduction of representation to the representation of a restricted range of personality types.

The second result from this assault on the privacy of the public official is that that official loses his appreciation for the meaning of the right to privacy. This lack of appreciation of the realm of the private is particularly dangerous to the average citizen because it may find its way into legislation through which the citizen loses his privacy rights.[60] This is no small matter in this technological age in which there is so much information on every citizen in numerous computer databases. One of the major functions of the citizenship frontier is to maintain the distinction between public and private. It is an easy matter for a public official who has lost her appreciation of the right to privacy to engage in an assault on the citizenship frontier. If the citizenship frontier is breached by such assaults, the public will overwhelm the private and the representation of the citizen in public space will be replaced by the absolute representation of the sovereign in what was formally private space.

Election Results in Hubris

The fact that election campaigns are highly contentious results in the phenomenon which I will call "the hubris of electoral victory". Quite simply this is the attitude that since the legislator was victorious in the electoral campaign, she deserves the office, and that the office is hers. This attitude includes the idea that the electoral victory confers a right to hold the office upon the victor. One result

---

[60] The issue of privacy is central in the last two attempts to impeach the President. In the current attempt, the issue has to do with the President's personal privacy. Most citizens were deeply offended by the President's actions; but they were equally offended by the invasion of his privacy by both prosecutors and representatives motivated by their personal animosity toward the President rather than protecting the republic from a "high crime or misdemeanor". In the Watergate affair, on the other hand, one of the major allegations against the President was his use of his office and other executive branch agencies to violate the privacy rights of individual citizens.

of this is hubris–that arrogance of power that is all too common in politics.[61]

In a democracy, public offices belong to the citizens. They have a right *to* the office since they may seek it themselves through election and they have a right *in* the office since they determine who shall occupy it *to serve them*. They also pay for the office through taxation. The office belongs to them. The holder of the office has no inherent right to or in the office other than the same rights held by every other citizen. In a sense, public offices are property rights of citizens held in common. In theory those rights to and in the office are exercised through election. In practice election violates this right, a violation that the hubris of electoral victory makes most evident.[62]

---

[61] The current scandal in Washington that has led to impeachment hearings is a result of this phenomenon. This episode provides ample examples of hubris in general on the part of the vast majority of all the participants, but it was the Clinton administration that exhibited hubris arising out of the assumption that the President has a right to the office he holds. An example that is virtually unknown outside Minnesota (and inside as well) is the "phonegate" scandal that occurred during the early 90's. This was a prime example of hubris in that it involved legislators assuming the attitude that they were exempt from laws they themselves had passed. Democracy is associated with the idea that the citizens are to be the authors of the laws that are addressed to them. In this case the opposite occurred– laws were addressed to the citizens and the legislators assumed that they were exempt. Had state employees in the executive branch committed the same offense, the sanctimonious blather emanating from the legislature would have been unceasing over a period of months. It was out of this episode that I got the original idea for writing this book. I had had jury duty the year before and began thinking that while jury duty is an inconvenience, it did bring people from all walks of life together who appeared to take it seriously. Why not choose legislators the same way?

[62] The issue in the current hearings and investigations into the possible impeachment of the President illustrate this point. President Clinton has no inherent right to the Office of President. Rather what is at stake is the right of the people in the office. For better or worse, they chose this President twice through election. To constitutionally negate that right through impeachment requires a showing that the President used the powers of the office to abuse the citizens' right

Election Emphasizes the Cult of Personality Instead of the Merit of Ideas

Max Weber (Weber, 1958) described the evolution of authority as proceeding from traditional authority, to charismatic, to rational or bureaucratic. In traditional societies authority resided in the customs and beliefs that were universally shared. Most of these had their origin in religious or supernatural beliefs. With the rise of monarchy, the authority of tradition was transferred to the person of the monarch, but eventually the actual personality of the monarch became a factor. Charismatic authority is that authority that arises out of "charisma" or personality traits that enable one individual to command respect from others and assume leadership roles. Bureaucratic or rational authority is that authority that arises out of hierarchy and is vested in highly structured organizations with well-defined rules and regulations. Bureaucratic authority in some form is prevalent in most of the present-day world societies. However, during elections in those societies which allow for some form of political competition, there is a reversion to charismatic authority which is reflected in the widespread media attention to the

---

in the office. My own personal view on this matter is that what the President did showed an incredible lack of judgment and common sense, but the acts he committed did not rise to the level of impeachment. There is no comparison between this President's lying to save face because of marital infidelity and President Nixon's using the power of the office to actually abuse, not only the citizens' right in the office, but other rights as well through such things as burglarizing the Democratic Party headquarters, violating the civil rights of those people on his "enemies list", the use of executive branch agencies such as the FBI and CIA to abuse citizen rights, etc. President Clinton should have resigned the office because his lack of judgment calls into question his ability to govern and raises the very real possibility that similar lack of judgment in the future could violate the citizens' right in the office. But future possibility is not proof of an actual offense, and at this stage of the investigation nothing has been shown that the citizens' right in the office has been violated by an inability to govern.

personalities involved which tends to eclipse the policies that they propose.

The emphasis on personality distorts the political process by shifting the focus from the merit of ideas to the person of the candidate. The characteristic that is deemed a "superiority" in the selection of the "natural aristocracy" quite often involves charisma rather than traits such as integrity, foresightedness, the ability to compromise, and the ability to generate new ideas. Since personality is filtered through the media, charisma has become detached from the actual personality of the candidate. The manipulation of images through the media has led to the creation of an artificial personality endowed with an artificial charisma, and it is for this artificial personality that the voter casts his ballot. The fact that charisma is more easily manipulated by the media than these other traits magnifies its distorting impact. What is lost with this focus on personality is any serious consideration of the quality of the candidate's ideas.

Election Results in the Political Manipulation of Citizenship

Another problem with election is that it induces politicians to manipulate citizenship for electoral advantage. In the past this practice was evident in manipulating eligibility for the franchise through such things as literacy tests that were specifically designed to maintain segregation and exclude blacks from voting. Today, these manipulations have become inclusive instead of exclusive in the form of get out the vote drives. But more cynical manipulations of citizenship occur in the form of granting citizenship to alien groups solely because it is presumed that these groups will vote for a particular party or candidate.[63]

---

[63] Granting expedited citizenship to the Hmong was the most recent example of this. The justification was that they deserved expedited citizenship because they

When Election is Appropriate

Before moving on to a consideration of the advantages of random selection, I must briefly mention that, in theory, election is an appropriate selection method at the local level of government. What is assumed here, however, is that there is something that approaches a genuine community at the local level. The assumption of community means that the individuals running for local office will be well known to the electors in their community and that their selection will be free of corrupting influences. This assumption is obviously not valid for most communities today because residential communities are no longer functioning communities for the following reasons: (1) most residents no longer work in them, (2) the distance between home and work has increased, (3) they have become culturally diverse, (4) they have a high population turnover, (5) mothers are no longer at home during the day, (5) the automobile has reduced pedestrian interaction, (6) security problems have led to increased privatization, (7) with fewer people home, the household has become less attached to the locality. (Popenoe, 1995) As a result of these conditions local government has become the province of real estate interests as evidenced by the proliferation of strip malls and retail chain stores of the same company and competing companies on virtually every other corner.

In spite of these problems, the idea of random selection should be applied to the state level as opposed to the local level. Local government involves overlapping jurisdictions and different types of local structures which create too much confusion to set up the administrative structure for random selection. In addition, much of local government tends to be executive and administrative type

---

assisted the United States in the Vietnam War. Using this justification to obscure the fact that they were presumed to vote democratic in an upcoming election emphasizes the cynical nature of the practice.

functions as opposed to purely legislative functions. Random selection is not appropriate for executive type functions which require specialization. The idea of citizenship applies to the nation, but because of the peculiar development of the American federal system, it applies to the state as well. The state is the ideal setting within which to develop the ideas of citizenship. After state citizenship is developed, the model of citizenship can them be applied to the federal government. Local government, however, will remain an arena of voluntary participation. However, it is certainly reasonable to provide that service at the local level exempts the citizen so serving from further service in the state legislature. It is also a hope that, as a byproduct of a vibrant state citizenship, the assumption of a genuine community at the local level will become valid.

Election at the federal level will have to continue until the citizenship role at the state level is sufficiently developed such that randomness can be applied to the selection of national legislators. Hopefully the experience in the various states will provide insight into the most appropriate way to apply the idea to the federal government. One possibility is that citizens who have served in the state legislature may volunteer for random selection to the House of Representatives, leaving the Senate elective during the transition. Federal service will probably have to have to be voluntary because of the sacrifice required, but the challenge will be to introduce a random element into the selection process.

Since lot is the democratic selection method *par excellence*, a review of its advantages is in order. The definition of random selection that I am using includes not only the random selection of representatives from the population of public citizens at large, but the requirement of selection without replacement - i.e., once a citizen is chosen for representative service, that citizen cannot be chosen again. In other words, there is a requirement of absolute rotation in office. Public offices may be viewed in two ways. In an elective system they are viewed as scarce goods for which candidates compete. In the view presented here, they are viewed as a burden or an obligation of citizenship like jury duty. I will now consider the idea of random selection. A discussion of how to apply the idea in practice is taken up in Chapter IV.

The Idea of Random Selection

The idea of randomness is fundamental in both the physical and social sciences. In mathematics it refers to a set of objects each of which has an equal probability of occurring. It is this idea of equal probability or chance that is used in statistics to measure the degree of association between events. It is against this standard of equal probability that statistical relationships are inferred. In chemistry the idea of the ideal gas is used, one property of which is that its molecules move about at random and each one has an equal probability of being at one place in one point in time. In biology the idea of randomness is fundamental in genetics and evolution. Random variations or mutations in genes is what drives evolution. In the social sciences statistics is used to test hypotheses about social phenomenon and to make inferences about social processes.

The idea of randomness is often associated with disorder which is captured in the concept of entropy from thermodynamics. The idea here is than in any system there is an inherent tendency toward randomness and disorder. The addition of energy to a system is required to counteract this tendency. The idea of randomness is also associated with fairness as exemplified in the traditional toss of the coin. A random procedure is unbiased, and in that sense always produces a fair result. This idea of being fair is applied to election in the precept that each citizen's vote is to count equally. But election, as we have seen, is hardly a random process. It is subject to all sorts of voluntary and involuntary actions that affect the outcome, the negative effects of which were examined above.

The idea of random selection in politics has the same potential that it does in biological evolution, that is, random variants can lead to new forms that are more suitably adapted to the environment. In biology this process occurs naturally, as opposed to the artificial breeding of select forms.[64] In politics the purpose of randomness applies to the expression of ideas. Its purpose is not to achieve representation in the form of resemblance in which the legislature is a sample of the population. This is the result, but it is not the purpose. The purpose is to ensure the greatest probability that all political ideas are expressed and taken into consideration, a condition that can only obtain when legislators are selected randomly. The objective here is the same that occurs in natural selection–to provide adaptability to the natural, social, and political environment. When the expression of political ideas is blocked by interest, both society as a whole and the individuals of which it is composed, lose their ability to adapt. A disease free, permeable citizenship frontier is necessary for a healthy society precisely because it provides the greatest probability of adaptability.

The idea of the random selection of citizens for service in the legislature is the most radical, and most necessary, element of citizenship. It is obviously radical because it has never been tried. It

---

[64] The idea of random selection is a fundamental concept in genetics which is used to explain evolution. Current developments in microbiology and genetic engineering could lead to the reduction of randomness in the human genome. Even though the intent is to reduce disease and suffering, the long-range consequences are not only unknown, but potentially very dangerous. The opposite of randomness is uniformity. The search for genetic perfection could lead to the development of a humanity that at best could be described as boring and at worst is unable to adapt and becomes extinct. It is precisely because of the potential dangers of technological developments such as this that randomness needs to be introduced into the political process to provide a check on rushing off into the unknown without fully assessing the potential consequences.

requires an element of trust in our fellow citizens[65] which, in an individualistic, competitive society that revolves around group differences and is inherently distrustful, will be difficult to muster. This is also the reason that it is necessary. There is no doubt that there is risk in the idea, because the idea of randomness is inherent in the concept of risk. The idea will require not only transition and change which is fearful to most people, but the unpredictability of the burden will be disruptive to individual citizens. It will also require citizens to prepare themselves to accept the burden in terms of education, keeping themselves informed, and readjusting their lives when called to serve. Ultimately, it will require the individual citizen to reconceptualize himself and herself. The role of citizen will assume a much greater importance and serve to integrate and unify the individual's other roles. It is through this role transformation that citizenship will mediate and maintain balance in the tension between the individual and community.

The idea of randomness may take several institutional forms. The most basic is a one house legislature for which public citizens are selected on a random basis. The selection could be from a geographical district or at large. There is no inherent need for districts, because the duty of the representative is to represent him or herself. However, as a practical matter, districts may be useful,

---

[65] The issue of trust is obviously complex, the exploration of which requires separate treatment that cannot be dealt with here. However, a recent study by Putnam (1996) on our declining social capital exemplified by the observation that we are "bowling alone" suggests some rather compelling circumstantial evidence that indicts television as the culprit. "In short, television privatizes our leisure time." Through television we may be creating George Orwell's 1984 with an ironic twist. Instead of Big Brother watching us through the ubiquitous prying eyes of television cameras, we are voluntarily watching Big Brother through the ubiquitous presence of the tube, and by so doing, allowing Big Brother to exercise thought control in a far more efficient manner. Only in this case Big Brother is not the institution of government, but the ever present "market" with its incessant demands that we consume, consume, consume....

particularly as a transition device. The state legislature is the most appropriate place to try out this idea. The fact that there are fifty states allows for various forms of experimentation on which institutional arrangement is most effective. Theoretically, a one house legislature should be sufficient because the checks and balances that are provided by the two-house system will no longer be required. But there may be other reasons for a two-house system, particularly in the transition.

The idea of simple random selection may need to be modified, particularly in the transition, in which case districts will be required. Since there may be compelling reasons why a particular individual cannot make the commitment required for legislative service, simple random selection can be modified in the following way. Instead of simply selecting a representative at random from the pool of public citizens, a group of public citizens from the district will be selected, and they in turn will choose the representative *from within their own group*. This latter element is necessary to prevent outside influences from corrupting the selection process. This procedure loses the quality of pure randomness, but it provides a compromise between randomness and the fact that particular individuals may have legitimate reasons why they cannot serve. It may, therefore, be a useful alternative in the transition to a purely random system. Citizens born into a society in which random selection is the norm will have much less difficulty in accepting the idea. But in the interim, this compromise may be necessary.

A two-house legislature may also be desirable in the interim. In this case the idea of random selection will be applied to the House of Representatives while maintaining an elected Senate. The main advantage of this arrangement is that it allows for a gradual phase in of the new selection method while preserving institutional stability. Democracy does not just happen. It involves learning and practice on the part of the citizenry. That is why the ideas advocated here cannot be applied to the Federal government until they have been tried out at the state level first to both provide an opportunity to iron out bugs and make improvements and to provide a learning opportunity for the citizens. A gradual phase in at the state level may also be necessary for the same reasons. Maintaining the dual house legislature will allow for this gradual phase in

I have said virtually nothing about the selection of the executive, but the procedure will be a revival of the electoral college idea. However, there is one major difference. The executive does not represent him or herself. He or she represents the state in the form of re-presenting the will of the citizens as expressed by the legislature in the form of executive action. He or she brings the will of the citizens to life. The electoral college can take several forms. Initially, it will have to consist of a group of citizens selected at random, either at large or from districts, but eventually, after the number of citizens who have served in the legislature has built up, it could be selected from the body of former legislators. At any rate, the electoral college will search for the most qualified candidate for the chief executive from the body of public citizens. However, there is the danger that it could be open to corrupting influences, and therefore it is imperative that the electoral college conduct its work in public. While citizen legislators serve for one term only, it may be desirable to allow the executive to serve for more than one term. This decision will have to come from a new electoral college.

Judges of the state supreme court and lower courts should be appointed by the executive and ratified by the legislature. Election is not desirable, and, in this case, direct or indirect random selection is inappropriate. Since judicial independence is a necessary requirement for the judicial power to be an effective check on the legislature and executive, the term of office for judges should be relatively long, but they should not be eligible for a second term. However, they may be eligible for a term in a higher court.

Jury Duty

      The one area of government where we do not elect is in choosing the jury. Although the jury may have faults, these are not the result of the selection method, but the various machinations of the legal profession. To see why, imagine the type of justice that would obtain were the jury chosen by election. Lawyers would have a heyday in their designs to manipulate the process. Since the jury is the only available model of a system based on random selection, I need to examine the jury before turning to consideration of other advantages of the idea of random selection.

      Juries composed of citizens can be traced back to ancient Greece and probably consisted of six members is most cases, but in the trial of Socrates for corrupting the youth of Athens the total reached as high as 501. (Reid, Penrod, & Pennington, 1983) In England the practice probably derived from the Norman institution of recognition by sworn inquest in which 12 knights were chosen as reconitiors who had the duty to inquire into matters of interest to the new rulers of England that might be the object of public inquest such as the taxation of a subject. As early as the 12th century it became common for suitors in certain real estate matters to apply to the Kings Court for the summoning of recognitors who would determine the truth of the matter either from their own knowledge or the knowledge of others. If the verdict was unanimous, it was accepted by the court. This practice was gradually extended to other matters of common law. (Encarta, 1995) In criminal trials the unanimous decision rule probably originated in the 14th Century English practice of *afforcement*, in which a jury of twelve started to decide the case and additional jurors were added until at least twelve could agree on a verdict. (Reid, *et al.*, *op. cit.*) Originally jurors were selected because they were witnesses or had special knowledge of the facts, suitors, and customs of the people, but by the 15th Century their role was limited to judging factual matters based on the evidence presented.

The practice of trial by jury was carried over into the American colonies in various forms. Connecticut, Rhode Island, Massachusetts, and New Hampshire blended law, equity, and admiralty jurisdictions and thus extended the right of trial by jury further than the other colonies. They also had a peculiar feature in which the verdict of one jury could be appealed to another until two out of three agreed. (Hamilton, Federalist #83) The original Constitution did not specify a right to trial by jury, but this was added for criminal cases in the 6th Amendment and it was preserved in civil cases where the value in controversy exceeded twenty dollars by the 7th Amendment. De Tocqueville praised the wisdom of the jury system, particularly when applied in civil cases. The jury system had a republican character in that it put the control of affairs into the hands of the ruled.

Juries, especially civil juries, instill some of the habits of the judicial mind into every citizen, and just those habits are the very best way of preparing people to be free.

It spreads respect for the courts' decisions and for the idea of right throughout all classes. With those two elements gone, love of independence is merely a destructive passion.

Juries teach men equity in practice. Each man, when judging his neighbor, thinks that he may be judged himself. That is especially true of juries in civil suits; hardly anyone is afraid that he will have to face a criminal trial, but anybody may have a lawsuit.

Juries teach each individual not to shirk responsibility for his own acts, and without that manly characteristic no political virtue is possible.

Juries invest each citizen with a sort of magisterial office; they make all men feel that they have duties toward society and that they take a share in its government. By making men pay attention to things other than their own affairs, they combat that individual selfishness which is like rust in society.

Juries are wonderfully effective in shaping a nation's judgment and increasing its natural lights. That, in my view, is its greatest advantage. It should be regarded as a free school which is always open and in which each juror learns his rights, comes into daily contact with the best-educated and most-enlightened members of the upper classes, and is given practical lessons in the law, lessons which the advocate's efforts, the judge's advice, and also the very passions of the litigants bring within his mental grasp. I think that the main reason for the practical intelligence and the political good sense of the Americans is their long experience with juries in civil cases. (de Tocqueville, 1968:274-5)

The jury is the only institution in which the people are entrusted with the power of government, and it functions in two roles that may be contradictory - as an institution of democratic representation and an institution of democratic deliberation. (Abramson, 1994) Unfortunately the jury has been eviscerated from an institution that assumed ordinary citizens were competent to make independent judgments about the law to the opposite assumption that they know nothing about the law. In addition, in the name of impartiality, the ideal juror is virtually ignorant about everything.

A minister, intelligent, esteemed, and greatly respected; a merchant of high character and known probity; a mining superintendent of intelligence and unblemished reputation; a quartz-mill owner of excellent standing, were all questioned in the same way, and all set aside. Each said the public talk and the newspaper reports had not so biased his mind but that

177

sworn testimony would ... enable him to render a verdict without prejudice and in accordance with the facts. But of course, such men could not be trusted with the case. Ignoramuses alone could mete out unsullied justice. (Mark Twain, quoted in Abramson p. 45)

The one element that preserves the democratic character of the modern jury is selection by lot which produces a representative cross section of the community. Unfortunately, even this last remaining vestige of democracy is being eroded by justifying the cross sectional ideal in terms of interest group politics where the representative jury is used to mediate among interest groups.[66] The cross-sectional ideal was a response to the fiction that jurors represent pure disembodied reason, but it has been carried too far. Now all that is expected is the balancing of competing biases rather than deliberation aimed at delivering justice. In spite of its imperfections, jurors are still proving that twelve persons of diverse backgrounds are capable of achieving a wisdom that one individual is incapable of achieving along. (Abramson, *op. cit.*)

The unanimous decision rule that applies in criminal cases distinguishes the jury as a deliberative, as opposed to a merely representative, body. A jury is deliberative when its members realize that their goal is not to represent or protect the interest of their own group, but to join with others in the search for truth and shared justice. In their study of the jury, Hastie, *et al* (1983) found that the "social climate" of deliberation became adversarial or even combative when the decision rule was changed from unanimity to

---

[66] A variant of this erosion is the "death qualified" jury in capital cases. A death qualified juror is one who has no a priori qualms in applying the death sentence in the statutorily specified circumstances. Obviously if "death qualified" jurors are more prone to convict the representativeness of the jury is lost. In election the "litmus test" phenomenon that pertains to certain social issues is somewhat analogous to a "death qualified" jury.

majority rule. Their explanation for this phenomenon was that the larger factions realized it was not necessary to respond to all opposition arguments when their goal was to achieve a faction size of eight or ten members.

The Hastie study is instructive because it examined the social dynamics that occur within small groups. Although a legislative body is larger than a jury, the dynamics of jury deliberation may point to potential problem areas in the legislative setting. Hastie and his colleagues were attempting to assess jury adequacy in terms of cross-sectional representativeness, counter balancing of biases, accurate fact finding, accurate application of the law, and accurate verdicts. The decision rule affected each of these factors except for representation and composition. In terms of individual juror performance, the education of the juror was the predominant predictor of performance. There was a wide amount of variance in terms of participation on the part of individual jurors. This variance is typical of that found in many types of discussion groups and probably results from a combination of factors that include individual differences in talkativeness, a dominance hierarchy within the group, and social conventions governing polite debate. What the authors found disturbing was that a number of the juries included members that didn't participate at all other than in voting. However, they were usually a part of the majority factions and their views may have been expressed by other members of the faction. Jury decision processes did not get hung up on abstract legal concepts and they managed to display an impressive amount of common sense. In the view of at least one judge, the jury verdict, upon reflection, was correct in most cases.[67]

---

[67] Charles W. Joiner (in Simon,1975:146-7) This judge upon reflection considered the jury verdict correct in every case but one, even though he initially did not always agree with the verdict. He points out that when jurors are deliberating, they are teaching one another about the facts, rationale of the case, and the law all of which helps to prevent error in the final decision.

It is difficult to compare jury deliberations and the deliberations of a randomly selected legislative body because (1) the size of the two are radically different, (2) the decision rules are radically different, and (3) jury deliberations are conducted under conditions of secrecy (which has severely limited the ability to study jury behavior) while legislative sessions are conducted under conditions of public scrutiny. Nevertheless, the jury is a real-life example of ordinary citizens from all walks of life coming together on a random basis to perform a function of government. When we consider that the jury system still manages to work fairly well even under conditions where the ideal juror is the uninformed juror, where interest group representation has been injected into the selection process, and where jurors are presumed ignorant of the law and restricted to the role of fact finders only, the vision of ordinary citizens performing as reasonably effective legislators on a randomly selected basis is not outside the realm of the possible. The fact that the jury system needs reform does not obviate the fact that it does show the potential of the citizen legislator as a reasonable alternative to the elected "professional" career politician.[68]

---

[68] A relatively recent variation on the idea of jury duty is the "citizen jury". This involves a random selection of a panel of citizens who then meet to discuss and make recommendations on issues of public policy. The Governor of Minnesota is using this idea to resolve the issue of property taxation. A panel of randomly selected citizens will meet and hear testimony on this complex issue and will then make recommendations on how it can be reformed. The Jefferson Center has conducted 26 Citizens Jury® projects since 1974. A typical jury consists of 18 randomly selected individuals who hear testimony from expert witnesses and on the final day present their recommendations to the public. Although there is random selection in the selection of the panel, the decision to serve is voluntary.

Advantages of Random Selection

While the experience with jury duty exemplifies the importance of the idea of random selection in providing justice, the idea has other advantages that are particularly appropriate in the legislative setting. I will now outline the legislative advantages of the idea.

Maximizes Liberty

Representative democracy radically expands the obligations of citizenship. In this model participation in the legislature is a fundamental obligation of citizenship. This obligation cannot be voluntary because that would defeat representation. Since this obligation does not exist anywhere at present, it will have to be created, and it can only be created by constitutional amendment. Thus it will originate from a *political* contract. This obligation creates a new responsibility - the responsibility to respond to political ideas with other political ideas in the legislative forum. The creation of this new obligation raises the issue of liberty.

The idea of liberty is a paradox because too much freedom can lead to too little. If people can do what they like, what happens is that the strong arbitrarily impose their will on the weak. This can be seen in certain progressive school settings where, in the absence of adult authority, there is notorious peer group pressure and compulsive rule enforcement by the children themselves. (Peters, 1987) People are not free in a situation like this.[69] They are only free because there is some rule that is enforced that allows them to be free. Rousseau argued that the general will is what allowed man to

---

[69] People are also not free when the rule of law breaks down. We like to think that we are free, but a people afraid to walk down the street because of crime is not free. A people hidden behind walled gates out of fear of crime is not free.

be free, and anyone who would not conform to the general will would have to be forced to be free. What man lost by entering the social contract was his natural liberty for which he gained civil liberty in return. Natural liberty is bounded by the strength of the individual, but civil liberty is limited by the general will. When man acquires civil liberty, he also acquires moral liberty which makes him master of himself and frees him from impulse and appetite. (Rousseau, 1993)

The compulsory component of citizenship which includes the obligation to serve in the legislature is an extension of this paradox. To maximize their political liberty, citizens may be called upon to sacrifice some non-political liberty. This is consistent with Rawlsian justice which requires a lexical ordering of the principles of justice in which liberty can only be restricted for the sake of liberty and it is only the political liberties that are guaranteed their fair value. (Rawls, 1976,1997) To develop this argument, I need to start by considering what is meant by political liberty. I will then need to show that the involuntary nature of the requirement that citizens serve as legislators produces greater political liberty.

The essence of political liberty centers around freedom of conscience and expression. It involves the free expression of ideas in general, but, since it is political ideas that it is most tempting for the intolerant to suppress, there is a particular emphasis on the freedom to express political ideas. Political ideas, as I have said, have to do with those ideas about the type of society we want to live in. The four benefits of free expression to mankind have been concisely expressed by Mill. First, an opinion that is forced into silence may be true, and to silence it is to assert infallibility. Second, the silenced opinion, although basically false, may contain a part of the truth, and since the prevailing opinion rarely contains the whole truth, it is only through confrontation with adverse opinions that the remainder of the truth can be supplied. Third, if the prevailing opinion is in fact the whole truth, it will lose its force and become more of a prejudice without understanding unless it is contested. And related to this, fourth, the doctrine will be in danger of losing its meaning preventing the development of conviction based on reason and experience. (Mill, 1993:120-1)

Liberty is a property of individuals, and liberty of expression is the freedom of individuals to express themselves without restriction. The search for truth, in the political sense, is a search for those ideas that address the questions of what constitutes a desirable society and how it can be achieved. These ideas are the raw material out of which it becomes possible to construct the desirable society. [70] Since ideas arise in the minds of individuals, it is the liberty of individual expression that is of ultimate importance. The group and society itself can become tyrannical in overt and covert ways. Mill referred to the despotism of custom as one of the great hindrances of human advancement.[71] There is much talk of diversity these days, but this is not the type of diversity to which Mill referred. Millian diversity is the diversity of opinion which is an expression of individuality. The diversity that is defended today is the diversity of groups. While there is value in the recognition and appreciation of group differences, it is important not to lose sight of the fact that liberty can be lost when the emphasis is on group differences. When the emphasis is on group differences, the result is often the suppression of potentially innovative individual ideas by group ideology.

Individuals are not born in freedom because they had no choice over the circumstances of their birth. They did not choose

---

[70] One of these ideas is citizenship. Citizenship is an idea that we inherit from the past, but it is also politically constructed and reconstructed through time. What is being suggested here is a model for its reconstruction in the next stage of its evolution.

[71] A people afraid to participate in politics because of fear of criticism is not free. A people unable to participate in politics because of economic pressure is not free. An individual unable to think for himself is not free.

their parents, the society they were born into, and the historical period they happen to be in. They also had no choice in the outcome of the genetic lottery. But, if they can develop the ability to think for themselves and give expression to their ideas, they can alter these initial conditions and contribute to social evolution. In short, they can become free. The social conditions they are born into are given; their continuance is not. Social conditions are not the product of nature; they are created by human agency and they can be changed by human agency. Political ideas are the means through which this change can and does occur. Therefore, for there to be progress, there must be a diversity of political ideas. Some ideas may be inappropriate under current conditions but may be very useful when conditions change. To lose these ideas is to rob the future. Some ideas may be inappropriate under any circumstances. To lose these ideas is to lose the opportunity to replace them with better ideas. Some ideas may contain a solution to a pressing problem. To lose these ideas is to rob the present. Some ideas may enlighten the past. To lose these ideas is to rob the past, present, and future. To lose any of these ideas is to rob our culture.

The liberty that is lost when an individual citizen is required to serve in the legislature is an opportunity cost to that individual and to society. I do not mean to minimize these costs, but it is important to recognize that they are limited. The term of legislative service is limited to a single term once in an individual's lifetime. It is possible that during that time the individual may lose some fantastic opportunity that could even have untold benefits to society. But it is much more likely that the opportunity will be displaced into the future. The liberty that is gained is in the expansion of the political ecology of ideas. Herein it is expected that the benefits will outweigh the costs, at least in the long run. It is possible that some of the benefits may only be realized by future generations. If so, that is a gift that we bequeath to the future. The point is that the cost of the non-political individual liberty that is lost is more than compensated for by the gain in individual political liberty. In this sense the citizen is in fact being forced to be free. She is not being forced to accept the general will, but to participate in its creation. And since the general will is never static, it must be continually recreated.

Integrative Effects

The most obvious integrative effect of the random selection of representatives is that over the long run the representative body will resembles the body of citizens. Although integration in the form of resemblance is not the objective, it does provide the opportunity for individuals from diverse backgrounds to confront one another and learn to work together which will lead to a gradual erosion of the racial and ethnic stereotypes that have been built up over the years. This will occur not only among the individual members of the legislature itself, but in the public at large as it views the process. Since the main source of racial and ethnic animosity is ignorance, the random selection of legislators will provide an education to the public about other people of different backgrounds. This education will occur because the legislative forum is a *public* forum. The fact of publicity will also have a moderating effect on the expression of extreme ideologies and behaviors. Although legislators will not be motivated by reelection concerns, most of them will still be desirous of public esteem.

The more important type of integration that will occur is the integration of political ideas. The integration of political ideas is a hermeneutic endeavor that results in homeostasis. A true integration of political ideas cannot occur when the range of the political is restricted to the relatively undifferentiated ideologies of the two political parties. One of the basic dimensions along which political integration must occur is the tension between the individual and community which is difficult enough in homogeneous social settings

185

but becomes far more complex when there are multiple communities. To eliminate the multiple community problem, it is necessary to create a political community that includes all. The tension to be resolved, then, is between the individual and the political community, and the way to resolve it is for the individual to represent him or herself to the political community. Representation means the presentation of political ideas to the political community. It is this continuing presentational process that results in a dynamic integration of political ideas. For it to succeed, it must occur within the context of public reason. Individuals representing themselves *qua* individuals unhindered by group obligation gives expression to individualism as a value. The integration of individual ideas with other individual ideas which together help resolve public problems gives expression to pluralism as a value.

Random Selection Will Replace the Cult of Personality with Representational Authority

I mentioned above that election emphasizes the cult of personality. The selection of candidates by random selection will result in a new type of authority that may serve as a correcting mechanism to bureaucratic authority and will displace the cult of personality. I will call this new type of authority "representational authority" because it is derived directly from the species of representation advanced here in which the citizens are the authors of the laws that address them. The authority of public policy will be derived from the quality of the political ideas upon which it is based rather than the personality traits of a charismatic leader. The formalization of these ideas in law and policy will also redirect the founding principle of the bureaucracy away from its rationalization in obtuse rules and regulations that usually have a self-perpetuating character linked to a hidden interest, toward a genuine public purpose based on serving the policy objectives authored by public

186

citizens. The executive and administrative branches of government will become much more fluid and adaptable to the needs and wishes of the citizens they are supposed to serve.

Long Range View

Even though they are limited to a single term, randomly selected legislators are more likely to take a longer-range view of public policy. In the electoral system, legislators are always acting within the constraint of the next election. This constrains them in two ways. First, they must frame legislative proposals with an eye toward the next election if they hope to get reelected. This fact alone virtually guarantees a short-sighted view of legislation. Unfortunately, this fits right in with the general American cultural trait of desiring instant results. In the corporate world the focus in on the financial results for the next quarter. In the society at large, the focus is on various forms of instant gratification. But when it comes to public policy, there are issues that require a long-term view. The degradation of the natural environment and the explosion of the human population are issues that will affect the survival of our species on this planet. But because of the short-term view which elections force upon the representatives in the legislature, issues such as these, if they are considered at all, are considered in terms of their short-term economic consequences. There is no guarantee that a randomly selected legislature will consider issues such as these with a long-range view, but the probability is higher in a legislative body that is not focused on re-election.

The second constraint imposed by re-election is that the process of re-election distracts the legislator from his or her legislative duties. The process of election is a costly enterprise which can be compared to an entrepreneur running a business. (Mondale Policy Forum, 1992:39) This not only takes time away from legislative duties, but it means that the legislator is not accountable

187

to his or her electorate. While the randomly selected legislator is not accountable to an electorate either, at least all of his or her time and energy will be spent on the job of legislating.

Minimizes the Tyranny of the Majority and the Evils of Faction

> What I find most repulsive in America is not the extreme freedom reigning there, but the shortage of guarantees against tyranny.
>
> When a man or a party suffers an injustice in the United States, to whom can he turn? To public opinion? That is what forms the majority. To the legislative body? It represents the majority and obeys it blindly. To the executive power? It is appointed by the majority and serves as its passive instrument. To the police? They are nothing but the majority under arms. A jury? The jury is the majority vested with the right to pronounce judgment; even the judges in certain states are elected by the majority. So, however iniquitous or unreasonable the measure which hurts you, you must submit.
>
> ..., the majority has such absolute and irresistible sway that one must in a sense renounce one's rights as a citizen, and, so to say, one's status as a man when one wants to diverge from the path it has marked out.
>
> Alexis De Tocqueville

As we have seen Madison's solution to the problem of the tyranny of the majority and faction was a large republic. The reason a large republic prevents these evils is that the proportion of fit characters is not less in a large republic than a small one and that in a large republic a representative is chosen by a larger number of citizens. Madison recognized that "[M]en of factious tempers, of local prejudices, or of sinister designs, may, by intrigue, by corruption, or by other means, first obtain the suffrages, and then betray the interests, of the people." (Madison, *Federalist*, #10) He also deplored direct democracy because "[A] common passion or interest will, in almost every case, be felt by a majority of the whole; and there is nothing to check the inducements to sacrifice the weaker party or an obnoxious individual. Hence it is that such democracies have ever been spectacles of turbulence and contention; have ever been found incompatible with personal security or the rights of property; and have in general been as short in their lives as they have been violent in their deaths. Theoretic politicians, who have patronized this species of government, have erroneously supposed that by reducing mankind to a perfect equality in their political rights, they would, at the same time, be perfectly equalized and assimilated in their possessions, their opinions, and their passions." (*Ibid.*) Obviously de Tocqueville was not impressed that the solution had been found.

Madison assumes that in a direct democracy a permanent majority will arise that will inflict its tyranny on the rest. This is a distinct possibility in a direct democracy that can only exist in a small republic. But it is also a distinct possibility under any system of election as Madison also recognized. His argument was that it was least likely to occur in a large republic. Since the idea of lot was never seriously considered at the time Madison wrote, he did not discuss it. However, under a system of lot, any majority that forms will exist only for the duration of the legislative session, and when a new session begins with new members, a new majority will form. Madison also implies that the majority is the same over a range of issues. It is doubtful that a randomly selected legislature will produce a monolithic majority on all issues. Rather, the more likely scenario is different majorities will form depending upon the issue under consideration.

Madison's underlying concern was with protecting the institution of property and he feared that a democratic form of government that seeks to create equal political rights will also seek to create equal economic status. Perhaps the type of majority he anticipated under direct democracy would be inimical to the institution of property. However, when the majority is in a constant state of flux, this danger is greatly reduced. The far greater danger is the susceptibility of elective systems to invasion by commercial interests and the concomitant concentration of economic wealth in few private hands as a direct result of their economic influence in the electoral mechanism. Marshall's distinction between welfare and democracy is relevant here. Welfare stresses need and the right to receive; democracy the duty to participate. Therefore, the welfare principle cannot be derived from majority rule because its objective is to provide what minorities need, not what majorities want. (Marshall, 1994b:47) A representative legislature is most likely to both provide what minorities need and determine what majorities want. It is most likely to do this because the majority that rules in one session will be ruled once it leaves office by the new majority that forms in the next session. Madison's disease of faction, while not eliminated in its entirety, is contained and controlled so that its deleterious effects are drastically reduced. And controlling faction brings us one step closer to a well-ordered society.

Representation of all Personality Types

Random selection achieves resemblance between the represented and represented in an even more subtle way. Not only are the various major societal groupings represented, but various personality types will also be represented. Manin has explicitly shown how election selects candidates that have a trait that stands out when compared to the public at large which he terms a superiority. But election also selects individuals who constitute a particular personality type, namely, that of "politician". It is well known that conducting an exhaustive political campaign requires a particular personality type. What this also means is that the composition of the legislature consists of this same personality type which affects not only the process of legislation, but the content of legislation. For example, some recent work in psychoanalysis and moral development has found that women have different personality traits than men that revolve around responsibility and relationships. They tend to focus more on the needs of particular situations than the application of general rules of conduct. These differences have been termed an "ethic of care" as opposed to the male "ethic of justice". This is a personality type that could be termed "maternalist".(Dietz, 1994:450) Since women are under-represented in legislative bodies, this personality type will be under-represented. It is highly unlikely that those women who do run for the legislature possess this personality type. Likewise, there are other personality types, both male and female, that are under-represented. The point is that the predominance of a particular personality type is one element that has a direct bearing on the content of legislation.

Representation of all Age Groups

When it comes to age, legislative bodies across the country under-represent younger age groups. According to the Congressional Research Service the at the beginning of the 116th Congress the average age of House members was 57.6 and the average age of Senators was 62.9. The National Council on State Legislatures found that the average age of state legislators was 56 while the average age of the population was 47 in 2015. The problem with this under representation of younger age groups is that the mistakes of the older generation are passed on to the young who will have to live with them for decades while lacking the legislative power to provide a corrective. Climate change is the most obvious example. In addition, the interests of the younger generations are inadequately represented. Education is one obvious example. Younger people offer fresh ideas that are often disparaged by the older generation. Younger people deserve adequate representation because the future belongs to them and they have the right and responsibility to play a major role in shaping it. It is my generation that has bequeathed a political, economic, and environmental mess to the younger generations.

Reduce the Complexity of Government and Strengthen Local Political Communities

Unfortunately, the complexity arising out of the division of labor becomes magnified several fold when corruption and parasitism enter in. The various forms of rent seeking and other types of parasitism lead to complexity in legislation as bills are introduced to satisfy various interest groups. Often these bills are attached to unrelated pieces of legislation to ensure passage when the bill cannot stand on its own merits. This type of maneuvering complicates the legislative process and creates a legislative product that is incomprehensible to all but the few involved in its creation. It also creates increased opportunities for litigation and may lead to the creation of an entire class or profession that makes its living off the legislation.[72] These effects are unavoidable with almost any piece of legislation, but the proliferation of legislation geared toward narrow

---

[72] Workers compensation and the Americans with disabilities act are prime examples of growth industries sprouting up around legislative enactments. The fact that lawyers are one of the prime beneficiaries is of obvious concern. The superfund legislation is a prime example of resources being diverted into transaction costs rather than being directed toward cleaning up polluted sites.

particularistic interests only magnifies the problem. The symptom of this type of complexity is its disorderliness.

Another source of complexity is maintaining the facade of citizen participation. This has led to the creation of numerous boards, commissions, and task forces created to monitor a narrow specialty or to study a particular area of concern which results in a report being issued that does nothing but consume paper and gather dust. At the local level it is one cause of overlapping jurisdictions such as counties, cities, towns, townships, school districts, conservation districts, watershed districts, etc. This myriad of overlapping jurisdictions is justified on the grounds of local control and citizen participation. With genuine citizen participation in the state legislature, there may no longer be a rationale for all these governmental entities. If this is so, then a randomly chosen legislature may very well help to reduce the complexity of government. It may also reduce the complexity of the legislature itself, because the checks and balances of a two-house body will no longer be needed. For those areas of legislation that may require extra "due diligence", the requirement that the legislation pass two successive legislative sessions will provide an adequate check.

I mentioned above that election, in theory, is appropriate at the local level. In reality, of course, local elections have been as corrupt and dominated by special interests as election at any other level of government. What is being assumed here is that without campaigns for state offices, the citizenry may begin to focus more of its attention on local campaigns and issues. This assumption may not have much validity given the difficulties mentioned above about developing a sense of community in many of today's residential communities. However, without the diversion of campaigns for state office, citizens may begin to pay more attention to local issues. It is also possible that citizens who have served in the legislature may have developed a greater interest in public policy issues which will lead them to become more active at the local level. Thus, the replacement of election with random selection at the state level may, over time, result in the strengthening of the local political community.

Free Up Resources Used in Election for Use Elsewhere in the Economy

I mentioned above that a whole ecology has evolved around the institution of election which consumes a fairly substantial amount of societal resources, not in producing anything, but in seeking and preserving private interest or maintaining the institution of election itself. These resources range the gamut from highly paid lobbyists, to polling organizations, to political science departments. All of these are involved in election either in manipulating its outcome or analyzing it. These are resources that would be freed up for use elsewhere, and perhaps the one area where they could most fruitfully be applied is in education. Although the human species has achieved a high degree of technological and economic progress, it has done so at a correspondingly high environmental cost which poses real threats to our long-term survival on this planet. Social evolution has not matched technological evolution, and the only way to close this gap is through the political construction of a meaningful citizenship. Since this requires education, this is the area, I suggest, where the resources squandered on election should be applied.

The Involuntary Aspect of Random Selection

The idea that citizenship has a compulsory component is contrary to contemporary political thought with its emphasis on rights, but a compulsory component has always been present to some degree. The most obvious until recently was compulsory military service in the form of the draft, and it has been suggested that some form of compulsory volunteer service be substituted in place of the

194

draft as a means of "promoting good citizenship". Obviously, the term "compulsory volunteer service" is an oxymoron. Jury duty, which was discussed above, is compulsory in theory, but unfortunately in practice it has been extremely easy to evade. And, of course, some form of taxation has always been compulsory. The idea of compulsory representation is new and contrary to contemporary social thought. Both John Rawls and Jürgen Habermas view citizenship primarily as a source of rights rather than obligations. Habermas explicitly states that a "legal duty to make active use of democratic rights would have something totalitarian about it; we would feel it to be alien to modern law." (Habermas, 1994) Yet he goes to great lengths to establish that the addressees of positive law must also understand themselves to be its authors.

> According to the discourse-theoretic reading of the system of rights, positive law, because it depends on the decisions of a legislature, must split up the autonomy of legal persons into the complementary relation between private and public autonomy, so that the addressees of enacted law can at the same time understand themselves as authors of lawmaking. Both sides of autonomy are essentially incomplete elements that refer to their respective complement. This nexus of reciprocal references provides an intuitive standard by which one can judge whether a regulation promotes or reduces autonomy. According to this standard, enfranchised citizens must, in exercising their public autonomy, draw the boundaries of private autonomy in such a way that it sufficiently qualifies private persons for their role of citizen. (Habermas, 1996,417)

Habermas envisions political opinion and will formation arising out of communicative action which occurs in the Tocquevillian realm of voluntary associations and informal settings such as coffee houses. He rejects the civic republican emphasis on the obligations of citizenship, but he has an appreciation for the duty to participate, an appreciation that distinguishes him from Rawls, but which nonetheless is not made explicit. (Stevenson, 1998:375) Rawls would not support the idea that citizenship has a compulsory component because he asserts that for citizens there is no political obligation because it is not clear what the requisite binding condition is (Rawls, 1971:113-4), but he does recognize that to preserve equal liberty, certain random elements may be required (*op cit.*, 223). These are not specified, however.[73]

The idea of compulsory legislative service is hardly totalitarian. In fact, it is far less onerous than the idea of compulsory military service which may cost one his life and certainly restricts one's liberty during the period of service. What it does do is impose a heavy moral obligation upon the citizen. What authoritarian and totalitarian societies *do not do and cannot do* is allow moral autonomy on the part of their "citizens". The assumption of moral obligation is the hallmark of liberty. Liberty–the freedom and ability to think for oneself and to apply this thinking by participating in the governing of society as an equal member–should not be conflated with egoism–the satisfaction of one's desires. Liberty involves moral choice. Compulsory representation may be burdensome, but it is not onerous in the authoritarian or totalitarian sense unless it forces the citizen into a morally unacceptable position like forcing someone who objects to war on moral grounds into military service. It is a duty that arises out of the acceptance of citizenship rights and its

---

[73] Both Habermas and Rawls argue that the addressees of law should also be its authors, but to accomplish this they have developed elaborate devices of representation–the original position in the case of Rawls and the ideal speech situation in the case of Habermas. I wonder if they are using these devices as a means of avoiding the fact that random selection is implied by their arguments. If so, then these devices simply become another one of the fictions of democracy, and a democracy based on fiction cannot, in the long run, maintain its legitimacy.

exercise is necessary to preserve those rights. For when citizens fail to legislate a vacuum is created in which some other entity will legislate in their stead. In addition to creating the conditions for corruption, liberty is lost.

While compulsory legislative service may not result in every participant assuming moral obligation, it is expected that it will occur in most cases, an expectation that is based on citizen participation on juries. Compulsory legislative service also cannot be imposed by some external agency but must arise out of citizen choice and can be abolished by citizen choice. Constitutional amendment is the only means available to create the obligation and it can be dissolved by constitutional amendment. The creation of the duty is a voluntary act of those citizens that undertake it, and it can be revoked by citizens at any time in the future. This is a collective act and an obvious case of majority rule, but this single decision is not the tyranny of the majority. It is an act of asserting citizenship rights to create a duty that will expand and preserve those rights. It creates a procedure that gives substance to citizenship.

If Habermas, when he refers to the enforcement of democratic rights as having something totalitarian about it, means making voting in elections compulsory, then this would have a totalitarian element. The anomaly of enforced voting being totalitarian while the much more burdensome requirement that citizens legislate is not explained on the basis of choice and legitimacy. Enforcing a citizen to vote in an election in which there is no choice is to force him into giving his assent to the regime in power. This is a typical ploy used in totalitarian regimes to claim legitimacy based on citizen approval. The typical "election" in such regimes is where there is one political party that receives an overwhelming majority of the votes cast in an election in which over 90% of the citizens participate. Compelling a citizen to give the appearance of assent to a regime which she finds morally abhorrent is totalitarian. As elections become more democratic in terms of the range of choice, the totalitarian element of compulsory participation is reduced, but not eliminated. The United States is notorious for its low voter turnouts in its elections. It is an open question, however, as to whether the low turnout is a result of pure apathy or if there an element of protest involved. The 1998 election in Minnesota suggests that there is an element of protest in low voter turnouts.[74] The payment of taxes to a government engaged in activity that the taxpayer finds morally abhorrent has a similar totalitarian element in it.

This anomaly illustrates the difficulty that arises out of the rights-responsibility nexus–the paradox of Rousseau in which the citizen is forced to be free. Habermas uses the terms "legal duty to make use of a citizenship right" as having a totalitarian quality. Rawls says there is no such thing as political obligation because the requisite binding condition is unclear. Other writers such as Walzer (1970) and Etzioni (1996) view obligation as arising out of a voluntary act or choice, and Walzer discusses situations in which the citizen may have an obligation to disobey. It is the voluntary element that supplies the binding condition, and in the case of disobedience the citizen is voluntarily accepting the consequences. What is it about compulsory representation that is different than these other cases and what supplies the binding condition?

The first part of the question has already been alluded to. Compulsory representation is similar to, and is predicated upon, compulsory education. The citizen is compelled to be present in the

---

[74] Minnesota, as we shall see later, has conditions that are favorable to third parties compared to most other states. In 1998 the Reform Party candidate for governor won the election over two politically established candidates with 37% of the vote. His candidacy was not taken very seriously by the other two candidates or the media. Although toward the end of the campaign it was becoming clear that the race would be close, the surprise victory of the Reform Party candidate was due, in no small part, to the participation of eligible voters who were non-participants in prior elections and many of whom registered on the day of the election.

legislative forum just as the student is compelled to be present in the classroom. In both instances the individual is forced into a particular social setting with her peers. Compulsory education prepares the individual for citizenship; compulsory representation engages the individual in citizenship. Education was made compulsory toward the end of the nineteenth century and was justified not only on the grounds that the exercise of free choice is a right for mature minds, but that a political democracy needs an educated electorate. "The duty to improve and civilize oneself is therefore a social duty, and not merely a personal one, because the social health of a society depends upon the civilization of its members. And a community that enforces this duty has begun to realize that its culture is an organic unity and its civilization a national heritage." (Marshall, 1994:11) Representation, like education, is both a right and an obligation. Just as education was made compulsory at the end of the 19th Century, so representation needs to be made compulsory as we approach the end of the 20th. Compulsory education is a substantial investment of society in its citizens. It is funded through a tax burden that falls on most citizens, a burden that is justified on the grounds that educated children benefit the entire citizenry, not just the children that receive its immediate benefits. Representation is the process through which this investment is returned to society, a benefit that is maximized only if representation is compulsory. Education prepares the individual to be free, representation makes him free.

The idea of compulsory legislative service raises the question of the source of political obligation in a liberal society. Obligation generally arises out of our recognition of the unique identity of others and the fact that they, like us, have rights which we may not transgress. This is part of the socialization process in which we begin to define our own identities through our relatedness to others. We learn that there are social norms that define behavioral expectations, and it is through adherence to these norms that our membership in society is formed. At some point in the socialization process we begin to question why it is necessary to adhere to the norm–i.e. we ask for the reasons for the norm. It is at this point that the development of moral reasoning begins. If the reasons given for a norm convince us of its legitimacy, we will tend to voluntarily adhere to the norm. We may adhere to norms when we have not been convinced of their legitimacy, but such adherence is based on factors other than reason such as peer pressure or various other types of coercion. In these instances, the individual cannot be said to be behaving as he is out of a sense of moral obligation. Moral obligation arises out of what we call "free will". Its force may be compelling, but it is incurred voluntarily.

Political obligation arises out of our relationship to the state and its institutions and involves various forms of compulsion that range from the payment of taxes to fighting in war. These restrictions on liberty are perceived as legitimate so long as the citizen was "represented" in the decisional process that created the obligation. But when it comes to the obligation of the citizen to represent herself, the argument appears to be tautological because the assertion that the citizen has an obligation to represent herself is derived from her having been represented. But the point is the citizen has not been represented by the process of election. She has had a voice of sorts, but she has not been represented.

The obligation of representation exists in rudimentary form in our relationships–both with ourselves and with others. We have an obligation to ourselves to represent ourselves to ourselves. This is an integral part of the process of individual development in which we represent our past selves to our present selves and when we represent our ideas to ourselves. We evaluate ourselves through our self-representation. We also represent ourselves to others whenever we interact with them and this representation occurs on many levels from subtle non-verbal communications to the communication of highly abstract ideas. In other words, representation is communication. When we communicate, we are presenting ideas and making them present. By virtue of our being in society we have the obligation to communicate.

To raise this rudimentary obligation of representation to self and others to the level of political obligation will require a political contract. This political contract is the device through which citizenship is politically constructed. Unlike the more mythical social contract, this political contract is real. It is initially enacted through the consent of the citizens and may be revoked in the future through their consent. In this sense, the obligation of representation can be said to be voluntary. The obligation is created by plebiscite and may be revoked by plebiscite. But for the individual, the obligation is both involuntary and burdensome. If it is not involuntary, the very idea of representation is defeated. And it is burdensome in moral terms because it places political responsibility where it rightfully belongs–with the individual citizen.

Chapter III

Education for Citizenship

The long run solution is education, but in the long run we are all dead.
John Meynard Keynes

...the test of a man's education is what he chooses to do when he is not obliged to do anything.
George Newman

The system of education is the template which society uses to reproduce itself. As such, the system of education tends to be a mirror which reflects the values of society at large into the next generation. The current system is merely a template for work; the challenge is to change it into a template for citizenship - i.e., to teach the 3R's of representation: rights, responsibility, and reason. It is important to emphasize the direction of change. The system of education cannot and will not change until there is a change in the larger society for it to reflect. The view that changes in the system of education will be reflected later in the larger society is an excuse for avoiding change in the larger society. It is a covert way to deny citizens their citizenship. What I want to explore here is what the template of citizenship will look like after the first steps toward representative democracy have been taken.

Education vs. Training

The purpose of a *free, compulsory* education is to teach the student to be able to think for him or herself and to instill those values and behaviors that enable the student to work with and resolve differences with others. A distinction needs to be made here between *education* and *training*. Education consists of the acquisition of basic knowledge, values, and behaviors which are necessary to function as a citizen. With education the student learns how to use and acquire knowledge within an ethical context that enables critical thinking and effective functioning in various social groups. Training consists of the acquisition of specific knowledge and skills necessary to perform tasks that constitute a job or profession. Education is the process whereby the individual student is socialized into his or her role as a citizen; training is the process through which an individual develops in his or her career.

Education in the Context of the Citizenship Model

Since the system of education must be the template of citizenship if the culture of democracy is to reproduce itself, the system of education will reflect the model of citizenship. The function of the system of education is to prepare the future citizen for both membership and participation in the political community. Its success in this is measured by the extent to which representation as opposed to ideology determines public policy. The homeostatic dimension mediates the tension between the individual and community. It is along this dimension that the role of the individual citizen as a functioning member of the political community is developed. The hermeneutic dimension links the past to the future. It is along this dimension that the citizen interprets and reinterprets her past culture history on its evolutionary path to the future. In

203

education the homeostatic dimension involves the development of personal traits that enable the individual to function in the community. The hermeneutic dimension involves the acquisition of substantive knowledge within the historical context of the culture to enable the student to interpret her role both in society and in history. The general model is displayed in Figure I.

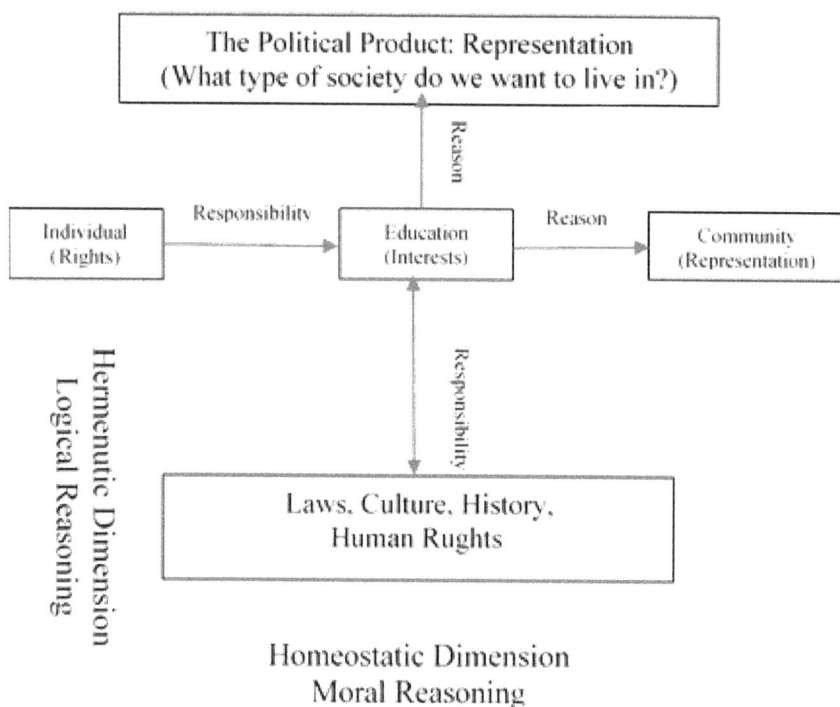

Figure I
The Template of Citizenship

The Political Product: Representation
(What type of society do we want to live in?)

Reason

Individual
(Rights)

Responsibility

Education
(Interests)

Reason

Community
(Representation)

Hermenutic Dimension
Logical Reasoning

Responsibility

Laws, Culture, History,
Human Rughts

Homeostatic Dimension
Moral Reasoning

The system of education, if it is successful, will produce public citizens which I have defined as citizens able to represent themselves in the political community. This is a two-dimensional concept that involves the moral dimension and the intellectual dimension. The essence of the system of education is the transformation of rights and responsibility into representation through reason. The development of reason is the primary rationale for the system of education. Reason, like many concepts, is binary,

205

and its moral and intellectual dimensions must be distinguished. Moral reasoning has its origins in the sentiments which means that it has a strong emotional and intuitive component which is exemplified by the sense of justice.[75] In an individual in which the sense of justice is acute, an act that is perceived as unjust will result in feelings of "violation". These feelings are often difficult to explain, but their occurrence provides the stimulus to attempt an explanation which is how moral reasoning originates. Intellectual reasoning, on the other hand, arises out of the sense of curiosity. Curiosity invokes feelings of "wonderment" which provides the stimulus to explain phenomena that occur in both the natural and social world. The system of education needs to tap both these sources of reasoning and link them to the individual's natural abilities so that she can develop into a fully functioning person. The development of moral reasoning lies primarily along the homeostatic dimension and the development of intellectual reasoning lies primarily along the hermeneutic dimension.

The system of education is shown as the intersection of the homeostatic and hermeneutic dimensions. One of the main functions of education involves interest in both meanings of the term that Pitkin (1967) discussed–one having to do with attention or concern and the other welfare. These meanings mirror the moral and intellectual dimensions to a certain extent. The first meaning is the psychological concept of what one finds interesting. With respect to this meaning the system of education is to assist the student in identifying and developing her own unique talents and abilities, that is, develop those things she finds interesting. It is with this first meaning of interest that the system of education has been primarily

---

[75] John Rawls suggests that the sense of justice is acquired at an early age as discussed in Chapter I and again below. Noam Chomsky suggests that the there is a 'genetically inherited moral system' that enters into the formation of moral values including our varying concepts of justice. (Burchill, 1998)

focused. But it also needs to focus on the second which has to do with the student's welfare–i.e. what she has at stake in society. This second meaning has to do with the student acquiring the ability to know what her interests are such that her wishes and welfare coincide. This means that she will not be dependent upon another to determine what is objectively in her best interest; she will be able to do it herself. One major component of being able to represent herself, then, is the ability to be able to articulate her interest in both meanings of the term.

The Homeostatic Dimension

The homeostatic dimension is where the nexus of rights, responsibility, and reason are developed and integrated to provide the student with the moral tools of citizenship that mediate the tension between the individual citizen and the political community of citizens. This dimension is primarily involved in the moral development of the student and it proceeds roughly from the development of the recognition of rights and responsibility to the exercise of reason all of which is eventually manifested in representation. The development of responsibility begins with the student responding to her sense of justice in the educational setting. This can occur within the student's own personal experience when her rights are violated by a fellow student or she witnesses the violation of a fellow student's rights. It may also occur in the student's exposure to the lessons of history when she experiences a vicarious sense of violation. Both instances are manifestations of the students' capacity for empathy with her fellow human beings. The student's response to this violation is an opportunity for the teacher to introduce the rudiments of moral reasoning. It is also an opportunity for the teacher to begin to instill habits of etiquette.

Rights, responsibility and reason are linked in a dialectic that becomes increasingly complex as the student progresses through the system of education. It is out of this linkage that representation is developed. The interaction of rights, responsibility and reason enables the student to justify her responses to moral issues, and when she presents these justifications to her fellow students, she is representing herself. Representation is the presentment and re-presentment of these justifications as they become increasingly refined as a result of the interaction of rights, responsibility and reason in response to the justifications of others. Representation becomes political when it addresses the question of the type of society we want to live in.

The task of the homeostatic dimension is for the student to develop the ability to represent herself in all social situations, not just the political. But political representation is the most complex and difficult form of representation because it interjects the individual into the public forum of the political community where her values and interests bump up against the values and interests of others. Thus, education for citizenship is not a minimalist enterprise. In addition to all the elements of character that are developed through moral reasoning along the homeostatic dimension, it also requires intellectual development that is the primary focus of the hermeneutic dimension.

The Hermeneutic Dimension

The hermeneutic dimension of education is where knowledge is developed within its cultural and historical context to equip the student with the intellectual tools of citizenship. These intellectual tools span the major disciplines of the sciences and humanities and are necessary for informed choice. They need to be taught within the context of representation which provides their underlying unity. Just as one of the functions of the citizenship role is to provide a unifying context for the various other roles an individual occupies in society, in education this translates into representation providing the unifying focus for the various academic disciplines. Each discipline has an intellectual history that provides insight into the interpretation of our culture and civilization, and each discipline raises questions for public choice. It is through the representation of ideas both within and between disciplines that the evolution of civilization occurs. Therefore, citizenship requires a broad overview of the various disciplines.

One of the main functions of the type of education advocated here is to counteract the trend toward narrow specialization in one's career. Career specialization is one of the main dimensions along which modern society is fractured, others being religious, racial, and ethnic groupings. Specialization tends to restrict choice by narrowing one's point of view. If it occurs without exposure to other fields of knowledge, options open to the individual may be foreclosed which will not only result in talents being misapplied but will also reduce individual liberty. The larger danger, however, is political. A fractured society is unable to achieve a unifying focus on issues of common concern.[76] The lack of a unifying focus on common issues creates a political vacuum within which narrow special interests achieve dominance, and this dominance severely restricts the political field of view.[77] A liberal education is the antidote for this tendency because a conspicuous element in liberal education is the

---

[76] Note that I said focus. The use of the term "unifying focus" does not imply agreement on the resolution of the issue, but it does imply agreement that the issue is of concern to a large segment of the public.
[77] The dangers of specialization were captured by Mill:
"Experience proves that there is no one study or pursuit which, practiced to the exclusion of all others, does not narrow and pervert the mind, breeding in it a class of prejudices special to that pursuit, besides a general prejudice, common to all narrow specialties, against large views, from an incapacity to take in and appreciate the grounds for them." (Mill,1993:206)

notion of balance. It fosters a broad range of potential allowing no one aspect of human nature to predominate. It excludes none of the principal modes of experience - i.e. it is aimed at cultivating the mind and body, person and citizen. It gives due weight to the sciences and the arts and has opposed specialization and vocational training as inimical to a balanced, proportioned development. (Garforth, 1979:218)

The Issue of Liberty

Parents Rights and Children's Rights

It used to be that wives and children were regarded as proprietary economic assets. Aristotle made it quite clear that citizenship was available only to those who could rule themselves and ruling themselves included the ability to rule the persons and things in the household. Thus, citizenship was open only to a few select males. (Pocock, 1994) This idea of the proprietary nature of women and children has survived in various forms up until the latter part of the 20th Century, and vestiges of it still exist. It finds expression in various ideologies that fall under the rubric of "family values". In one form or another, it raises the issue of liberty. The particular aspect of liberty that I need to examine here is the tension between the liberty of parents to raise their children as they see fit and the liberty of children to become fully functioning citizens. Since education is the template of citizenship, the resolution of this tension is central to the system of education.

John Rawls (1993:199-200) walks a tightrope when it comes to this issue. Since various religious sects oppose the culture of the modern world, a problem arises about their children's education and the requirements the state may impose. He argues that his version of political liberalism, since it is not a comprehensive doctrine, only requires that their education include such things as knowledge of

210

their constitutional and civic rights and that it prepares them to be fully cooperating members of society and to be self-supporting. To the objection that even these minimal requirements may be, in effect if not intent, an attempt to educate them into a comprehensive liberal doctrine, he replies that these unavoidable consequences of reasonable requirements may have to be accepted, often with regret.

Eamonn Callan (1997) specifically applies Rawlsian ideas to the issue of common vs. separate schooling after examining and rejecting several other schools of thought in the context of subsidiary issues. His objective is a conception of parent's rights that will not license the oppression of children and will also do justice to the hopes parents have and the sacrifices they make in raising their children. A moral theory that says only children have rights inverts the despotism of patriarchy. The issue involves the moral autonomy of children. To be denied a sympathetic understanding of ethical diversity by parents who seek to preserve an unswerving identification with the primary culture of birth is to be denied the resources for democratic deliberation under conditions of pluralism which requires independent thought about the right and good. Callan examines how far this argument for moral autonomy can be repudiated before it results in a condition he calls "ethical servility"– a condition of moral impotence in which the individual is unable to make ethical choices for himself. The point is not to teach children which points of view are right or wrong, but to empower them to make the choices for themselves. The argument against ethical servility is based on the fundamental moral equality of persons in the family. For parents to veto a child's exposure to ethical diversity–a conception of liberal education that is captured in the term 'the great sphere'–is to render that child ethically servile under any credible interpretation of the child's prospective interest in her personal sovereignty.

The danger of pluralism with respect to common education is that, in the minimalist form of common education, the more diversity

211

there is, the lower the common denominator becomes. This is because the whole point of the minimalist conception is to avoid those disagreements that divide us. But since it is impossible even under minimalist conditions to accommodate all objections, even this minimalist conception fails to meet the standard of impartial teaching that the minimalist conception requires. Since a common education that will enjoy unanimous consent is an impossibility, some other conception of common education is called for. This conception begins to emerge, according to Callan, if we look within Rawls's morality of association which can provide a link between the moral life of the child in the family and the role of the just citizen in the public culture of democracy. This is the second step in the acquisition of the sense of justice that proceeds from the morality of authority, to the morality of association, to the morality of principles. It bridges the gap between family and polity. In the school the child gains increasing sophistication in perceiving other people through a succession of more demanding roles with more complex rights and duties. This can only occur in common schools that reflect the diverse ethical voices represented in pluralism.

Callan does argue, however, that even given a well-structured common schooling, some parents still will want separate schools because they want no part of reasonable pluralism. He argues that the ideal of tolerance suggests letting them go their way. This argument is based on the fact that the blunt instrument of coercive law is not necessarily the best means of enforcing even the more modest ends of common education against those who would oppose them. Such coercion may only intensify the political alienation of those who are on its receiving end with unfortunate consequences for their children, and it may encourage the continuance of those illiberal values that would gradually fade in a more tolerant environment. There is no virtue in a self-defeating intransigence in the imposition of common educational ends.

The conception of citizenship that I am advancing extends the Rawlsian conception of a fully cooperating member of society over a complete life to include within the definition of "fully cooperating member" the requirement to be available to perform the duties of representation. Representation, as I argued in the last chapter, is an act of original self-presentation. To be able to present oneself politically, the citizen to be needs an education that gives him the ability to think for himself and, in political settings, to express his thoughts as political ideas. It is education that prepares the citizen to cross the citizenship frontier. Obviously, any form of ethical servility will fail to meet this threshold. However, the ability to make ethical choices requires the citizen to attain a certain level of both intellectual and moral development. This raises an extremely difficult problem–*what will determine the content of the education that makes this development possible and what level of attainment is required to cross the citizenship frontier?* This is the issue of competence and it is so potentially contentious that it may be, quite frankly, unresolvable. This issue is taken up below. But the issue of competence itself is separate from, although related to, the issue of *the right and duty of the child* to become educated for citizenship. It is the latter issue that I am considering here.

Education, in its current form, may contain some minimalist exposure to "citizenship" as a "unit" required for graduation. The content of this unit may range anywhere from a form of indoctrination designed to instill feelings of patriotism to some detailed instruction on the mechanics of how government works. There may be some emphasis on voluntarism and community service. But education in its current form is a template for work, and as such its primary focus is to prepare students to enter the market. The campaign slogan "Its the economy, stupid" is directly translated into the enterprise of education. The political question of what kind of society do we want to live in is never seriously raised because the answer is given in the orientation to the market. The political use of education as a device to produce "human resources" for the economy is a subtle way to exclude citizens from political participation. By focusing on their future role in the market, students fail to give serious consideration to their role as citizens. This is most unfortunate because their role in the market may be rather short lived and uncertain, but their role as citizen is permanent and has the potential to give them some control over the uncertainties of the market.[78] The study of politics is reduced to an extension of the study of marketing, and the challenges of pluralism to the idea of representation are avoided under the guise of "political correctness".

Education, as I defined it earlier, has to do with developing citizens and training has to do with the development of careers. Education has two basic goals: (1) to enable the student to think for herself and to present her ideas, and (2) to identify and develop her unique talents and abilities. These two objectives represent the homeostatic dimension that mediates the tension between individual and community. The ability to think for oneself is a necessary requirement for individuality to have any meaning at all. Presentation is a socially constituted act which occurs in a community of some sort. One presents oneself to others. The purpose of education is to develop individuality so that it can express itself in community with others. Thus, education is required for moral autonomy of the individual and the development of the community. Since this is what maximizes political liberty, the liberty

---

[78] The ideology of the market also finds expression in the debate over public vs private schooling. The work of Myron Liberman (1993) is an example of market oriented approaches to education in which the idea of for profit private schools competing with public and nonprofit schools is strongly endorsed. What is interesting about this work is that in its focus on the virtues of competition, it fails to mention citizenship at all.

of parents to raise children as they see fit must, if it conflicts with education, yield to education.[79]

Ideological Indoctrination and Representational Freedom

The state of being indoctrinated is a form of ethical servility. Indoctrination is not education and it has no place in any democratic system of education. Indoctrination into a particular ideology involves cultural and historical distortions such that culture-history is made to fit the ideological interpretation. Indoctrination represents a corruption of the hermeneutic dimension of education which in turn interferes with the homeostatic dimension. Callan sheds light on how this corruption occurs in his discussion of the contrast between excessive moral criticism of the past and a sentimental interpretation of it. The view of American history as a moral wasteland in which Americans are incapable of transcending racism and the brutality it engenders leaves no room for a rational belief that they can forge bonds of commitment required for a just community in the future. The more likely error, according to Callan, is the sanitization of history as a foundation for civic virtue that occurs in sentimental civic education.

An emotion is sentimental if it is unearned which means it comes about through some misrepresentation of reality in the evaluative judgments it evokes. The task of sentimental civic education then becomes the inculcation of strong and abiding beliefs in the moral purity of the nation's founders which confers legitimacy on the institutions they created. The moral liabilities of the tasks that

---

[79] The changing nature of the family raises a number of subsidiary issues when addressing the issue of the liberty of parents. In the case of divorce, the parents may have conflicting views on how they want to raise the child. The changing structure of the family is raising the question of what, if any, is the role of the parent. And, of course, there are continuing problems of providing support for children. For a detailed discussion of these issues see Coontz (1992,1997)

sentimental civic education must undertake to buttress the faith in these fictions pose three difficulties for the defense of sentimental civic education. First, in order to protect the relevant fictions of moral purity from falsification, the historical imagination must be constricted in ways that blind us to the contemporary relevance of the values that were rejected in the choices not taken. Second, the simplification of reality that is necessary to maintain the fictions of moral purity requires the supportive simplification of judgments that relate even indirectly to the object of emotion. Third, the recipients of sentimental civic education must be inclined to see themselves as inheritors of political projects which, at least in their initial conception, are perfection itself. Thus, any significant innovation becomes a threat to perfection. This is a trend that even conservatives should find troubling.

A belief that there is no redeemable value in the historical past of one's nation leads to a nihilistic ideological outlook which makes it impossible to form bonds of community. Sentimentality leads to the opposite ideological outlook that one's nation and culture is the embodiment of moral purity that makes it impossible to confront and correct the horrors of the past. Ideological indoctrination can arise out of any one or combination of the misrepresentations that are necessary to support either view. The task of education as a hermeneutic endeavor is to develop the capacities of critical reason so that the student can steer her way between these two poles on her way to the citizenship frontier.

While ideology can corrupt the hermeneutic dimension of citizenship by distorting history, it can also corrupt the homeostatic dimension by introducing unreasonable pluralism. The homeostatic dimension represents a resolution of the tension between individual and community. Unreasonable pluralism makes it difficult, if not impossible, to resolve this tension. Pluralism in its reasonable form is a dialog between and among groups of diverse cultural backgrounds that signals the need for thoughtful moral discrimination in the way we respond politically to the fact of diversity. It is an adjudicatory process between different views each of which elicits a robust respect. (Callan, *op. cit.*) Out of this process ties are developed between individuals that transcend group difference and make possible the formation of a political community. Ideological thinking restricts thoughtful moral discrimination by introducing intolerance. It is not possible to form ties between individuals where there is intolerance to ideas, persons, or both, except for those ties that form between the members of the intolerant group. Thus, intolerance abruptly truncates the homeostatic dimension such that the individual, instead of becoming integrated into the political community where his individuality is expressed in the form of a presentation of political ideas to his fellow citizens, loses his individuality within the confines the group's ideology. Adherence to the ideology promotes membership in the group at the expense of membership in the political community of citizens. The task of education on the homeostatic dimension is to instill those interpersonal skills and virtues that make it possible for the student to pass through the citizenship frontier.

The task of education on both dimensions is representation. At the point where the dimensions intersect, the task of education is political representation. Representation is the presentation of ideas in original form and the re-presentation of ideas as they are refined through reason. In political representation reason occurs within the context of rights and responsibility. The focus of education is on the representation of reality so that the student can gain an understanding of the environment within which she finds herself and adapt to it. The political aspect of education is to enable the student to represent herself so that she can participate in the ongoing creation of the society within which she lives. It is in political representation, where the moral and intellectual meet, that the challenge of ideology must be confronted. When the challenge is successfully met, ideological misrepresentation is transformed into political representation.

The Role of Authority

The school is an institution of democracy, but it is not itself a democratic institution. It develops citizens which means that it cannot be a forum of citizens. It is a place where future citizens learn those skills and habits necessary to assume their sovereignty, it is not a place where that sovereignty is expressed without restriction. Therefore, authority does not reside in the body of students; it must come from elsewhere, and that elsewhere is in the professional staff of teachers as delegated to them by the political community of citizens. This authority corresponds directly to the dimensions of education–i.e., there is intellectual authority and moral authority.

There are two basic types of authority: (1) personal or substantive which derives from authorship–a person is an authority on a subject, and (2) formal or positional–authority is vested in a position or office. A subtype may be derived from these two types of authority in the notion of authorization or agency. (Flathman, 1995) The first aspect of authority with respect to education is the fact that it is compulsory. There is a positive duty for parents to educate their children and for the child to become educated. The school is authorized–i.e. is the agency–which executes this authority. The authority to establish a compulsory education is an instance of political authority the source of which is in the various state constitutions.[80]

---

[80] For example, the Minnesota Constitution requires a uniform system of public schools (Article 13 § 1) which states: "The stability of a republican form of government depending mainly upon the intelligence of the people, it is the duty of the legislature to establish a general and uniform system of public schools. The legislature shall make such provisions by taxation or otherwise as will secure a thorough and efficient system of public schools throughout the state." The next

The education of children is the first instance of the compulsory aspect of citizenship. Education in some form is necessary if society is going to reproduce itself and continue the development of its cultural heritage. The public school has been the primary vehicle through which this process of cultural reproduction is initiated. The school must have the authority to require attendance and to maintain order such that individual students are able to develop their personal sovereignty of citizenship to the fullest. This contradictory demand to provide for the development of personal sovereignty within an ordered environment reflects the tension between the individual and political community in the larger society and is one aspect of what is meant by saying that the system of education is the template for citizenship. The teacher is endowed with formal authority by virtue of his position and with substantive authority by virtue of his knowledge of his subject and ability in the art of transmitting that knowledge to his students. His formal authority is an extension of the school's authority to maintain order and require attendance. His substantive authority is the tool kit he uses in building the framework within which his students can become citizens. The teacher's ability to use his formal and substantive authority reflects the intersection of moral and intellectual reasoning, and it is his ability to develop these capabilities in his students that enables society to reproduce itself through representation.

One important aspect of a student's education is to learn how to relate to authority itself. Ultimately the relationship to authority becomes the relationship of the citizen to her fellow citizens because it is out of this relationship, made manifest in the process of

---

section prohibits state funding of sectarian schools. Minnesota Statutes 120.101 provides for compulsory instruction and makes the parent responsible for ensuring that the "child acquires knowledge and skills that are essential for effective citizenship".

representation, that authority arises. The art of teaching is the art of authoritative presentation. From it the student acquires not only substantive knowledge of the subject presented but practical knowledge in presenting ideas. The process of education, then, becomes a dialectic in which the teacher presents material to the student which the student re-presents to the teacher and her fellow students and thereby acquires skill in representing herself. At some point in this process the student's re-presentation will be in the form of a challenge to the authority of the teacher. Teaching is an art because there are no firm rules as to how to direct this dialectical process so that the student learns to use knowledge to think for herself and to present her ideas. What is clear, however, is that this process cannot begin in an institution that is democratic. Authority is needed to initiate the process, and in the beginning this authority rests in the institution and the teacher. As the dialectic continues, however, there is a gradual transfer of authority from the institution to the body of students which takes place in the form of the students learning how to govern themselves. This transfer of authority, however, is never complete.

The Issue of Equality

The idea of equality in democratic theory has been extremely troublesome because of the muti-dimensionality of the idea and the fact that it can conflict with other democratic ideas such as liberty. There are three dimensions to the term equality: equality of conditions, equality of means, and equality of outcomes. (Bell, 1994) Equality of conditions refers to the equality of the political liberties, equality of means refers to opportunities, and equality of outcomes refers to equality in terms of income, status, etc. The paradox of equality is that increasing the equality of opportunity guarantees an inequality in outcome. Since it is impossible and not even desirable to attain equality of outcomes, the emphasis has shifted to equality of opportunity. This is nowhere more evident than in the educational setting because it is here that the citizen to be acquires the skills that will enable her to maximize her life chances. Unfortunately, the application of the idea of equality has been inimical in the educational setting because it is misapplied in a way that redefines equality as the achievement of the lowest common denominator. I need to examine the idea of equality and its application to the educational setting.

Equality is the source of social solidarity. It refers to that which is held in common which is what enables members of a society to form bonds with one another. It is an idea that contains inherent tension because of the problem of finding commonality in diversity. Equality does seek a common denominator, but the challenge for the system of education is to use commonality as a source of enriched diversity rather than reducing it to triviality. Since citizenship is what is held in common, the task of education is to enrich this common possession. This implies an educational core that is essential to citizenship. It also implies the equal opportunity to achieve the educational core of citizenship and the additional education that enables the citizen to be to discover and develop her unique abilities and talents.

The educational equivalent of equality of conditions is the common core of citizenship coursework, the equivalent of equality of means is equal educational opportunity for all, and the equivalent of equality of outcomes refers to the development of each student's unique abilities and talents. The common core of education for citizenship is that aspect of the curriculum that prepares the student to be able to represent himself by presenting his political ideas to his fellow citizens. It is this common core that all students must master to be effective citizens. A common language is at the heart of this core because it is through the common language that ideas are presented. Thus, proficiency in reading and writing English is an absolute necessity. A certain level of mathematics is also included in

221

the idea of a common language because the ability to use numbers in today's world is an essential aspect of communication. The core must also provide the basis of a liberal education which includes the natural sciences, humanities and arts, and social sciences. The common core is that aspect of the student's education that prepares him to assume his political liberties.

Equality of opportunity means that each student gets the same chance to attain the common core of citizenship and to develop her unique talents and abilities. Equality of opportunity for the citizenship core implies common public schooling. Equality of opportunity to develop one's unique abilities and talents implies special schooling, but equal opportunity for special schooling for all. The latter need not necessarily be provided by public schools. However, what is implied here is funding at the state level instead of through local school districts. Since the purpose of education is to create citizens, the common core should be provided by the state and both the common core and special education should be funded by the state.[81] As Walzer points out, the community has an interest in the education of children and so do the children and that interest is not adequately represented by entrepreneurs nor parents. (Kahne, 1996:103-4) Neither, we might add, by the authoritative state which ideologically transforms citizen into subject. That interest can only be adequately represented by the democratic state in which the "creation of citizens" means providing an educational environment within which the student learns to think for herself. A citizen is "a fully cooperating member of society over a complete life" capable of representing herself in the collective shaping of society.

---

[81] Education is not a service to homeowners and other owners of real estate. Therefore, it makes little sense to use the property tax as a means of financing education. Education is investment in the future, and we should all share in this investment to some degree.

Equality of outcomes is only possible when educational outcomes are reduced to the lowest common denominator. Therefore, this type of equality is not a desirable educational objective. What can be provided is the opportunity for the student to discover what her talents and abilities are and the environment within which they can be developed to the fullest. This aspect of her education is what will provide her with the basis to develop her individuality - i.e., her own unique socio-political niche the political dimension of which is manifested in representation. Equality of outcomes means that each student should be given an equal chance to compete with herself. Current educational practice employs *norm-referenced* evaluation in which the student strives for a position on a curve. Being in competition with oneself is what produces mastery learning and it employs *criterion-referenced* evaluation. Mastery learning strategies shift the primary motivation for learning away from aversive motivation associated with low grades to cognitive drive motivation associated with recognized units of subject matter. Current educational practices make it difficult for teachers because it is difficult to foster warm relationships among students when they view themselves in competition and it is difficult for staff members to be sympathetic facilitators of learning when they are identified with ranking students on tests that label one fourth or more as failures. (Novak, 1977:85-7)[82]

---

[82] Novak goes on to point out that there is evidence that shows that enriching the learning environment in physics and providing adequate time for mastery of concepts can serve to reduce or eliminate much of the disadvantages of poor prior preparation. This raises the question that if all students can get A's, who will judge which students should be admitted into medical or graduate school. The move toward egalitarianism that results from enriched learning that removes the advantages conferred by the adequacy of prior schooling is not preferred by many teachers, parents, administrators, and students.

The Issue of Competence

The idea of equality in education is not meant to imply that all citizens will be able to represent themselves upon completion of their schooling. At some point the system of education must be able to certify that the student has become what I have called a public citizen–a citizen who can cross the citizenship frontier because she is able to represent herself in the political community. Obviously, not all citizens will become public citizens. The mentally ill cannot effectively represent themselves and criminals should not be allowed to represent themselves. These cases may be obvious, but the educational task of certifying competent citizenship certainly is not. The intellectual side of citizenship can be measured to some degree by testing, but testing becomes extremely difficult, if not impossible, when it comes to the moral side. The point is, however, that citizenship has both an ascriptive and an earned component. The citizenship minimum includes all citizens but crossing the citizenship frontier for the purpose of representation requires a level of competence that must be earned through participation in the system of education. The certification that the student meets the standards that constitute what it means to be a public citizen are best left to an agency independent of the system of education. (Lieberman, 1993)

John Stuart Mill addressed the issue of competence by proposing a system of plural voting in which the more educated would have more votes. Since England did not have national education at the time he wrote, he thought occupation could serve as a surrogate for education. However, he did think that a voluntary national examination would be a useful means to determine those individuals that should receive a plurality of votes.[83] He was fearful

---

[83] There is a real danger in the use of standardized tests in education, particularly the true-false and multiple-choice types. The danger is in the implication that there

of two things: (1) the danger of class legislation and (2) too low a standard of political intelligence. "It is not useful, but harmful, that the constitution of the country should declare ignorance to be entitled to as much political power as knowledge." (Mill, 1993:312) And there was a further danger, namely, that those who attained power would no longer need to use reason to preserve it. "The position which gives the strongest stimulus to the growth of intelligence is that of rising into power, not that of having achieved it; and of all resting-points, temporary and permanent, in the way to ascendancy, the one which develops the best and highest qualities is the position of those who are strong enough to make reason prevail, but not strong enough to prevail against reason." (*Ibid.*:313)

Whatever means is chosen to determine competence, what must be measured is reason in all its nuances. Intellectual reasoning involves the ability to use logical argument and an understanding of the scientific method the antecedent for which is background information acquired through inquiry and discussion, not rote memorization. Moral reasoning involves the ability to justify moral judgments which requires knowledge of the humanities and social sciences to provide the contextual background. Both types of reasoning are needed for the effective presentation of political ideas. In the final analysis, the only practical way to determine representational competence may be an instrument that can somehow measure the student's ability to express herself in standard English. There is no instrument that is suitable for the measurement of moral reasoning and testing the various dimensions of intellectual

---

are right and wrong answers to everything which is related to the problems associated with ideological thinking. The reality is that every discipline is fraught with ambiguity and paradox and learning how to work one's way through such confusion is one of the principal tasks of education. Spitting out answers on tests may demonstrate factual and perhaps some operational knowledge, but it does not demonstrate the ability to reason with ideas. The ability to represent oneself is not amenable to measurement.

ability is simply not practical, nor necessarily relevant. Representation is achieved through each citizen that comes to the legislative forum applying her own unique abilities and talents in the process. Representation involves the integration of differences. But this integration cannot occur unless the participants are able to communicate with one another. Therefore, the ability to present oneself in English is the only common denominator.

Conclusion

The above discussion is intended to illustrate in broad outline the parameters of the system of education within a culture of democracy. It requires repeating that the system of education reflects the culture within which it is embedded. It is much more a means of social reproduction, particularly at the lower levels, than it is a means of social change. It is a mistake, therefore, to assume that changing the system of education will be reflected in social change. The casual chain works in the opposite direction, and therefore it is necessary to develop citizenship politically which will eventually find its reflection in the system of education.

It is quite remarkable, given all the political pressures which are brought to bear upon the system of education, that it is able to work as well as it does. Somewhere along the line the system of education manages to find itself being blamed for virtually every social ill–from dysfunctional families to "lack of competitiveness" in the economic market. It is the whipping boy of politicians of every political persuasion. It finds itself under assault not only in the secular sphere, but in the religious as well. It is blamed not only for the individual's failure in the economic market, but for his failure to get into heaven as well. Given the fact that this recriminatory political environment exists on top of a social environment within which educational practitioners often find themselves working under conditions of physical assault as well, it is a testament to their fortitude that they not only go to work every day, but that in the process of so doing, they are often successful in creating citizens. A culture of democracy will liberate educational practitioners to do the job of education–insuring the viability of our future through the social and political reproduction of an ethic of citizenship.

Chapter IV

Praxis

*We live in a time of transition, an uneasy era which is likely to
endure for the rest of this century. During the period we may be
tempted to abandon some of the time-honored principles and
commitments which have been proven during the difficult times of
past generations. We must never yield to this temptation. Our
American values are not luxuries, but necessities - not the salt in our
bread, but the bread itself.*

Jimmy Carter

Introduction

My main argument in this book is that democratic citizenship
is socially and politically constructed.[84] This construction has been
going on throughout history, but a hermeneutic perspective can be
employed in which the development of citizenship from its first
inceptions to the present is interpreted in the context of present-day
reality. This interpretation can then be used to build upon the past to

---

[84] The social construction of citizenship is associated with social contract theory
and it involves the citizenship minimum which defines membership. The political
construction of citizenship involves the citizenship frontier which defines
participation. The citizenship minimum has already been constructed in some
form. It may require remodeling, but as a structure it already exists. The
citizenship frontier as conceptualized here requires political construction de novo
which will require some form of political contract. The constitutional amendments
suggested here lay the basis for such a contract.

construct a citizenship the practice of which will result in the creation of a culture of democracy. As Alegandro has pointed out, we are not beginning with a clean slate, but we are free to discover our own truths. The United States has achieved an electoral government that has been somewhat representative of the governed. It has also achieved a high degree of economic development and a population that is fairly well educated. Although there are signs that serious social decay is beginning to become endemic, there are other conditions that still exist that make the transition to a culture of democracy, while not necessarily probable, at least possible. The point is that if the type of citizenship outlined above cannot be created within the United States, then it is doubtful that it will be created anywhere.

The United States is favorably suited for this citizenship project because it is a federal system which affords a range of opportunities for experimenting with various aspects of the model. It is also a society of immigrants so, in a very important sense, it reflects the diversity of the world at large, but within the unifying context of the nation state. If the project is successful within the United States, then this society may serve as a "reference society" for other nation states that are struggling with their own ideas on the type of citizenship they want to create for the future. The American experience could be particularly germane to the citizenship issues that are arising out of the formation of the European Union.

The model developed here is to be applied at the level of state government which in turn will provide the evolutionary impetus to further development at the local and federal levels. Local government consists of a complex mixture of overlapping jurisdictions some of which were created specifically to provide for citizen participation and local control. As state government becomes a citizen enterprise, local jurisdictional complexity may lose its rationale. For this reason, local government is not specifically addressed here, but it is anticipated that over time local government will become less complex and more rational in the sense that jurisdictions will align themselves by function and territory in such a way as to effectively use resources to the maximum benefit of the citizens. As explained above, election is appropriate at the local level in theory. What will occur in practice will depend in large part on the developments within the legislature at the state level.

The federal level is also not specifically addressed, but here it is anticipated that the states may serve as a model for federal changes. The fact that there are fifty states provides the room for experimentation. Once experience has been acquired at the level of state government, then it will become possible to consider the appropriate changes to the federal government. Some states are more corrupt and less representative than the federal government, others less so. But working out the transition issues at the level of state government will provide the blueprints for applying the practice of citizenship to the federal government. In the following Minnesota is used as an example of the political construction of citizenship at the state government level in the transition toward a culture of democracy.

Minnesota is well suited for this citizenship project because it consists of a population that is well educated, it is fairly homogeneous (although becoming less so), and its citizens are politically active in terms of participation. Out of a total 1996 population of 4,657,758, 362,689 or 7.8% were classified as minorities, an increase from 6.2% in 1990 (Minnesota State Demographic Center). In terms of education, 87.9% of the population aged 25 and over has a high school degree and 26.3% aged 25 and over has a bachelor's or higher degree for a US rank of 7 and 12 respectively. Minnesota has one of the most open means of voter registration anywhere, and registration is actively encouraged. In 1996 there were 3,412,000 eligible voters, of whom 2,211,161 or 64.81% participated in the general election. Participation in the primary election was considerably lower–450,120 or 13.19% (MN

Secretary of State). In the 1998 general election, Minnesota voters exhibited the type of independent thinking that may make the state receptive to the idea of a genuine citizen legislature. Both major party candidates for governor were rejected in favor of the Reform Party candidate. This is a remarkable outcome considering the fact that the major party candidates vastly outspent the third-party candidate and that they both had much greater name recognition. In fact the candidate with the greatest name recognition ended up third in the race. While the actual assumption of the obligations of citizenship outlined here is a long way from protest voting, the election outcome does indicate that there may be some receptivity to the idea of reform.

Minnesota is also showing the same signs of social decay that have afflicted the rest of the nation which are reflected in increased poverty, crime, racism, the formation of inner-city ghettos, etc. Crime in Minnesota was 4,443 per 100,000 in 1994 compared to a national rate of 5,374. Within the Twin Cities Metropolitan area there are some interesting socio-economic indicators. Of the 24 largest metropolitan areas, the Twin Cities ranks 5th and 6th with respect to median family income and median household income respectively and 7th with respect to the percent of households with incomes over $50,000. However, when it comes to income per worker, its rank is 20 and with respect to the overall poverty rank it is 24 (Metropolitan Council). These rankings indicate that there may be a wide income disparity in the Twin Cities metropolitan area.

An organization that may be unique to Minnesota that affords an opportunity for citizen involvement in framing public policy issues is the Citizens' League. This organization was founded in 1952 as a non-partisan citizens group that frames policy issues and links citizen involvement to positive policy changes. It meets in the Twin Cities metropolitan area and performs public affairs research by convening volunteer committees from among its members that study an issue in depth which results in the issuance of a report that often plays a significant role in the development of legislation. Thus, even though Minnesota is beginning to experience the social problems that have afflicted the rest of the nation for some time, of the 50 states, it provides one of the most suitable environments in which to initiate the transition to a representative democracy.

The Minnesota Constitution was adopted in 1857 and was generally revised in 1974. It follows the federal model, but one major difference is the placement of the bill of rights at the very beginning as Article I. Representatives are chosen for a term of two years and senators for a term of four. Legislators are prohibited from holding any other office, federal or state, with the exception of postmaster or notary public. Legislators must be qualified voters and a resident of the state for one year and the district from which elected for six months immediately preceding the election. Qualified voters are persons 18 years of age or greater who have been citizens of the United States for three months and who have resided in the precinct for 30 days preceding the election. Persons not entitled to vote are those who have been convicted of treason or felony unless restored to civil rights, a person under guardianship, or a person who is mentally insane or incompetent. Eligible voters who are at least 21 years of age are eligible for any elective office from the district in which they reside except as otherwise provided in the constitution. (Constitution of the State of Minnesota)

The executive offices of the State of Minnesota consist of the governor, lieutenant governor, secretary of state, treasurer[85], attorney general, and state auditor. The terms of all of these offices is four years. The supreme court consists of one chief judge and not less than six nor more than eight associate judges as the legislature may

---

[85] This office was just abolished by a constitutional amendment passed by the voters during the 1998 election. The office will cease to exist in 2003 and its duties will be assumed by other executive branch agencies, mainly the Department of Finance.

determine. The legislature may establish a court of appeals, a district court, and other courts of lesser jurisdiction. Judges of the supreme court, court of appeals, and district courts "shall be learned in the law". Judges are elected and hold office for a term of six years. (*op. cit.*)

The Minnesota Constitution may be amended by proposals which are approved by a majority of the members elected to each house and ratified by the majority of the voters at the next general election. If two or more amendments are submitted at the same time, each is voted upon separately. (*op. cit.*) Minnesota does not have the initiative, referendum, and the constitution was amended in 1966 to provide for recall. Minnesota is a two-party state consisting of the Independent Republicans and the Democratic Farmer Labor parties. There have been attempts to form third parties, and the Reform Party is the latest such attempt. If the model of citizenship that has been developed above is to be applied in Minnesota, it will have to occur through the mechanism of a third political party even though third parties have been historically unsuccessful. I will call this third party the Transition Party because its sole purpose is to initiate the transition from elective government to representative democracy, and the initiation of this transition requires a constitutional amendment.

The Transition Party

The basic idea behind the Transition Party is a citizen political initiative to replace election with random selection. The Transition Party has no other purpose and will not take a stand on substantive political issues. Its sole purpose is to institute a new selection procedure, and since its purpose is amending the constitution, it will not be successful until such time that it achieves a majority in both houses. Once it achieves such a majority, it will propose a constitutional amendment that will: (1) set the standard of competence for service in the legislature, (2) establish selection of representatives from the body of public citizens on the basis of random selection, (3) set the standard of competence for service as an elector for the constitutional officers, (4) establish the selection of the constitutional officers on the basis of a randomly selected electoral college, and (5) establish the selection of judges on the basis of appointment by the governor with approval of the legislature (or one house thereof, if the legislature is uni-cameral). Once these proposed amendments are submitted to the voters, the Transition Party shall establish the rules of procedure for the new legislature so that the new legislature has a framework within which to operate at the beginning of the session. Upon approval by the voters of the new selection procedures, the Transition Party will cease to exist. I will call candidates running on the Transition Party platform "transitional candidates".

Unlike conventional campaigning in which a candidate must take a stand on a host of issues and make contradictory promises, the transitional candidate is pledged to submit the proposed constitutional amendment below to the voters. Transitional candidates will not take positions on substantive policy issues. The purpose of this restraint is to limit the range of issues only to the constitutional questions. The Minnesota Constitution also provides a mechanism for calling a constitutional convention by a two-thirds vote of each house with ratification by a majority of the electorate participating in the election. Any proposed changes must then be approved by three-fifths of all eligible voters voting. (Constitution of the State of Minnesota, Art. IX, Sec. 3) The convention approach is not recommended here, because it is not the purpose of the Transition Party to re-write the constitution, but only to change the method of selecting legislators and constitutional officers. Thus, the legislative session in which the Transition Party has achieved a majority in both houses will be of limited scope.

The fact that transitional candidates will not take a stand on substantive policy issues will make it somewhat easier for them to conduct their campaigns. Voters need to be informed of the proposed amendment and its implications without the distracting influence of subsidiary social and special interest issues. Thus, a transitional candidate only needs to identify herself as a member of the Transition Party pledged to bring the proposed constitutional amendments to the voters. This restricted focus will lower the cost of the campaign for transitional candidates assuming that the party platform is well known. The dissemination of these ideas can occur through discussion in and among the various associations located in political private space. As a general consensus coalesces around these ideas, the conditions favorable for the formation of the Transition Party will emerge. The Transition Party is envisioned as emerging as a citizen initiative after the idea of representative democracy has gone through a germination period in which the voters have become educated as to its meaning and implications.

There will be several practical problems associated with the session in which the Transition Party secures a majority in both houses. The first arises out of the fact that the session will be dealing only with the proposed constitutional changes. Since the Minnesota Legislature is biennial, this means that the process of running the day to day operations of state government will be in a holding pattern similar to the continuance of the federal government under the conditions of a continuing resolution. The state budget will need to be modified to take into account the effects of inflation and other economic changes, but no new proposals that have the potential to generate controversy can be initiated. It also means that legislators may need to be vigilant with regard to the executive so that the governor does not take advantage of the restricted range of focus to secure some benefit on behalf of a special interest. For this reason, and because they will need to conduct an election campaign to get elected, transitional candidates will need to be familiar with the political system they are seeking to change–i.e. they will need to possess many of the attributes of the politician. Another problem will arise during the election cycle in which the voters approve the constitutional amendments. They will be voting for candidates to the legislature under the electoral system while at the same time voting to replace that system. This means there will be a lag of one session after the amendments are approved, but before they can take effect. There is a heightened risk of corruption occurring during this final electoral session depending upon the quality of candidates selected.

On top of these issues, there are the general risks associated with any transition to something new. New procedures mean a new way of doing things which requires learning. Thus, there will be an inevitable lag in legislative effectiveness until institutional experience has accumulated to some degree. Even though the institutional membership is continually renewed, the institution itself goes through a learning process and accumulates knowledge and experience that transcends its membership. The constant renewal of membership, however, does require an informed public that serves as a background reservoir for this knowledge and experience. Transitional risks are not to be taken lightly, but the important point is that unwillingness to take these risks still involves risk–the risks associated with remaining in the dystopia of the present. Democracy has always been considered somewhat of an experiment. What is proposed here is a continuance of the experiment as a conscious effort to achieve a closer approximation of the democratic ideal.

General Ideas

So far, I have proposed the idea of simple random selection from the pool of *public citizens*. This is the simplest and most democratic selection procedure, but it may not be the most appropriate in all cases, and even if it is appropriate, it may not be appropriate until after the transition period. Before proceeding to the details of a constitutional amendment, I will briefly explore a few different institutional arrangements: (1) simple random selection at large, (2) simple random selection from districts, (3) random selection of electors by district, and (4) a randomly selected House with an elected Senate. Simple random selection at large from the statewide pool of public citizens is most consistent with the idea of citizens representing themselves as unique entities. It removes any vestige of the idea of geographic representation. In the past there was a much closer association of the citizen with his community as a distinct social entity tied to a geographic location. Today the idea of community is becoming tied to more fluid entities located in social space instead of physical territory. These communities take the form ranging from Tocquevillian voluntary associations to multi-national corporations. An individual citizen may be more closely associated with his profession and its association than the local community where he resides. She may be more closely associated with the community that has grown up around a particular cause than the local community where she lives. Some of these associations are trans-national in scope. Multi-national corporations and their international activities has stimulated the development of non-governmental organizations (NGOs) that have arisen in response to particular issues that are international in scope such as environmental degradation and child labor.[86] Individuals may also identify

---

[86] The rise of non-government organizations is a world-wide phenomenon that began recently–within the last 20 or 30 years but mushrooming since the 1980's. De Tocqueville and others have written about the vital role of citizen's groups (those groups that make up what is referred to as civil society) in democracies, but the NGO phenomenon is seen by some as a distinct sector that combines the attributes of both government and business–i.e. they serve essential social functions but have entrepreneurial qualities. They were major players in such recent events as the demise apartheid in South Africa, the overthrow of Communist regimes in Central Europe, the establishment of an international criminal court, the international treaty on land mines, the political transformation of the Philippines, and the end of dictatorship in Chile. (Bornstein, 1999) The

themselves more closely with a religious or ethnic group than their local community. All these changes have given rise to ideas such as group representation and multi-national citizenship. Simple random selection without territorial reference maintains the fundamental meaning of citizenship as the political identity of the individual natural person. It is for this reason that it is not only the simplest of the selection methods, but also the most democratic.

Simple random selection from a geographical district retains the idea of geographic representation. Even though the representative is obligated to represent himself, the fact that he is chosen from a district will inevitably exert a subtle, or perhaps not so subtle, influence on his approach to representation. The merit in retaining districts is that during any one legislative cycle, no area of the state will appear to be underrepresented. It also maintains consistency with the election of members of congress which is by congressional district. The main problem with using districts is the risk of allowing them to become a subterfuge for group representation instead of geographic representation. Therefore, how the districts are set up such that their geographical identity is maintained while keeping them numerically equal will be a challenge. The issue of districts is related to the issues surrounding local government which, as I mentioned above, will change as citizen control of the legislature takes hold. The issue of regional representation has valid arguments on both sides. Therefore, this is an issue that falls within the scope of the Transition Party as it decides upon the exact form of the amendment to the constitution.

A variant of simple random selection by district is the idea of selecting a group of electors by district who would then choose the representative. (This is simply the electoral college idea applied to

---

exponential expansion in the numbers of these organizations and their influence raises some interesting questions with respect to the perceived decline of civil society.

the legislative district.) The danger here is that this is a form of election and the problems associated with election will enter in. But there is one variant that may avoid some of the evils of election while at the same time avoiding some of the burdens of simple random selection. This is the idea of selecting a random group of public citizens by district who would then select the representative *from within the group*. This allows the introduction of a potential voluntary element in that members of the group could offer themselves as candidates and allow the group to decide who should serve. Limiting the selection to members of the group will avoid many, but not necessarily all, non-random influences. However, because of the potential hardship imposed by simple random selection of a single legislator, this alternative may be attractive.

All the proposals considered so far support the idea of a unicameral legislature. The reason for this is that the checks and balances of a two-house body are no longer necessary when selection is done randomly. Under conditions of electoral politics, members of the legislature introduce bad legislative proposals intentionally to satisfy a special interest knowing that the other body will kill the proposal. There are times, however, when responsible proposals have unintended consequences that are checked by the other body. One way to provide a check for unintended consequences is to require certain critical types of legislation to pass two successive legislative sessions or two separate constitutions of the legislature. (A factor that will enter in here is whether or not the entire legislature is replaced in toto during each cycle.) In this instance the second review provides a check similar to review by the other house. There may be valid reasons for maintaining a bicameral legislature. However, a bicameral legislature complicates the selection process, particularly if the two houses have terms of different length.

A variant of the selection process that maintains a bicameral body is a randomly selected house with an elected senate. The main problem with this proposal is that it maintains election and all the evils associated with it regarding the elected senate, even though these evils are eliminated with respect to the house. However, this idea does mitigate these evils and it can be structured to mitigate them further. One way to do this is to provide that the senate serve as the source of legislative proposals, but none can become law without passing the house. In this instance the house serves as a sort of citizen jury and the senate must persuade it that a particular proposal has merit. This is a compromise position between special interest and representation as I have defined it.

The above are suggestions of various types of random selection for legislators. The constitutional officers will be selected by an electoral college of randomly selected electors. This is a revival of the original idea of the electoral college with the only difference being that electors are randomly selected rather than being elected by voters. The issues regarding the electoral college are whether it is selected at large or by district, whether a single electoral college selects all the constitutional officers or if there is a separate group of electors for each office, and whether service as an elector exempts the elector from future service in the legislature. The one constitutional office that is of particular interest regarding these proposals is the Secretary of State, because, in Minnesota, this office has had jurisdiction over elections. Under the system proposed here, this office will be charged with the actual operation of the lottery used to select both legislators and electors. Therefore, it may be desirable to select this particular officer in isolation from, and at different times than, the others. It may also be desirable to provide a separate term of office for this officer.

In addition to the form of the selection process itself, there are the issues of the definition of a *public* citizen, the term of legislative office, and legislative compensation. The first issue is of critical importance which was considered above in the theoretical discussion. A public citizen is a citizen who has the ability to cross the citizenship frontier and assume the obligations of representation through the integration of rights, responsibility and reason. In practical terms this theoretical construct means that the private citizen, through the process of education, has become competent to legislate. Since education is the template for citizenship, it means he has become educated. John Stuart Mill recommended various proxies for determining whether a particular citizen should receive greater voting power in his system of plural representation. He settled on examination as the best determinant. Until such time that the system of education reflects the changes proposed here, examination may have to be used to determine whether a citizen is capable of being a public citizen. If examination is to be used, it is important that its administration be kept simple and that it not be discriminatory on any criterion except competence. I suggest that, since English is the medium of communication and since representation involves self-presentation, the ability to communicate in standard English is the best proxy for competence to legislate. The administration of this examination will fall within the purview of the Secretary of State which provides another reason that this officer may need to be selected separately from the other constitutional officers.

The second issue is the length of the legislative cycle which may affect the legislative term of office. Minnesota uses a biennial legislative cycle which originally consisted of a single session every two years but has been extended to annual sessions with a biennial budget. This has resulted in what is known as the long and short sessions in which budget matters are considered during the biennial long session and other items in the short session. The idea of the biennial budget cycle should be reconsidered as part of the amendment process. It may be possible to retain it and return to a single session every two years, or it may be necessary to replace it with an annual budget cycle. The final issue, compensation, is of particular importance. Randomly selected legislators are having a heavy burden placed upon them both in terms of the disruption of their personal lives and the difficulty of the task of representation.[87] Therefore, they must be compensated highly, and the terms of the compensation must be constitutionally specified along with other protections such as job security while in legislative service. Also the state will have to provide and maintain housing for those legislators that have to travel to St. Paul from distant parts of the state. These costs will replace the costs of publicly financing election campaigns.

A final issue is the mechanics of the selection procedure. The office of Secretary of State, since it currently has jurisdiction over election returns and voter registration, is the logical place to house this function. Random selection procedures are already in place for selecting jury pools, so a model for the mechanics of the process already exists.[88] The mechanics will vary depending upon whether selection is at large or by district, and the procedure will need to provide both legislative candidates and electors for the constitutional offices. What is important here is that, unlike jury duty, there should

---

[87] The argument here also applies to jury duty to a lesser extent. Jurors are woefully undercompensated and in many jurisdictions are not afforded the simple niceties, such as having parking provided, that make the performance of their task easier and a more rewarding experience. Hopefully the idea of the citizen legislature will lead to improvement in the treatment of jurors.

[88] This does not imply that jury selection methods are without problems, however. A complex system in Atlantic County, NJ that used computer tapes of licensed drivers and registered voters to select jurors appeared random but managed to introduce some systematic errors that resulted from the maze of lists, interval numbers, and alphabetizing schemes. Sometimes an inordinate number of people with Jewish names were selected, other times Italian names were selected. Out of 4366 jurors, 292 had another family member on the list. These errors resulted from improperly merging the lists which caused some people to be listed twice, the interval number was four times larger than it should have been, and the starting number was not random. The alphabetizing scheme combined with the other problems meant that many people in the same panel would have the same 5th letter in their last name. (Hans and Vidmar, 1986,56-7)

be very few grounds for exemption. This is an extremely difficult issue. If exemption is to be permitted, it must be permitted in such a way as not to make the process voluntary and thus defeat representation. One implication of this is that a citizen selected for legislative service must receive constitutional protection with respect to his employment. Democracy has costs, and this is a cost that will have to be borne by employers. For the self-employed there could be a significant cost which may require special provision, such as a business re-establishment allowance like the readjustment allowance that is provided to volunteers returning from the Peace Corps.

The main difficulty will be establishing the pool of public citizens from which names are to be drawn. The system of education will eventually be the source of these candidates, but certification of competence will be determined by the Secretary of State. I say "eventually" because the current system of education is not the template for citizenship. A system of education that is a template for citizenship can only arise out of a culture of democracy that has a vibrant practice of citizenship. There is no ideal standard that can be applied to determine legislative competence since moral and intellectual reasoning, although related, are two separate dimensions. There also is no ideal method of accurately assessing intellectual reasoning and there is virtually no assessment that is reliable with regard to moral reasoning and behavior. Therefore, the only reliable indicator of competence with regard to representation is the ability to express oneself and communicate with others in standard English. Until such time that this need can be met by the system of education, an examination or other proxy will be needed. The administrative difficulties associated with the idea of a standard examination established by the Secretary of State obviate against it. Therefore, another proxy, such as graduation from a college or university, may have to be used in the interim. The process of obtaining this information presents further difficulties. One idea is to collect the information through the individual tax return and/or the application process for a driver's license. The information would not need to be verified until an individual is selected for service. This means that more names will have to be drawn from the pool than will be needed to allow for contingencies such as inaccurate information and possible exemption.

The purpose of the above discussion is to illustrate some of the issues that will arise before a constitutional amendment can be properly drafted. These are the types of issues that will receive initial consideration when the Transition Party drafts its platform and final consideration during the legislative session in which the proposed constitutional amendment is drafted for presentation to the voters.

Creation and Platform of the Transition Party

Purpose: The Transition Party of Minnesota is established for the sole purpose of achieving the transition from an elective government to a representative democracy. By representative democracy is meant a government of citizens, by citizens, and for citizens in which the burden of governing is an obligation of citizenship. Legislators and executive officer electors are chosen by lot from the body of public citizens. The Transition Party shall exist for the sole purpose of amending the constitution of the state of Minnesota to incorporate this change in selecting legislators and constitutional officers.

These changes are intended to initiate the political construction of a new conception of citizenship–a citizenship which will provide the secular ethical context for political competition. Over time the citizen will evolve from the passive occupant of a status primarily associated with rights to an active participant in a role that, in addition to rights, assumes the obligations of governing. The construction of citizenship will not occur *ex nihilo*. Although it requires an affirmative act of initiation, what is being initiated is the further development of citizenship–a development from status to active practice. The Transition Party will initiate the constitutional changes to begin this constructive process.

Membership: Membership in the Transition Party is open to any citizen of the state of Minnesota committed to creating a government of the state that derives its legitimacy from a conception of citizenship within which the citizen assumes the responsibility of representation through the integration of rights, responsibility, and reason.

Creation: The Transition Party shall be created by a convocation of citizens convened for the purpose of drafting its constitution and bylaws. It shall come into being once a constitution is approved by two-thirds of those present. The constitution and bylaws shall define the internal governance of the Transition Party and shall specify the method of selecting its candidates for legislative office. The party constitution shall also specify that the Transition Party will cease to exist upon implementation of the constitutional amendment as specified below.

Platform: The following items constitute the platform of the Transition Party.

Item 1: To amend the constitution of the State of Minnesota to provide for the selection of legislators by lot, to provide for a college of electors chosen by lot that will select the executive branch officers, to change the terms of office for certain officers, and other matters as specified in the proposed amendment below.

Item 2: To maintain the state budget at its current level with provision for inflation until the legislature selected according to item 1 has taken office.

245

Item 3: To refrain from all policy initiatives unless legislative action is required in response to a bona fide emergency. To monitor the executive branch during this transition period to provide a check on potential corruption of the public interest.

Item 4: To draft proposed rules and procedures for the new legislature which it may adopt, modify, or reject.

Item 5: To draft proposed rules and procedures for the first panel of electors which that panel may adopt, modify, or reject.

Item 6: To initiate a study of the system of education to generate recommendations and proposals on how it may be changed such that its primary objective is the creation of citizens.

Constitutional Amendment

Below is an example of an amendment to the Constitution of the State of Minnesota. The amendment will apply to several articles in the constitution. The example is based on simple random selection from legislative districts and a unicameral legislature. Legislative terms will be staggered. If some of the ideas discussed above were to be introduced, the amendment will obviously become more complicated. The principle changes apply to the article that pertains to the legislative department. Selection of judges is changed to appointment by the governor with the approval of the legislature. The terms of office for the executive officers are increased, and the definition of "elector" in that article has a new meaning. A new article pertaining to citizenship and representation is added. Other minor changes, such as in the article pertaining to impeachment, will have to be made to reflect the fact that the legislature is a unicameral body. The duties of the secretary of state are expanded to include jurisdiction over the process of selection by lot. It is appropriate, therefore, to make this an appointive office by the legislature for a four year term that begins with the convening of the next legislature.

Proposed Constitutional Amendment

To achieve a more representative democracy, the constitution of the State of Minnesota shall be amended as follows:

I. **Preamble.** To secure and perpetuate the blessings of a representative democracy, which includes our civil, religious, and political liberties, for ourselves and our posterity, we the people of the state of Minnesota do ordain and establish this Constitution of the state of Minnesota.

Annotation: This change removes the reference to "God" to reflect the fact that a constitution is a secular document that pertains to all the people and their diverse religious views. It adds the term "representative democracy" since that reflects the subject matter of the proposed changes. It also specifically adds "political liberties" since it is through the exercise of the political liberties that the blessings of a representative democracy are secured. Liberty, as discussed above, implies the acceptance of moral responsibility. It must be emphasized again that citizenship carries with it the obligation to exercise one's political liberty.

II. **Legislature.** Article IV–Legislative Department–shall be amended as follows:

ARTICLE IV
LEGISLATIVE DEPARTMENT
Section 1. **Composition of legislature.** The legislature shall consist of a single house composed of representatives. Each representative is

selected by lot from among the citizens in the legislative district within which he resides.

Section 2. **Apportionment of members.** The number of members who compose the legislature shall be prescribed by law. Representation shall be apportioned equally throughout the different sections of the state in proportion to the population thereof.

Section 3. **Census enumeration apportionment; congressional and legislative district boundaries.** At its first session after each enumeration of the inhabitants of this state made by the authority of the United States, the legislature shall have the power to prescribe the bounds of congressional and legislative districts. Legislative districts shall be numbered in a regular series.

Section 4. **Terms of office; vacancies.** Representatives shall be chosen for a term of two years, except to fill a vacancy. Vacancies shall be filled by lot from among the citizens of the district within which the vacancy occurs. Legislative terms shall be staggered with representatives from even numbered districts being selected in even numbered years and representatives from odd numbered districts being selected in odd numbered years.

Section 5. **Restriction on holding office.** No legislator shall hold any other office under the authority of the United States or the state of Minnesota or subdivision thereof, except that of notary public. A legislator may not seek election to, or be appointed to, another office during his term as legislator.

Section 6. **Qualifications of legislators.** Legislators shall be citizens of the State of Minnesota who have been deemed qualified for legislative service as enumerated in Article VII.

Section 7. **Rules of government.** The legislature may determine the rules of its proceedings, sit upon its own adjournment, punish its members for disorderly behavior, and with the concurrence of two-thirds expel a member; but no member shall be expelled a second time for the same offense.

Section 8. **Oath of office.** Each member and officer of the legislature before entering upon his duties shall take an oath or affirmation to support the Constitution of the United States, the constitution of this state, and to discharge faithfully the duties of his office to the best of his judgment and ability.

Section 9. **Compensation; job security; other income.** The compensation of legislators shall be set at 2.5 times the median income of the State of Minnesota for the year immediately preceding legislative service. Legislators shall be granted a leave of absence from their place of employment for the duration of the term of the legislature and shall be allowed to return to their place of employment in the same or comparable position at the same rate of compensation received before the leave adjusted for any cost of living or other allowances provided to other comparable positions within the organization during the absence. Self-employed legislators may be granted a business re-establishment allowance if their absence while in legislative service was a direct cause of lost business. Legislators shall receive no compensation from their place of employment while in legislative service. Housing will be provided at the seat of government for those legislators whose districts are outside a reasonable commuting distance therefrom.

Section 10. **Privilege from arrest.** The members of the legislature in all cases except treason, felony and breach of the peace, shall be privileged from arrest during the session of the legislature and in going to or returning from the same. For the purpose of this section acceptance of compensation or other reward to promote a particular piece of legislation shall constitute a felony. For any speech or debate in the legislature, legislators shall not be questioned in any other place.

Section 11. **Protest and dissent of members.** Two or more members of the legislature may dissent and protest any act or resolution which they think injurious to the public or to any individual and have the reason of their dissent entered in the journal.

Section 12. **Biennial meetings; length of session; special sessions; length of adjournments.** The legislature shall meet at the seat of government in regular session in each biennium at the times prescribed by law for not exceeding a total of 120 legislative days. The legislature shall not meet in regular session, nor in any adjournment thereof, after the first Monday following the third Sunday in May of any year. After meeting at a time prescribed by law, the legislature may adjourn to another time. "Legislative day" shall be defined by law. A special session of the legislature may be called by the governor on extraordinary occasions.

Section 13. **Quorum.** A majority constitutes a quorum to transact business, but a smaller number may adjourn from day to day and compel the attendance of absent members in the manner and under the penalties it may provide.

Section 14. **Open session.** The legislature shall be open to the public during its sessions except in cases in which in its opinion require secrecy.

Section 15. **Officers; journals.** The legislature shall elect its presiding officer and other officers as may be provided by law. The legislature shall keep a journal of its proceedings, and from time to time publish the same, and the yeas and nays, when taken on any question, shall be entered in the journal.

Section 16. **Elections via voce.** In all elections by the legislature members shall vote via voce and their votes shall be entered in the journal.

Section 17. **Laws to embrace only one subject.** No law shall embrace more than one subject, which shall be expressed in its title.

Section 18. **Reporting of bills.** Every bill shall be reported in the legislature on three different days, unless, in case of urgency, two-thirds of the legislature deem it expedient to dispense with this rule.

Section 19. **Enrollment and certification of bills.** Every bill passed by the legislature shall be enrolled. The legislature by rule shall provide the manner in which a bill shall be certified for presentation to the governor.

Section 20. **Passage of bills on last day of session prohibited.** The legislature shall pass no bill on the day prescribed for adjournment. This section shall not preclude the enrollment of a bill or its transmittal to the executive for his signature.

Section 21. **Majority vote of all members to pass a law.** The style of all laws of this state shall be: "Be it enacted by the legislature of the state of Minnesota". No law shall be passed unless voted for by a majority of all the members of the legislature, and the vote entered in the journal of the legislature.

Section 22. **Approval of bills by governor; action on veto.** Every bill passed in conformity to the rules of the legislature shall be presented to the governor. If he approves a bill, he shall sign it, deposit it in the office of the secretary of state and notify the legislature of that fact. If he vetoes a bill, he shall return it with his objections, and his objections shall be entered in the journal. If, after reconsideration, two-thirds of the legislature agree to pass the bill, it shall become law and shall be deposited in the office of the secretary of state. In such cases the votes shall be determined by yeas and nays, and the names of the persons voting for or against the bill shall be entered in the journal. Any bill not returned by the governor within three days (Sundays excepted) after it is presented to him becomes a law as if he had signed it, unless the legislature by adjournment within that time prevents its return. Any bill passed during the last three days of a session may become law if the governor signs and deposits it in the office of the secretary of state within 14 days after the adjournment of the legislature. Any bill passed during the last three days of the session which is not signed and deposited within 14 days after adjournment does not become a law.

If a bill presented to the governor contains several items of appropriation of money, he may veto one or more of the items while approving the bill. At the time he signs the bill the governor shall append to it a statement of the items he vetoes and the vetoed items shall not take effect. If the legislature is in session, he shall transmit a copy of the statement, and the items vetoed shall be separately reconsidered. If on reconsideration any item is approved by two-thirds of the members of the legislature, it is a part of the law notwithstanding the objections of the governor.

Section 23. **Presentation of orders, resolutions, and votes to governor.** Each order, resolution or vote except such as relate to the business or adjournment of the legislature shall be presented to the governor and is subject to his veto as prescribed in case of a bill.

Section 24. **Disorderly conduct.** During a session the legislature may punish by imprisonment for not more than 24 hours any person not a member who is guilty of any disorderly or contemptuous behavior in its presence.

Section 25. **Banking laws; two-thirds votes.** Passage of a general banking law requires the vote of two-thirds of the members of each house of the legislature.

Annotation: This article is completely rewritten to reflect the selection of legislators by lot and the establishment of a one house legislature. Legislative districts are retained, and the term of office is two years. Terms are staggered to promote institutional learning. The view taken here is that legislative service is a burden upon the citizen called to serve and therefore it is necessary to remove as many difficulties as possible from the conditions of service. Legislators are to be provided a fairly high level of compensation, job protection while in service, and housing if they must travel long distances to the seat of government. Special provision is made for self-employed legislators whose businesses may be interrupted during their absence.

III. **Executive.** Section 1 and 2 of Article V–Executive Department–shall be amended as follows:

Section 1. **Executive officers.** The executive department consists of a governor, lieutenant governor, secretary of state, auditor, and attorney general. The executive officers, with the exception of the secretary of state, shall be chosen by the electors of the state. The secretary of state shall be chosen by the method prescribed below.

Section 2. **Term of executive officers; qualifications.** The term of office for the executive officers is six years and until a successor is chosen and qualified. Each shall have attained the age of 25 years and shall have been a bona fide resident of the state for one year next preceding his election and shall be a citizen of the United States and the state of Minnesota. The executive officers shall serve for a single term only.

Annotation: The terms of office for the executive officers is changed to six years without the possibility of a succeeding term. The reason for this change is to provide for a term of sufficient length to allow the executive officers a chance to implement their programs while maintaining the principle of rotation in office.

III. **Judiciary.** Section 7 of Article VI–Judicial Department–shall be amended as follows:

Section 7. **Term of office; appointment.** The term of office of all judges shall be ten years and until their successors are qualified. District court judges shall be appointed by the governor. Appellate and Supreme Court judges shall be appointed by the governor with approval of a two-thirds vote of the legislature. Judges shall be limited to a single term in the office to which they were appointed, but they may be appointed for a term in a superior court.

Annotation: The purpose of these changes is to have judges appointed by the governor instead of elected. Appellate and supreme court judges require legislative approval. The term of office is increased to ten years to maintain judicial independence while providing rotation in office.

IV. **Citizenship and Representation.** Article VII–Citizenship and Representation–shall be added to the Constitution of Minnesota as a new article.

ARTICLE VII
CITIZENSHIP AND REPRESENTATION

Section 1. **Citizenship.** Every person who has been a citizen of the United States for three months and who has permanently resided in the State of Minnesota for a period of three months shall be deemed a citizen of Minnesota.

Section 2. **No loss of citizenship; exemptions from legislative and electoral service.** No person loses Minnesota citizenship solely by reason of his absence while employed in the service of the United States; nor while engaged upon the waters of this state or of the United States; nor while a student in any institution of learning; nor while kept at any almshouse or asylum; nor while confined in any public prison. Any citizen who is absent or engaged in the above enumerated activities is exempt from legislative and electoral service for the duration of the absence or activity. No soldier, seaman or marine in the army or navy of the United States is a citizen of this state solely in consequence of being stationed within the state.

Section 3. **Legislative eligibility.** Every person who is a citizen of Minnesota and has attained the age of 21 years shall be deemed eligible for legislative service from that legislative district within which he resides unless that person has been convicted of treason or felony, is a person under guardianship, a person insane or not mentally competent, or a person unable to communicate using acceptable standard English. Eligibility is for the duration of residence as a citizen within the State of Minnesota but ceases upon having served once as a legislator or elector within the state of Minnesota. Selection for legislative service is by lot, and during each legislative cycle, one legislator shall be selected from each even numbered legislative district in even numbered years, and one legislator shall be selected from each odd numbered legislative district in odd numbered years.

Section 4. **Electoral eligibility.** Every person who is a citizen of Minnesota and has attained the age of 21 years shall be deemed eligible to serve as the elector from the legislative district within which he resides for the constitutional officers of the State of Minnesota, with the exception of the secretary of state, unless that person has been convicted of treason or felony, is a person under guardianship, a person insane or not mentally competent, or a person unable to communicate using acceptable standard English. Eligibility is for the duration of residence as a citizen within the State of Minnesota but ceases upon having served once as a legislator or elector within the state of Minnesota. Selection for electoral service is by lot, and in each electoral cycle, one elector shall be selected from each legislative district.

Section 5. **Duties of Electors.** Electors shall convene at the seat of government not later than March 1 of the year in which they are selected for the purpose of selecting the constitutional officers of the state of Minnesota with the exception of the secretary of state. Constitutional officers must be selected by Nov. 1 of the year before which they are to begin service. Electors shall determine their own rules and procedures including how often they shall meet, and they shall keep a journal within which these procedures and the minutes of their meetings are recorded. Electors shall determine the factors they will use in the selection of the constitutional officers. These factors shall be announced publicly through the office of the secretary of state. The electors may solicit nominations and/or the submission of applications for the constitutional offices. This solicitation, the format for nominations and applications, and the procedures for submission shall be announced by the secretary of state. Nominations and applications shall be submitted to the secretary of state in the time frame specified for transmittal to the electors. Selection of constitutional officers shall be by majority vote of all electors. Upon selection of the constitutional officers the electors shall submit the journal and any other records of their proceedings to the secretary of state and shall then disband. The secretary of state shall maintain the journal and records of the electoral proceedings as permanent records available to the public.

Section 6. **Jurisdiction over selection process rests with secretary of state.** The secretary of state shall determine and administer the process of random selection to be used in the selection of legislators and electors. The process shall be administered by legislative district and the citizens selected so informed by official notice bearing the seal of the secretary of state. The selection of legislators shall occur in January of the year preceding the term of service. The selection of electors shall occur in January of the year of service.

Section 7. **Compensation of electors.** Electors shall receive $10,000 compensation in addition to per diem and travel expenses. Electors may not be penalized as a result of absence from their place of employment and their salaries may not be diminished except for the periods of absence. Such diminishment of salary may not exceed 5% of gross salary. After the first electoral cycle, the secretary of state shall recommend, and the legislature shall set a new level of compensation for electors based upon the actual effort required in selecting constitutional officers. Thereafter, the level of compensation shall be adjusted to account for increases in the cost of living.

Section 8. **Selection of the secretary of state.** In the year that the term of office for the secretary of state expires, a nominating committee of three legislators shall nominate a slate of three candidates to the legislature and the legislature shall choose from among these three by preference voting. The candidate receiving the highest number of votes shall be chosen. The secretary of state shall be chosen for a single term.

Annotation: This is a completely new article that is a radical departure from the present constitutional practice in that it specifically defines state citizenship and provides for the direct random selection of legislators and the selection of constitutional officers by a randomly selected panel of electors. The office of secretary of state is selected by a separate method because that office has jurisdiction over the operation of the random selection process for both legislators and electors. That office also serves as a liaison between the electors and the public. The use of an electoral college is new. Therefore, the compensation for electors is arbitrarily set until the secretary of state can monitor the process to determine the level of effort required. Legislators are selected one year before they are to begin service to allow them time to prepare for such service. Electors are to choose constitutional officers by Nov. 1 of the year before they begin service. This follows current practice, but it may be desirable to move up these dates to allow more time for the constitutional officers to prepare for office. This is particularly important with respect to the task of selecting agency heads and other appointive officers.

V. **Elective Franchise.** Article VII–Elective Franchise–will be renumbered as Article VIII and a new section will be added as follows:

Section 1. **Election.** Election is reserved for non-appointive federal and local offices. Election occurs in the precinct within which the citizen resides.

All other sections will be renumbered accordingly.

Annotation: It is necessary to retain this section since random selection applies to state constitutional officers and legislators. Election is still used to choose federal and local officials.

VI. **Impeachment.** Article VIII–Impeachment and Removal from Office –shall be renumbered as Article IX. Section 1 shall be amended as follows:

Section 1. **Impeachment Powers.** The legislature has the sole power of impeachment through a concurrence of two-thirds of all its members. All impeachments shall be tried by a panel of nine district judges selected at random by the chief justice of the supreme court except when the chief justice is the object of impeachment in which case the secretary of state shall make the selection. No person shall be impeached except upon concurrence of seven members of the judicial panel.

Annotation: These changes are required to reflect the establishment of a unicameral legislature. The power of impeachment is changed from a majority to a two-thirds vote of the legislature and impeachments are tried by a nine-member panel of randomly selected district court judges. Conviction requires concurrence of seven of these nine members. The intent here is to make impeachment apply to cases in which the conduct in question is clearly impeachable. Public offices belong to the citizens of the state of Minnesota and not to the occupant as a vested right. However, impeachment must not be employed in a frivolous manner.

VII. **Renumeration.** All other succeeding articles shall be renumbered accordingly.

VIII. **Reaffirmation**. Twenty years after the approval of this amendment by the voters of the state of Minnesota, the voters shall reaffirm these amendatory changes through referendum.

Annotation: This amendment is an experiment in constitutional practice which could result in unanticipated consequences. Therefore, the citizens, in their capacity as voters, will need to reaffirm the practice after a period of twenty years. Twenty years is suggested to allow sufficient time for citizens to adapt to the practice, institutional learning to occur, and the resolution of transitional problems while at the same time keeping the period short enough to abandon the idea if it is becoming obvious that it is failing to achieve representative democratic practice. In approving this amendment citizens will need to accept the fact that transitional difficulties will occur, and they must realize that they are accepting the obligations which these changes imply. Over time the practice of citizenship this amendment seeks to establish will become embedded in the political culture. A twenty-year period is suggested as a sufficient period of time to see if the anticipated changes are in fact manifesting themselves.

IX. **Approval and Non-severability.** This proposed constitutional amendment, although affecting various articles and sections, constitutes a single amendment and must be passed or rejected in its entirety by three-fourths of the voters participating in the election in which it is placed on the ballot.

Annotation: The above proposal constitutes a single proposal that must be approved or rejected by the voters in its entirety. Because of the importance of the proposal and its impact on the citizens of the state, it must be approved by three-fourths of the voters participating in the election. If voter participation is low, even this level of approval may not be sufficient, and it may be necessary to consider raising the level of support to two-thirds or three-fourths of the eligible voters. In this case non-participation in the election counts as a vote against the amendment.

Discussion

The proposals above are intended to illustrate the means by which a transition to a representative democracy can be initiated at the level of state government. These proposals are intended to be suggestive only. The actual details for any particular state will have to take into account the unique features of that state. The idea of the Transition Party is suggested as the vehicle through which interested citizens could come together to work out the procedural details of the constitutional amendment and the transition phase to the new form of governance. Obviously, before the idea of the Transition Party can take hold, there must be a general discussion and debate of these ideas among the citizens of the state–i.e. the idea of building a citizenship along the lines presented here must arise from within the citizenry itself. This is a radical first step that is similar to the radicality of the idea of choosing governors by election in place of monarchy.

Conclusion

The New Citizenship to which we commit ourselves is open, diversified, inclusive, and nonpartisan: a civic forum comprising every segment of America. But it is not a stand in for any and every kind of activity. It is the provenance neither of the "state-centered left" which thinks government can solve every problem nor the "market-centered right" which believes in the social power of the "invisible hand." It is skeptical both of the "technocratic center" where faith resides in experts and of talk show democracy, whose politics of grievance and self-righteousness distorts public discussion, confounding democracy with demagoguery.

Rather, the New Citizenship seeks a return to government of and by as well as for the people, a democracy whose politics is our common public work: where citizens are as prudent in deliberation as we expect our representatives to be; where all give life to liberty and rights are complemented by the responsibilities that make them real.

CIVIC DECLARATION: Call for a New Citizenship
http://www/cpn.org/sections/new_citizenship/civic_declaration.html

The end of a millennium is a good time to focus on where we, as a species, have been and where we desire to go. It is a good time to revisit ultimate questions such as: who are we? how did we get here? why are we here? and, where are we going? It is also a good time to revisit the political question that asks: What type of society do we want to live in? While it is possible to provide answers

261

to the ultimate questions based on individual belief,[89] the political question must be answered collectively. How to go about deriving that answer is what the argument above has been about.

Although the end of the millennium is witness to significant human progress when progress is measured in terms of technological development and economic growth, it is also witness to the cost of that progress in terms of the destruction of the natural and social environment. The bifurcation of our evolution in which our scientific and technological knowledge has outstripped our social and behavioral knowledge has contributed to the condition that the institution of government is incapable of dealing with the threat that technological and economic development, and the social dislocations they produce, pose to human survival on this planet. I do not believe that we can solve these environmental and social problems until something is done to close the evolutionary gap. It is also my belief that these problems cannot be solved in isolation from one another. Instead, it is first necessary to address the question of how government can be turned into an instrument of human evolution and flourishing. That question raises the further question of what it means to be a citizen. In my view, the political construction of a citizenship along the lines outlined above is necessary if our species is to not only survive but thrive.

The gap between the moral burden this conception of citizenship places on the individual and citizenship in its current form is enormous. It also requires a sense of trust in our fellow citizens that involves a leap of faith. This sense of trust must proceed from the assumption that on the whole people are more good than they are bad, and that acting collectively, the good will prevail in the

---

[89]Although belief is individual, "[T]he test of a belief is its capacity to explain and to organize human experience. Every belief must on demand accept the role of hypothesis and prove its adequacy to explain and to order such relevant facts as may be adduced to test it." (Griffin:1996: 90)

long run. As Pitkin pointed out, the position a theorist takes with respect to her view of representation depends upon her view of human nature. If we proceed with the view that man is inherently evil, not only is an authoritarian form of government called for, but quite frankly, if this view is correct, human life on this planet will not be worth living in the long run. Another dire possibility is that humanity simply does not possess the intelligence to survive long term in its own ecological niche. There are obvious elements of truth in both these views. The Twentieth Century horrors of the holocaust and the development of the capability of destroying all life on the planet attest to these elements of truth, and it may be that no form of government can be created that will promote long term human flourishing.

The view that collectively speaking man is more good than bad allows room for the further assumption of perfectibility in human evolution. This assumption does not imply that man will evolve into a god, but it does imply that his lot here on earth can be improved, not only or mainly in material terms, but socially, spiritually, and intellectually. It implies that he can develop the capability of governing himself such that he can survive and thrive in harmony with the rest of nature. It implies that he can develop the moral and intellectual ability to represent himself as an equal citizen in a government of equal citizens designed to nourish both private and public autonomy so that both the individual citizen and the political community flourish symbolically as a unified whole that allows humankind to express itself in all its potentiality. However, the idea of human perfectibility is not something that should be assumed; it is something that can only be sought after through conscious choice. Assuming it will occur is not the same thing as making it occur. It will not occur by the operation of some inexorable historical laws or by historical accident. If it is to occur, it can only occur through the development of a democratic citizenship that allows it to occur.

The model of citizenship developed here is not a model of ultimate citizenship nor is it equivalent to the Aristotelian ideal in which the citizen is wholly consumed in public business. It is merely a model for a potential next stage in the evolution of democratic citizenship. It provides a large space for private autonomy and the development of the individual. But it does call for the individual to be involved in the public business. Being a citizen asks the individual to be prepared for the obligation of representation. It asks him to be responsive to his fellow citizens who serve as representatives. It asks him to participate with them in the process of governing. The obligation of representation itself, however, occurs once, if at all, in a citizen's lifetime. In terms of inconvenience the burden lies more in its unpredictability than in the actual length of service. But in terms of moral responsibility during that period of service the burden is a heavy one indeed. It is important that the citizens be aware of this burden, so they know what they are obligating themselves to, should they amend their state constitution along the lines suggested above. The price of liberty is the burden of representation.

The purpose of politically constructing citizenship along the lines suggested here is to create a culture of democracy for the next millennium. Democracy is a system of government, but it is also a type of culture. Our current culture, however, it is labeled, derives part of its character from the institution of election. In the absence of election, the culture of democracy will be considerably quieter than at present. This implies that it will be considerably duller because the absence of election will mean the absence of a major source of entertainment. Instead of focusing on the personalities of political participants, the news media will have to focus on the content of political ideas. The arena of citizen action may shift to local government which could result in the strengthening of local communities. Much of what this culture will look like is difficult to predict, but most likely it will be a more fluid culture simply because

264

it will be much more adaptable to changes in the environment. Over time it should develop into a culture of far greater civility than at present. The one word that sums up what this culture will look like is "balance", and because it is adaptable, it will stay balanced. The idea of balance primarily refers to the balance between the private and public, but it also extends to other areas such as living in balance with the rest of nature. Balance is maintained by democratic citizenship because citizenship is both individual and collective. It is vested in the individual, but it is a collective endeavor. It defines the individual politically qua individual and endows him with rights. But it also integrates him into the political community through the obligation of representation. It is in the practice of citizenship that the paradox of freedom is resolved. By accepting the obligations of citizenship, the individual forces himself to be free.

To be *citizens*, or not to be. That is the question.
The choice is ours.
Mitakuye oyasin.[90]

---

[90] Lakota meaning "All My Relations"

References

Abbinnett, Ross (1998); "Politics and Enlightenment: Kant and Derrida on Cosmopolitan Responsibility", Citizenship Studies, Vol. 2. No. 2, July, 1998

Abramson, Jeffrey (1994); We, the Jury, Basic Books, New York, 1994

Abramson, Jill (1998); "The Business of Persuasion Thrives in the Nation's Capital", The New York Times, Sept. 29, 1998

Alcock, Pete (1994); "Why Citizenship and Welfare Rights Offer New Hope for New Welfare in Britain", in Turner, Bryan and Hamilton, Peter (eds.); Citizenship Critical Concepts, Routledge, London, 1994

Alegandro, Roberto (1993); Hermeneutics, Citizenship, and the Public Sphere, State University of New York, 1993

Ancelovici, Marcos, and Dupuis-Déri, Francis (1998); "Interview with Professor Charles Taylor", Citizenship Studies, Vol. 2. No. 2, July, 1998

Angell, Ann V. and Hahn, Carole L.(1996); "Global Perspectives", in Parker, Walter C. (ed.), Educating the Democratic Mind, State University of New York Press, 1996

Apple, Michael W. (1996); "The Hidden Curriculum and the Nature of Conflict", in Parker, Walter C. (ed.), Educating the Democratic Mind, State University of New York Press, 1996

Arendt, Hannah (1968); Between Past and Future Eight Exercises in Political Thought, Viking Press, NY, 1968

Arendt, Hannah (1979); "On Hannah Arendt", in Hill, Melvyn A. (ed), Hannah Arendt: The Recovery of the Public World, St. Maritin's Press, NY, 1979

Arendt, Hannah (1982); Lectures on Kant's Political Philosophy, edited with an interpretive essay by Ronald Beiner, University of Chicago Press, 1982

Aron, Raymond; "Is Multinational Citizenship Possible?" (1994); in Turner, Bryan and Hamilton, Peter (eds.); Citizenship Critical Concepts, Routledge, London, 1994

Bakan, Mildred (1979); "Hannah Arendt's Concepts of Labor and Work", in Hill, Melvyn A. (ed), Hannah Arendt: The Recovery of the Public World, St. Maritin's Press, NY, 1979

Baker, Keith Michael (1994); "Representation", in Turner, Bryan and Hamilton, Peter (eds.); Citizenship Critical Concepts, Routledge, London, 1994

Barbalet, J.M. (1993); "Citizenship, Class Inequality and Resentment", in Turner, Bryan S. (ed.); Citizenship and Social Theory, Sage Publications, Newbury Park, CA, 1993

Barbalet, J.M. (1994); "Citizenship Rights", in Turner, Bryan and Hamilton, Peter (eds.); Citizenship Critical Concepts, Routledge, London, 1994

Barry, Brian (1965); Political Argument, Routledge and Kegan Paul, London, 1965

Beiner, Ronald; ed. (1995); <u>Theorizing Citizenship</u>, State University of New York Press, Albany, 1995

Bell, Daniel (1994); "The Revolution of Rising Entitlements", in Turner, Bryan and Hamilton, Peter (eds.); <u>Citizenship Critical Concepts</u>, Routledge, London, 1994

Bellah, Robert N.(1994); "Are Americans Still Citizens", in Turner, Bryan and Hamilton, Peter (eds.); <u>Citizenship Critical Concepts</u>, Routledge, London, 1994

Bellah, Robert, *et al.*(1994); "Citizenship", in Turner, Bryan and Hamilton, Peter (eds.); <u>Citizenship Critical Concepts</u>, Routledge, London, 1994

Benestad, Brian (1995); "Ordinary Virtue as Heroism", in Glendon, Mary Ann and Blankenforn, David, (eds.) , <u>Seedbeds of Virtue Sources of Competence, Character, and Citizenship in American Society</u>, Madison Books, Lanham, MD, 1995

Berkowitz, Marvin W. and Oser, Fritz (eds.) (1985); <u>Moral Education: Theory and Application</u>, Lawrence Erlbaum Associates, Hillsdale, NJ 1985

Bernard-Powers, Jane (1996); "The 'Woman Question' in Citizenship Education", in Parker, Walter C. (ed.), <u>Educating the Democratic Mind</u>, State University of New York Press, 1996

Blakeslee, Sandra (1996); "Complex and Hidden Brain in the Gut Makes Stomachaches and Butterflies", <u>The New York Times</u>, Jan. 23, 1996

Blankenhorn, David (1995); "The Possibility of Civil Society", in Glendon, Mary Ann and Blankenforn, David, (eds.) , <u>Seedbeds of</u>

268

Virtue Sources of Competence, Character, and Citizenship in American Society, Madison Books, Lanham, MD, 1995

Blasi, Augusto (1985); "The Moral Personality: Reflections for Social Science and Education", in Berkowitz, Marvin W. and Oser, Fritz (eds.); Moral Education: Theory and Application, Lawrence Erlbaum Associates, Hillsdale, NJ 1985

Boeckelman, Keith and Corell, Gina (1996); "An Analysis of Term Limitation Elections", in Grofman, Bernard (ed.); Legislative Term Limits: Public Choice Perspectives, Kluwer Academic Publishers, Norwell, MA, 1996

Bornstein, David (1999); "A Force Now In the World, Citizens Flex Social Muscle", The New York Times, July 10, 1999

Bowers, C. A. (1987); Elements of a Post-Liberal Theory of Education, Teachers College Press, New York, 1987

Boyte, Harry C. and Kari, Nancy N. (1996), Building America The Democratic Promise of Public Work, Temple University Press, Philadelphia, 1996

Brion-Meisels, Steven and Selman, Robert L.(1985); "The Adolescent as Interpersonal Negotiator: Three Portraits of Social Development", in Berkowitz, Marvin W. and Oser, Fritz (eds.); Moral Education: Theory and Application, Lawrence Erlbaum Associates, Hillsdale, NJ 1985

Browning, Don S.(1995); "Altruism, Civic Virtue, and Religion", in Glendon, Mary Ann and Blankenforn, David, (eds.) , Seedbeds of Virtue Sources of Competence, Character, and Citizenship in American Society, Madison Books, Lanham, MD, 1995

Brubaker, William Rogers (1994); "Immigration, Citizenship, and the Nation-State in France and Germany: A Comparative Historical Analysis", in Turner, Bryan and Hamilton, Peter (eds.); Citizenship Critical Concepts, Routledge, London, 1994

Burchill, Scott (1998); "Human Nature, Freedom and Political Community: An Interview with Noam Chomsky", Citizenship Studies, Vol. 2, No. 1, Feb. 1998

Cagnon, Paul (1996); "History's Role in Civic Education: The Precondition for Political Intelligence", in Parker, Walter C. (ed.), Educating the Democratic Mind, State University of New York Press, 1996

Cain, Burce E. (1996); "The Varying Impact of Legislative Term Limits", in Grofman, Bernard (ed.); Legislative Term Limits: Public Choice Perspectives, Kluwer Academic Publishers, Norwell, MA, 1996

Callan, Eamonn (1997); Creating Citizens Political Education and Liberal Democracy, Clarendon Press, Oxford, 1997

Candee, Daniel (1985); "Classical Ethics and Live Patient Simulations in the Moral Education of Health Care Professionals", in Berkowitz, Marvin W. and Oser, Fritz (eds.); Moral Education: Theory and Application, Lawrence Erlbaum Associates, Hillsdale, NJ 1985

Capell, Elizabeth A.(1996); "The Impact of Term Limits on the California Legislature: An Interest Group Perspective", in Grofman, Bernard (ed.); Legislative Term Limits: Public Choice Perspectives, Kluwer Academic Publishers, Norwell, MA, 1996

Carbone, Peter F. Jr. (ed.) (1987); <u>Value Theory and Education,</u> Robert E. Krieger Publishing Co., Malabar, FL, 1987

Carbone, Peter F. Jr.(1987); "Reflections on Moral Education", in Carbone, Peter F. Jr. (ed.), <u>Value Theory and Education</u>, Robert E. Krieger Publishing Co., Malabar, FL, 1987

Carens, Joseph H.(1995); "Aliens and Citizens: The Case for Open Borders", in Beiner, Ronald; ed. , <u>Theorizing Citizenship</u>, State University of New York Press, Albany, 1995

Cattacin, Sandro and Tattini,Véronique (1997); "Reciprocity Schemes in Unemployment Regulation Policies: Towards a Pluralistic Citizenship of Marginalisation?", <u>Citizenship Studies,</u> Vol. 1, #3, Nov. 1997

Clark, John Ruskin (1984); <u>The Great Living System: The Religion Emerging from the Sciences</u>, Skinner House, Boston, 1984

Clarke, James, van Dam, Elsbeth, and Gooster, Liz (1998); "New Europeans: Naturalisation and Citizenship in Europe", <u>Citizenship Studies</u>, Vol. 2, No. 1, Feb. 1998

Cohen, Michael (1990); "Key Issues Confronting State Policymakers", in Elmore, Richard F. (ed.); <u>Restructuring Schools: The Next Generation of Education Reform</u>, Jossey-Bass Publishers, San Francisco, 1990

Coontz, Stephanie (1992); <u>The Way We Never Were American Families and the Nostalgia Trap</u>, Basic Books, New York, 1997

Coontz, Stephanie (1997); <u>The Way We Really Are Coming to Terms with America's Changing Families</u>, Basic Books, New York, 1997

Corboy, Philip H.(1975); "From the Bar" in Simon, Rita James; The Jury System in America, Sage Publications, Beverly Hills, 1975

Crick, Bernard (1979); "On Rereading the *Origins of Totalitarianism*", in Hill, Melvyn A. (ed), Hannah Arendt: The Recovery of the Public World, St. Maritin's Press, NY, 1979

Crowley, John (1998); "The National Dimension of Citizenship in T. H. Marshall", Citizenship Studies, Vol. 2. No. 2, July 1998

Dahrendorf, Ralf (1994); "Citizenship and Beyond: The Social Dynamics of an Idea", in Turner, Bryan and Hamilton, Peter (eds.); Citizenship Critical Concepts, Routledge, London, 1994

Davidson, Alastair (1968); "Norberto Bobbio, Liberal Socialism and the Problem of Language", Citizenship Studies, Vol. 2. No. 2, July 1998

De Tocqueville, Alexis (1994); "Democracy in America", in Turner, Bryan and Hamilton, Peter (eds.); Citizenship Critical Concepts, Routledge, London, 1994

De Tocqueville. Alexis (1969); Democracy in America, George Lawrence trans., Doubleday & Co., Garden City, NY, 1969

Delanty, Gerald (1997); "Models of Citizenship: Defining European Identity and Citizenship", Citizenship Studies, Vol. 1, #3, Nov. 1997

Delanty, Gerard (1998); "Review Essay Dilemmas of Citizenship: Recent Literature on Citizenship and Europe", Citizenship Studies, Vol. 2. No. 2, July, 1998

DeLeon, Peter (1979); Thinking About Political Corruption, M. E. Sharpe, Armonk, NY, 1993

Denneny, Michael (1979); "The Privilege of Ourselves: Hannah Arendt on Judgment", in Hill, Melvyn A. (ed), Hannah Arendt: The Recovery of the Public World, St. Maritin's Press, NY, 1979

Dewey, John (1987); "Aims in Education", in Carbone, Peter F. Jr. (ed.), Value Theory and Education, Robert E. Krieger Publishing Co., Malabar, FL, 1987

Dewey, John (1996); "The Democratic Conception In Education", in Parker, Walter C., Educating the Democratic Mind, State University of New York Press, 1996

Dick, Andrew R. and Lott, John R. Jr. (1996); "Reconciling Voters' Behavior with Legislative Term Limits", in Grofman, Bernard (ed.); Legislative Term Limits: Public Choice Perspectives, Kluwer Academic Publishers, Norwell, MA, 1996

Diderot, D. (1994); "Citoyen", in Turner, Bryan and Hamilton, Peter (eds.); Citizenship Critical Concepts, Routledge, London, 1994

Dietz, Mary (1994); "Context is All: Feminism and Theories of Citizenship", in Turner, Bryan and Hamilton, Peter; Citizenship Critical Concepts, Routledge, London, 1994

Dodds, Susan (1998); "Citizenship, Justice and Indigenous Group-specific Rights–Citizenship and Indigenous Australia", Citizenship Studies, Vol. 2, No. 1, Feb. 1998

Dore, Ronald (1994); "Citizenship and Employment in an Age of High Technology", in Turner, Bryan and Hamilton, Peter (eds.); Citizenship Critical Concepts, Routledge, London, 1994

Downing, Brian M.(1994); "Constitutionalism, Warfare, and Political Change in Early Modern Europe", in Turner, Bryan and Hamilton, Peter (eds.); Citizenship Critical Concepts, Routledge, London, 1994

Draenos, Stan Spyros (1979); "Thinking without a Ground: Hannah Arendt and the Contemporary Situation of Understanding", in Hill, Melvyn A. (ed), Hannah Arendt: The Recovery of the Public World, St. Maritin's Press, NY, 1979

Drew, Elizabeth (1983); Politics and Money the New Road to Corruption, Macmillian Publishing Co., New York, NY 1983

Edelstein, Wolfgang (1985); "Moral Intervention: A Skeptical Note", in Berkowitz, Marvin W. and Oser, Fritz (eds.); Moral Education: Theory and Application, Lawrence Erlbaum Associates, Hillsdale, NJ 1985

Eisler, Riane (1987); The Chalice and the Blade, Our History, Our Future, Harper and Row, Cambridge, MA, 1987

Elkin, Stephen L. and Soltan, Edward Karol (eds) (1999); Citizen Competence and Democratic Institutions, The Pennsylvania State University Press, University Park, PA 1999

Elmore, Richard F. (ed.) (1990); Restructuring Schools: The Next Generation of Education Reform, Jossey-Bass Publishers, San Francisco, 1990

Elmore, Richard F. (1990a); "Conclusion: Toward a Transformation of Public Schooling", in Elmore, Richard F. (ed.); Restructuring Schools: The Next Generation of Education Reform, Jossey-Bass Publishers, San Francisco, 1990
274

Elmore, Richard F. (1990b); "Introduction: On Changing the Structure of Public Schools", in Elmore, Richard F. (ed.); Restructuring Schools: The Next Generation of Education Reform, Jossey-Bass Publishers, San Francisco, 1990

Elshtain, Jean Bethke (1995); "The Communitarian Individual", in Etzioni, Amitai (ed.); New Communitarian Thinking, The University Press of Virginia, Charlottesville, VA, 1995

Etzioni, Amitai (1984); Capital Corruption: The New Attack on American Democracy, Harcourt Brace Javanovich, New York, 1984

Etzioni, Amitai (ed.) (1995); New Communitarian Thinking, The University Press of Virginia, Charlottesville, VA, 1995

Etzioni, Amitai (1995); "Old Chestnuts and New Spurs", in Etzioni, Amitai (ed.); New Communitarian Thinking, The University Press of Virginia, Charlottesville, VA, 1995

Etzioni, Amitai (1996); The New Golden Rule Community and Morality in a Democratic Society, Basic Books, NY 1996

Flathman, Richard E. (1995); "Citizenship and Authority: A Chastened View of Citizenship", in Beiner, Ronald; ed. , Theorizing Citizenship, State University of New York Press, Albany, 1995

Flynn, Rob (1987); "Quasi-welfare, Associationism and the Social Division of Citizenship", Citizenship Studies, Vol. 1, #3, Nov. 1997

Foucault, Michael (1994); "Governmentality", in Turner, Bryan and Hamilton, Peter (eds.); Citizenship Critical Concepts, Routledge, London, 1994

Fowler, Robert Booth (1995); "Community Reflections on Definition", in Etzioni, Amitai (ed.); New Communitarian Thinking, The University Press of Virginia, Charlottesville, VA, 1995

Frankel, Charles (1987); "Equality of Opportunity", in Carbone, Peter F. Jr. (ed.), Value Theory and Education, Robert E. Krieger Publishing Co., Malabar, FL, 1987

Frankena, William K. (1987a); "Ethics", in Carbone, Peter F. Jr. (ed.), Value Theory and Education, Robert E. Krieger Publishing Co., Malabar, FL, 1987

Frankena, William K. (1987b); "Meaning and Justification", in Carbone, Peter F. Jr. (ed.), Value Theory and Education, Robert E. Krieger Publishing Co., Malabar, FL, 1987

Frankl, Viktor (1992); Man's Search for Meaning: An Introduction to Logotherapy, Beacon Press, Boston, 1992

Frantz, Douglas (1999); "Plenty of Dirty Jobs in Politics and a New Breed of Diggers", The New York Times, July 6, 1999

Friedman, Daniel and Wittman, Donald (1996); "Term Limits as Political Redistribution", in Grofman, Bernard (ed.); Legislative Term Limits: Public Choice Perspectives, Kluwer Academic Publishers, Norwell, MA, 1996

Friloux, Anthony Jr. (1975); "Another View from the Bar", in Simon, Rita James; The Jury System in America, Sage Publications, Beverly Hills, 1975

Frohlich, Norman and Oppenheimer, Joe A.(1999); "Values, Policies, and Citizen Competence: An Experimental Perspective, in Elkin, Stephen L. and Soltan, Edward Karol (eds); Citizen
276

Competence and Democratic Institutions, The Pennsylvania State University Press, University Park, PA 1999

Fuss, Peter (1979); "Hannah Arendt's Conception of Political Community", in Hill, Melvyn A. (ed), Hannah Arendt: The Recovery of the Public World, St. Maritin's Press, NY, 1979

Galston, William A. (1995); "Liberal Virtues and the Formation of Civic Character", in Glendon, Mary Ann and Blankenforn, David, (eds.), Seedbeds of Virtue Sources of Competence, Character, and Citizenship in American Society, Madison Books, Lanham, MD, 1995

Garforth, F.W. (1979); John Stuart Mill's Theory of Education, Barnes and Noble, 1979

Gearing, Frederick and Sangree, Lucinda (1979); Toward a Cultural Theory of Education and Schooling, Mouton Publishers, New York, 1979

Gerber, Elisabeth R. and Lupia, Arthur (1996); "Term Limits, Responsiveness and the Failures of Increased Competition", in Grofman, Bernard (ed.); Legislative Term Limits: Public Choice Perspectives, Kluwer Academic Publishers, Norwell, MA, 1996

Gibson, Rex (1986); Critical Theory and Education, Hodder and Stoughton, London, 1986

Gideonse, Hendrik D. (1990); "Organizing Schools to Encourage Teacher Inquiry", in Elmore, Richard F. (ed.); Restructuring Schools: The Next Generation of Education Reform, Jossey-Bass Publishers, San Francisco, 1990

Gilder, George (1994); "The Collapse of the American Family", in Turner, Bryan and Hamilton, Peter (eds.); Citizenship Critical Concepts, Routledge, London, 1994

Gilmour, John B. and Rothstein, Paul (1996); "Term Limitation in a Dynamic Model of Partisan Balance", in Grofman, Bernard; Legislative Term Limits: Public Choice Perspectives, Kluwer Academic Publishers, Norwell, MA, 1996

Glazer, Amihai and Wattenberg, Martin P.(1996); "How Will Term Limits Affect Legislative Work?", in Grofman, Bernard (ed.); Legislative Term Limits: Public Choice Perspectives, Kluwer Academic Publishers, Norwell, MA, 1996

Glazer, Nathan (1994a); "Individual Rights and Group Rights", in Turner, Bryan and Hamilton, Peter (eds.); Citizenship Critical Concepts, Routledge, London, 1994

Glazer, Nathan (1994b); "The Limits of Social Policy", in Turner, Bryan and Hamilton, Peter (eds.); Citizenship Critical Concepts, Routledge, London, 1994

Glendon, Mary Ann (1995); "Forgotten Questions" (Introduction), in Glendon, Mary Ann and Blankenforn, David, (eds.) , Seedbeds of Virtue Sources of Competence, Character, and Citizenship in American Society, Madison Books, Lanham, MD, 1995

Glendon, Mary Ann and Blankenforn, David, (eds.) (1995); Seedbeds of Virtue Sources of Competence, Character, and Citizenship in American Society, Madison Books, Lanham, MD, 1995

Gouldner, A.W. (1994); "The War Between the Cities", in Turner, Bryan and Hamilton, Peter (eds.); Citizenship Critical Concepts, Routledge, London, 1994

Graham, Gene S. (1975); "From the Press", in Simon, Rita James; The Jury System in America, Sage Publications, Beverly Hills, 1975

Gray, Glenn (1979); "The Abyss of Freedom–and Hannah Arendt", in Hill, Melvyn A. (ed), Hannah Arendt: The Recovery of the Public World, St. Maritin's Press, NY, 1979

Green, Thomas Hill (1895); Lectures on the Principles of Political Obligation, Longmans, Green, and Co. London, 1895

Greve, Anni (1998); "Emile Durkheim Revisited: *Les corps intermédiaires*", Citizenship Studies, Vol. 2. No. 2, July, 1998

Griffin, Alan F. (1996); "Teaching in Authoritarian and Democratic States" in Parker, Walter C. (ed.), Educating the Democratic Mind, State University of New York Press, 1996

Grofman, Bernard (ed.) (1996); Legislative Term Limits: Public Choice Perspectives, Kluwer Academic Publishers, Norwell, MA, 1996

Grofman, Bernard and Sutherland, Neil (1996); "Gubernatorial Term Limits and Term Lengths in Historical Perspective, 1790-1990: Geographic Diffusion, Non-separability, and the Ratchet Effect", in Grofman, Bernard (ed.); Legislative Term Limits: Public Choice Perspectives, Kluwer Academic Publishers, Norwell, MA, 1996

Grofman, Bernard and Sutherland, Neil (1996); "The Effect of Term Limits When Competition is Endogenized: A Preliminary Model", in

Grofman, Bernard (ed.); Legislative Term Limits: Public Choice Perspectives, Kluwer Academic Publishers, Norwell, MA, 1996

Gunning, James Patrick (1998); Understanding Democracy an Introduction to Public Choice, http://web.nchulc.edu.tw/~gunning/pat/votehtm/vm-16.htm

Gutmann, Amy (1995); "The Virtues of Democratic Self-Constraint", in Etzioni, Amitai (ed.); New Communitarian Thinking, The University Press of Virginia, Charlottesville, VA, 1995

Gutmann, Amy and Thompson, Dennis (1996); Democracy and Disagreement, Belknap Press, Cambridge, MA, 1996

Habermas, Jürgen (1994); "Citizenship and National Identity: Some Reflections of the Future of Europe", in Turner, Bryan and Hamilton, Peter (eds.); Citizenship Critical Concepts, Routledge, London, 1994

Habermas, Jürgen (1996); Between Facts and Norms Contributions to a Discourse Theory of Law and Democracy, MIT Press, Cambridge, MA, 1996, William Rehg translator

Hamilton, Alexander; Jay, John; and Madison, James (1966); The Federalist Papers, Arlington House, New Rochelle, NY, 1966

Hans, Valerie P. and Vidmar, Neil (1986); Judging the Jury, Plenum Press, NY, 1986

Hastie, Reid; Penrod, Steven D. & Pennington, Nancy (1983); Inside the Jury, Harvard University Press, Cambridge, 1983

Hauerwas, Stanley (1985); "The Difference of Virtue and the Difference It Makes: Courage Exemplified", in Glendon, Mary Ann and Blankenforn, David, (eds.) , <u>Seedbeds of Virtue Sources of Competence, Character, and Citizenship in American Society</u>, Madison Books, Lanham, MD, 1985

Hegel, G.W.F. (1994); "Ethical Life: A constitutional Law", in Turner, Bryan and Hamilton, Peter (eds.); <u>Citizenship Critical Concepts</u>, Routledge, London, 1994

Heisler, B.S. (1994); "A Comparative Perspective on the Underclass: Questions of Urban Poverty, Race and Citizenship", in Turner, Bryan and Hamilton, Peter (eds.); <u>Citizenship Critical Concepts</u>, Routledge, London, 1994

Hewer, Alexandra (1985); "Moral Reasoning in the Assessment and Outcome of Suicidal Breakdown", in Berkowitz, Marvin W. and Oser, Fritz (eds.); <u>Moral Education: Theory and Application</u>, Lawrence Erlbaum Associates, Hillsdale, NJ 1985

Higgins, Ann and Gordon, Frederick (1985); "Work Climate and Socio-Moral Development in Two Worker-Owned Companies", in Berkowitz, Marvin W. and Oser, Fritz (eds.); <u>Moral Education: Theory and Application</u>, Lawrence Erlbaum Associates, Hillsdale, NJ 1985

Hill, Melvyn A. (ed) (1979); <u>Hannah Arendt: The Recovery of the Public World</u>, St. Maritin's Press, NY, 1979

Hill, Melvyn A. (1979); "The Fictions of Mankind and the Stories of Men", in Hill, Melvyn A. (ed), <u>Hannah Arendt: The Recovery of the Public World</u>, St. Maritin's Press, NY, 1979

Hindess, Barry (1993); "Citizenship in the Modern West", in Turner, Bryan S. (ed.); <u>Citizenship and Social Theory</u>, Sage Publications, Newbury Park, CA, 1993

Hirst, Paul H. (1987); "Moral Education in the Secular School", in Carbone, Peter F. Jr. (ed.), Value Theory and Education, Robert E. Krieger Publishing Co., Malabar, FL, 1987

Höffe, Otfried (1985); "Autonomy and Universalization as Moral Principles: A Dispute with Kohlberg, Utilitarianism and Discourse Ethics", in Berkowitz, Marvin W. and Oser, Fritz (eds.); Moral Education: Theory and Application, Lawrence Erlbaum Associates, Hillsdale, NJ 1985

Hofstadter, Richard (1965); The Paranoid Style in American Politics and Other Essays, Knopf, New York, 1965

Hollenbach, David S. J. (1995); "Virtue, the Common Good, and Democracy", in Etzioni, Amitai (ed.); New Communitarian Thinking, The University Press of Virginia, Charlottesville, VA, 1995

Hook, Sidney (1987); "The Ends of Education", in Carbone, Peter F. Jr. (ed.), Value Theory and Education, Robert E. Krieger Publishing Co., Malabar, FL, 1987

Howard, Rohda E. (1998); "Being Canadian: Citizenship in Canada", Citizenship Studies, Vol. 2, No. 1, Feb. 1998

Hunt, Maurice P. and Metcalf, Lawrence E. (1996); "Rational Inquiry on Society's Closed Areas", in Parker, Walter C. (ed.), Educating the Democratic Mind, State University of New York Press, 1996

Hyman, Harold M. and Terrant, Catherine M. (1975); "Aspects of American Trial Jury History", in Simon, Rita James; The Jury System in America, Sage Publications, Beverly Hills, 1975

Ignatieff, Michael (1995); "The Myth of Citizenship", in Beiner, Ronald; ed., Theorizing Citizenship, State University of New York Press, Albany, 1995

Janowitz, Morris (1994a); "Military Institutions and Citizenship in Western Societies", in Turner, Bryan and Hamilton, Peter (eds.); Citizenship Critical Concepts, Routledge, London, 1994

Janowitz, Morris (1994b); "Observations on the Sociology of Citizenship", in Turner, Bryan and Hamilton, Peter (eds.); Citizenship Critical Concepts, Routledge, London, 1994

Johnson, Susan Moore (1990); "Redesigning Teachers' Work", in Elmore, Richard F. (ed.); Restructuring Schools: The Next Generation of Education Reform, Jossey-Bass Publishers, San Francisco, 1990

Joiner, Charles W. (1975); "From the Bench" in Simon, Rita James; The Jury System in America, Sage Publications, Beverly Hills, 1975

Kahne, Joseph (1996); Reframing Educational Policy Democracy, Community, and the Individual, Teachers College Press, Columbia University, NY, 1996

Kalberg, Stephen (1993); "Cultural Foundations of Modern Citizenship", in Turner, Bryan S. (ed.); Citizenship and Social Theory, Sage Publications, Newbury Park, CA, 1993

Kant, Immanual (1994); "Excerpt from The Theory of Right, Part II: Public Right", in Turner, Bryan and Hamilton, Peter (eds.); Citizenship Critical Concepts, Routledge, London, 1994

Kessler, Joan B. (1975); "The Social Psychology of Jury Deliberations", in Simon, Rita James; The Jury System in America, Sage Publications, Beverly Hills, 1975

Keller, Monika and Reuss, Siegfried (1985); "The Process of Moral Decision-Making: Normative and Empirical Conditions of Participation in Moral Discourse", in Berkowitz, Marvin W. and Oser, Fritz (eds.); Moral Education: Theory and Application, Lawrence Erlbaum Associates, Hillsdale, NJ 1985

Kelly, George Armstrong (1994); "Who Needs a Theory of Citizenship", in Turner, Bryan and Hamilton, Peter (eds.); Citizenship Critical Concepts, Routledge, London, 1994

Kennebeck, Edwin (1975); "From the Jury Box", in Simon, Rita James; The Jury System in America, Sage Publications, Beverly Hills, 1975

Kiernan, Annabel K. (1997); "Citizenship–The Real Democratic Deficit of the European Union", Citizenship Studies, Vol. 1, #3, Nov. 1997

Kohlberg, Lawrence (1996); "Moral Reasoning", in Parker, Walter C. (ed.), Educating the Democratic Mind, State University of New York Press, 1996

Kohlberg, Lawrence (1985); "The Just Community Approach to Moral Education in Theory and Practice", in Berkowitz, Marvin W. and Oser, Fritz (eds.); Moral Education: Theory and Application, Lawrence Erlbaum Associates, Hillsdale, NJ 1985

Kohlberg, Lawrence (1987); "The Cognitive-Developmental Approach to Moral Education", in Carbone, Peter F. Jr. (ed.), Value

Theory and Education, Robert E. Krieger Publishing Co., Malabar, FL, 1987

Kuhn, Thomas; The Structure of Scientific Revolutions, University of Chicago Press, Chicago, IL 1962

Küng, Guido (1985); "The Postconventional Level of Moral Development: Psychology or Philosophy?" in Berkowitz, Marvin W. and Oser, Fritz (eds.); Moral Education: Theory and Application, Lawrence Erlbaum Associates, Hillsdale, NJ 1985

Kymlicka, Will and Norman, Wayne (1995); "Return of the Citizen: A Survey of Recent Work on Citizenship Theory", in Beiner, Ronald; ed. , Theorizing Citizenship, State University of New York Press, Albany, 1995

Lechner, Frank J. (1998); "Parsons on Citizenship", Citizenship Studies, Vol. 2. No. 2, July 1998

Lickona, Thomas (1985); "Parents as Moral Educators", in Berkowitz, Marvin W. and Oser, Fritz (eds.); Moral Education: Theory and Application, Lawrence Erlbaum Associates, Hillsdale, NJ 1985

Lieberman, Myron (1993); Public Education An Autopsy, Harvard University Press, Cambridge MA 1993

Linklater, Andrew (1998); "Cosmopolitan Citizenship", Citizenship Studies, Vol. 2, No. 1, Feb. 1998

Lister, Ruth (1994); "Women, Economic Dependency and Citizenship", in Turner, Bryan and Hamilton, Peter (eds.); Citizenship Critical Concepts, Routledge, London, 1994

Locke, John (1994); "Of the Beginning of Political Societies", in Turner, Bryan and Hamilton, Peter (eds.); Citizenship Critical Concepts, Routledge, London, 1994

Macedo, Stephen (1994); "Capitalism, Citizen and Community", in Turner, Bryan and Hamilton, Peter (eds.); Citizenship Critical Concepts, Routledge, London, 1994

MacIntyre, Alasdair (1995); "Is Patriotism a Virtue?", in Beiner, Ronald; ed., Theorizing Citizenship, State University of New York Press, Albany, 1995

Major, Robert W.(1979); "A Reading of Hannah Arendt's 'Unusual' Distinction Between Labor and Work", in Hill, Melvyn A. (ed), Hannah Arendt: The Recovery of the Public World, St. Maritin's Press, NY, 1979

Manin, Bernard (1997); The Principles of Representative Government, Cambridge University Press, 1997

Mann, Michael (1994); "Ruling Class Strategies and Citizenship", in Turner, Bryan and Hamilton, Peter (eds.) (1994); Citizenship Critical Concepts, Routledge, London, 1994

Marquand, David (1994); "Civic Republics and Liberal Individualists: The Case of Britain", in Turner, Bryan and Hamilton, Peter (eds.); Citizenship Critical Concepts, Routledge, London, 1994

Marsden, Chris and Andriof, Jörg (1998); "Towards an Understanding of Corporate Citizenship and How to Influence It", Citizenship Studies, Vol. 2. No. 2, July 1998

Marshall, Gordon, David Rose, Carolyn Vogler and Howard Newby (1994); "Class, Citizenship, and Distributional Conflict in Modern

Britain", in Turner, Bryan and Hamilton, Peter (eds.); Citizenship Critical Concepts, Routledge, London, 1994

Marshall, T. H. (1994a); "Afterthought on 'Value-Problems of Welfare Capitalism", in Turner, Bryan and Hamilton, Peter (eds.); Citizenship Critical Concepts, Routledge, London, 1994

Marshall, T. H. (1994b); "Citizenship and Social Class", in Turner, Bryan and Hamilton, Peter (eds.); Citizenship Critical Concepts, Routledge, London, 1994

Martin, Judith (1995); "The Oldest Virtue", in Glendon, Mary Ann and Blankenforn, David, (eds.) , Seedbeds of Virtue Sources of Competence, Character, and Citizenship in American Society, Madison Books, Lanham, MD, 1995

Marvin, Keith E.(1981); "Intergovernmental Implications for Evaluation Training", in Zweig, Franklin M. and Marvin, Keith E.; Educating Policymakers for Evaluation, Sage Publications, Beverly Hills, 1981

Marx, Karl (1994); "On the Jewish Question", in Turner, Bryan and Hamilton, Peter (eds.); Citizenship Critical Concepts, Routledge, London, 1994

Matthews, David (1996); "Reviewing and Previewing Civics", in Parker, Walter C. (ed.), Educating the Democratic Mind, State University of New York Press, 1996

Mead, Lawrence M. (1986); Beyond Entitlement–The Social Obligations of Citizenship, Free Press, NY 1986

Metropolitan Council (1998); http://www.metcouncil.org/metroarea/socioeco.htm, Oct. 18, 1998

Microsoft (1994), <u>Encarta'95</u>, 1992-1994

Mill, John Stuart (1994); "On Liberty: Chapter I, Introductory", in Turner, Bryan and Hamilton, Peter (eds.); <u>Citizenship Critical Concepts</u>, Routledge, London, 1994

Mill, John Stuart, (1993); <u>Utilitarianism, On Liberty, and Considerations on Representative Government</u>, Everyman, Rutland, VT, 1993

Miller, James (1979); "The Pathos of Novelty: Hannah Arendt's Image of Freedom in the Modern World", in Hill, Melvyn A. (ed), <u>Hannah Arendt: The Recovery of the Public World</u>, St. Maritin's Press, NY, 1979

Miller, Mark C. (1995); <u>The High Priests of American Politics</u>, The Role of Lawyers in American Political Institutions, University of Tennessee Press, Knoxville, 1995

Minnesota Secretary of State (1998); http://www.sos.state.mn.us/elections/elstat94.html, Oct. 18, 1998

Minnesota State Demographic Center (1998); http://www.mnplan.state.mn.us/demography/demog_3a_96.html, Oct. 27, 1998

Mitchell, Alison (1998); "A New Form of Lobbying Puts Public Face on Private Interest", <u>The New York Times</u>, Sept. 30, 1998

Moncrief, Gary F., Thompson, Joel A., Haddon, Michael & Hoyer, Robert (1996); "For Whom the Bell Tolls: Term Limits and State Legislatures", in Grofman, Bernard (ed.); <u>Legislative Term Limits:</u>

Public Choice Perspectives, Kluwer Academic Publishers, Norwell, MA, 1996

Mondale Policy Forum (1992); Political Parties in America: Who Needs Them?, University of Minnesota, May 7-8, 1992

Moynihan, Daniel Patrick (1994); "The Underclass–II: Toward a Post-Industrial Social Policy", in Turner, Bryan and Hamilton, Peter (eds.); Citizenship Critical Concepts, Routledge, London, 1994

Musgrave, Richard A. (1959); The Theory of Public Finance: A Study in Public Economy, McGraw-Hill, NY 1959

Narramore, Terry (1998); "Communities and Citizens: Identity and Difference in Discourses of Asia-Pacific Regionalism", Citizenship Studies, Vol. 2, No. 1, Feb. 1998

Newman, George (1928); Citizenship and the Survival of Civilization, Yale University Press, New Haven, 1928

Newmann, Fred M., Betrocci, Thomas A. and Landsness, Ruthanne M. (1996); "Skills in Citizen Action", in Parker, Walter C. (ed.), Educating the Democratic Mind, State University of New York Press, 1996

Nisbet, Robert (1994); "Citizenship: Two Traditions", in Turner, Bryan and Hamilton, Peter (eds.); Citizenship Critical Concepts, Routledge, London, 1994

Nock, Albert J. (1932); The Theory of Education in the United States, Henry Regnery Co., Chicago, 1932

Novak, Joseph D. (1977); A Theory of Education, Cornell University Press, Ithaca, 1977

Oldfield, Adrian (1994); "Citizenship: An Unnatural Practice?", in Turner, Bryan and Hamilton, Peter (eds.); <u>Citizenship Critical Concepts</u>, Routledge, London, 1994

Oliver, Donald W. and Shaver, James P. (1996); "Using a Jurisprudential Framework in the Teaching of Public Issues", in Parker, Walter C. (ed.), <u>Educating the Democratic Mind</u>, State University of New York Press, 1996

Parekh, Bikhu; "Hannah Arendt's Critique of Marx" (1979); in Hill, Melvyn A. (ed), <u>Hannah Arendt: The Recovery of the Public World</u>, St. Maritin's Press, NY, 1979

Parker, Glenn R. (1996); <u>Congress and the Rent-Seeking Society</u>, University of Michigan Press, Ann Arbor, 1996

Parker, Walter C. (ed.) (1996); <u>Educating the Democratic Mind</u>, State University of New York Press, 1996

Parker, Walter C.(1996); "Introduction", in Parker, Walter C., <u>Educating the Democratic Mind</u>, State University of New York Press, 1996

Parsons, Talcott (1994); "Full Citizenship for the Negro American: A Sociological Problem", in Turner, Bryan and Hamilton, Peter (eds.); <u>Citizenship Critical Concepts</u>, Routledge, London, 1994

Pateman, Carole (1994); "Feminism and Democracy", in Turner, Bryan and Hamilton, Peter (eds.); <u>Citizenship Critical Concepts</u>, Routledge, London, 1994

Peters, R. S. (1987); "Classical Theories of Justification", in Carbone, Peter F. Jr. (ed.), Value Theory and Education, Robert E. Krieger Publishing Co., Malabar, FL, 1987

Peters, R. S. (1987); "Freedom" in Carbone, Peter F. Jr. (ed.), Value Theory and Education, Robert E. Krieger Publishing Co., Malabar, FL, 1987

Petracca, Mark P and O'Brien, Kareen Moore (1996); "The Experience with Municipal Term Limits in Orange County, California", in Grofman, Bernard (ed.); Legislative Term Limits: Public Choice Perspectives, Kluwer Academic Publishers, Norwell, MA, 1996

Petracca, Mark P. (1996); "A History of Rotation in Office", in Grofman, Bernard (ed.); Legislative Term Limits: Public Choice Perspectives, Kluwer Academic Publishers, Norwell, MA, 1996

Pitkin, Hanna Fenichel (1967); The Concept of Representation, University of California Press, Berkeley, 1967

Pocock, A. (1995); "The Ideal of Citizenship Since Classical Times", in Beiner, Ronald; ed. , Theorizing Citizenship, State University of New York Press, Albany, 1995

Popenoe, David; "The Roots of Declining Social Virtue: Family, Community, and the Need for a 'Natural Communities Policy'", in Glendon, Mary Ann and Blankenforn, David, (eds.) , Seedbeds of Virtue Sources of Competence, Character, and Citizenship in American Society, Madison Books, Lanham, MD, 1995

Power, Clark (1985); "Democratic Moral Education in the Large Public High School", in Berkowitz, Marvin W. and Oser, Fritz (eds.); <u>Moral Education: Theory and Application</u>, Lawrence Erlbaum Associates, Hillsdale, NJ 1985

Pranger, Robert J. (1968); <u>The Eclipse of Citizenship Power and Participation in Contemporary Politics</u>, Holt, Rinehart, and Winston, Inc., New York, 1968

Putnam, Robert D. (1996); "The Strange Disappearance of Civic America", <u>The American Prospect</u>, no. 24 (Winter 1996), (http://www.epn.org/prospect/24/24putn.html)

Raths, Louis E., Merrill Harmin, Merrill and Simon, Sidney B. (1987); "Selections from *Values and Teaching*", in Carbone, Peter F. Jr. (ed.), <u>Value Theory and Education</u>, Robert E. Krieger Publishing Co., Malabar, FL, 1987

Rausch, John David Jr. and Copeland, Gary W. (1996); "Term Limits in Oklahoma, California, and Colorado in 1990", in Grofman, Bernard (ed.); <u>Legislative Term Limits: Public Choice Perspectives</u>, Kluwer Academic Publishers, Norwell, MA, 1996

Rawls, John (1971); <u>A Theory of Justice</u>, Harvard University Press, Cambridge, MA, 1971

Rawls, John (1993) <u>Political Liberalism;</u> Columbia University Press, New York, 1993

Raywild, Mary Ann (1990); "Rethinking School Governance", in Elmore, Richard F. (ed.); <u>Restructuring Schools: The Next Generation of Education Reform</u>, Jossey-Bass Publishers, San Francisco, 1990

Reed, Robert and Schansberg, D. Eric (1996a); "Impact of Congressional Tenure Restriction on Spending", in Grofman,

Bernard (ed.); Legislative Term Limits: Public Choice Perspectives, Kluwer Academic Publishers, Norwell, MA, 1996

Reed, Robert and Schansberg, D. Eric (1996b); "An Analysis of the Impact of Congressional Term Limits on Turnover and Party Balance", in Grofman, Bernard (ed.); Legislative Term Limits: Public Choice Perspectives, Kluwer Academic Publishers, Norwell, MA, 1996

Reigadas, Christina (1998); "The Public Household and New Citizenship in Daniel Bell's Political Thought", Citizenship Studies, Vol. 2. No. 2, July, 1998

Reinener, Larry R.; "Types of Authority", Jan. 31, 1999 http://cymru.web.cf.ac.uk/uwcc.socal/ugyear1/introsoc/WEBERW5. HTML,

Reisner, Marc (1986); Cadillac Desert: The American West and Its Disappearing Water, Viking Press, NY, 1986

Rest, James R. (1985); "An Interdisciplinary Approach to Moral Education", in Berkowitz, Marvin W. and Oser, Fritz (eds.); Moral Education: Theory and Application, Lawrence Erlbaum Associates, Hillsdale, NJ 1985

Riesenberg, Peter (1992); Citizenship in the Western Tradition Plato to Rousseau, University of North Carolina Press, 1992

Roche, Maurice (1994); "Citizenship, Social Theory, and Social Change", in Turner, Bryan and Hamilton, Peter (eds.); Citizenship Critical Concepts, Routledge, London, 1994

Rousseau, Jean-Jacques (1993); The Social Contract and Discourses, Everyman, Rutland, VT, 1993

Rousseau, J.J. (1994); "The Social Contract", in Turner, Bryan and Hamilton, Peter (eds.); Citizenship Critical Concepts, Routledge, London, 1994

Rowan, Brian (1990); "Applying Conceptions of Teaching to Organizational Reform", in Elmore, Richard F. (ed.); Restructuring Schools: The Next Generation of Education Reform, Jossey-Bass Publishers, San Francisco, 1990

Salins, Peter D. (1997); Assimilation American Style, Basis Books, NY, 1997

Sartori, Giovanni (1968); "Representational Systems", International Encyclopedia of the Social Sciences, David L. Shils (ed.), Macmillian, New York, 1968-1991

Saunders, Peter (1993); "Citizenship in a Liberal Society", Turner, Bryan S. (ed.); Citizenship and Social Theory, Sage Publications, Newbury Park, CA, 1993

Scheffler, Israel (1987a); "Justifying Curriculum Decisions", in Carbone, Peter F. Jr. (ed.), Value Theory and Education, Robert E. Krieger Publishing Co., Malabar, FL, 1987

Scheffler, Israel (1987b); "Moral Education and the Democratic Ideal", in Carbone, Peter F. Jr. (ed.), Value Theory and Education, Robert E. Krieger Publishing Co., Malabar, FL, 1987

Schell, Jonathan (1982); The Fate of the Earth, Avon Books, New York, 1982

Schmidt, Paul F. (1961); Religious Knowledge, Greenwood Press, Westport, CT, 1961

Seligman, Adam (1993); "The Fragile Ethical Vision of Civil Society", in Turner, Bryan S. (ed.); Citizenship and Social Theory, Sage Publications, Newbury Park, CA, 1993

Selznik, Philip (1995); "Personhood and Moral Obligation", in Etzioni, Amitai (ed.); New Communitarian Thinking, The University Press of Virginia, Charlottesville, VA, 1995

Shotter, John (1993); "Psychology and Citizenship: Identity and Belonging", in Turner, Bryan S. (ed.); Citizenship and Social Theory, Sage Publications, Newbury Park, CA, 1993

Sichel, Betty A. (1987); "A Critical Study of Kohlberg's Theory of the Development of Moral Judgments" in Carbone, Peter F. Jr. (ed.), Value Theory and Education, Robert E. Krieger Publishing Co., Malabar, FL, 1987

Simon, Rita James (1975); The Jury System in America, Sage Publications, Beverly Hills, 1975

Smith, Houston (1958); The Religions of Man, Harper, NY 1958

Smith, Rogers M. (1995); "American Conceptions of Citizenship and National Service", in Etzioni, Amitai (ed.); New Communitarian Thinking, The University Press of Virginia, Charlottesville, VA, 1995

Soltan, Edward Karol (1999); "Civic Competence, Attractiveness, and Maturity", in Elkin, Stephen L. and Soltan, Edward Karol (eds); Citizen Competence and Democratic Institutions, The Pennsylvania State University Press, University Park, PA 1999

Spragens, Thomas A. Jr.(1995); "Communitarian Liberalism", in Etzioni, Amitai (ed.); New Communitarian Thinking, The University Press of Virginia, Charlottesville, VA, 1995

Statham, Robert Jr.(1998); "US Citizenship Policy in the Pacific Territory of Guam", Citizenship Studies, Vol. 2, No. 1, Feb. 1998

Stevenson, Nick (1997); "Global Media and Technological Change: Social Justice, Recognition and the Meaningfulness of Everyday Life", Citizenship Studies, Vol. 1, #3, Nov. 1997

Stewart, John S. (1987); "Clarifying Values Clarification: A Critique", in Carbone, Peter F. Jr. (ed.), Value Theory and Education, Robert E. Krieger Publishing Co., Malabar, FL, 1987

Sullivan, William M.(1995); "Institutions and the Infrastructure of Democracy", in Etzioni, Amitai (ed.); New Communitarian Thinking, The University Press of Virginia, Charlottesville, VA, 1995

Sullivan, William M.(1995); "Reinstitutionalizing Virtue in Civil Society", in Glendon, Mary Ann and Blankenforn, David, (eds.) , Seedbeds of Virtue Sources of Competence, Character, and Citizenship in American Society, Madison Books, Lanham, MD, 1995

Sykes, Gary (1990); "Fostering Teacher Professionalism in Schools", in Elmore, Richard F. (ed.); Restructuring Schools: The Next Generation of Education Reform, Jossey-Bass Publishers, San Francisco, 1990

Tabarrok, Alexander (1996); "Term Limits and Political Conflict", in Grofman, Bernard (ed.); Legislative Term Limits: Public Choice Perspectives, Kluwer Academic Publishers, Norwell, MA, 1996

Talcott Parsons, Talcott (1994); "The Democratic Revolution", in Turner, Bryan and Hamilton, Peter (eds.); Citizenship Critical Concepts, Routledge, London, 1994

Taylor, Charles (1995); "Liberal Politics and the Public Sphere", in Etzioni, Amitai (ed.); New Communitarian Thinking, The University Press of Virginia, Charlottesville, VA, 1995

Taylor, David (1994); "Citizenship and Social Power", in Turner, Bryan and Hamilton, Peter (eds.); Citizenship Critical Concepts, Routledge, London, 1994

Tétreault, Mary Ann 1998); "Spheres of Liberty, Conflict and Power: The Public Lives of Private Persons", Citizenship Studies, Vol. 2. No. 2, July, 1998

Tichenor, Daniel (1995); "Immigration and Political Community in the United States", in Etzioni, Amitai (ed.) (1995); New Communitarian Thinking, The University Press of Virginia, Charlottesville, VA, 1995

Toulmin, Stephen (1972); Human Understanding, Princeton University Press, Princeton, NJ, 1972

Turner, Bryan and Hamilton, Peter (eds.) (1994); Citizenship Critical Concepts, Routledge, London, 1994

Turner; Bryan S. (1994a); "Outline of a Theory of Citizenship", in Turner, Bryan and Hamilton, Peter (eds.); Citizenship Critical Concepts, Routledge, London, 1994

Turner (1994b); "Outline of a Theory of Human Rights", in Turner, Bryan and Hamilton, Peter (eds.); Citizenship Critical Concepts, Routledge, London, 1994

Turner, Bryan S. (ed.) (1993); Citizenship and Social Theory, Sage Publications, Newbury Park, CA, 1993

Turner, Bryan S. (1993); "Contemporary Problems in the Theory of Citizenship", in Turner, Bryan S. (ed.); Citizenship and Social Theory, Sage Publications, Newbury Park, CA, 1993

Van Doorn, Jaques (1994); "The Decline of the Mass Army in the West: General Reflections", in Turner, Bryan and Hamilton, Peter (eds.); Citizenship Critical Concepts, Routledge, London, 1994

van Gunstern, Herman R.(1988); "Admission to Citizenship", Ethics, Vol. 98, #4, July 1988, pp. 731-741

Walzer, Michael (1970); Obligations: Essays on Disobedience, War, and Citizenship, Harvard University Press, Cambridge, MA, 1970

Walzer, Michael (1994); "Civility and Civic Virtue in Contemporary America", in Turner, Bryan and Hamilton, Peter (eds.); Citizenship Critical Concepts, Routledge, London, 1994

Walzer, Michael (1995a); "The Civil Society Argument", in Beiner, Ronald; ed. , Theorizing Citizenship, State University of New York Press, Albany, 1995

Walzer, Michael (1995b); "The Communitarian Critique of Liberalism", in Etzioni, Amitai (ed.); New Communitarian Thinking, The University Press of Virginia, Charlottesville, VA, 1995

Weber, Max (1958); <u>From Max Weber: Essays in Sociology</u>, Gerth, H. H. and Mills, C. Wright (eds.), Oxford University Press, NY 1958

Whitson, James Anthony and Stanley, William B. (1996); "'Re-Minding' Education for Democracy", in Parker, Walter C. (ed.), <u>Educating the Democratic Mind</u>, State University of New York Press, 1996

Wilson, James Q. (1995); "Liberalism, Modernism, and the Good Life", in Glendon, Mary Ann and Blankenforn, David, (eds.) , <u>Seedbeds of Virtue Sources of Competence, Character, and Citizenship in American Society</u>, Madison Books, Lanham, MD, 1995

Wolfe, Alan (1995a); "Human Nature and the Quest for Community", in Etzioni, Amitai (ed.); <u>New Communitarian Thinking</u>, The University Press of Virginia, Charlottesville, VA, 1995

Wolfe, Alan (1995b); "Social and Natural Ecologies: Similarities and Differences", in Glendon, Mary Ann and Blankenforn, David, (eds.) , <u>Seedbeds of Virtue Sources of Competence, Character, and Citizenship in American Society</u>, Madison Books, Lanham, MD, 1995

Wood, George H. (1992); <u>Schools that Work</u>, Dutton, NY, 1992

Young, Iris Marion (1994); "Polity and Group Difference: A Critique of the Ideal of Universal Citizenship", in Turner, Bryan and Hamilton, Peter (eds.); <u>Citizenship Critical Concepts</u>, Routledge, London, 1994

Zweig, Franklin M. (1981); "On Educating the Congress for Evaluation", in Zweig, Franklin M. and Marvin, Keith E.; <u>Educating</u>

Policymakers for Evaluation, Sage Publications, Beverly Hills, 1981

Zweig, Franklin M. and Marvin, Keith E. (1981); Educating Policymakers for Evaluation, Sage Publications, Beverly Hills, 1981

About the Author

The author was educated at Amherst College and the Maxwell School of Citizenship and Public Affairs at Syracuse University. He served as a Peace Corps Volunteer in the Philippines and has traveled rather extensively. He is now retired from his employment with the State of Minnesota. Under the pseudonym Claudius Proctus he authored the satirical novel **Combustion.** He resides in Lake Elmo, MN with his wife Susan and their canine Darwin.

www.ingramcontent.com/pod-product-compliance
Lightning Source LLC
Chambersburg PA
CBHW050108280326
41933CB00010B/1013